The Best Of **Fine WoodWorking**

Traditional Furniture
Projects

The Taunton Press

Cover photo by Jeff Gruver

...by fellow enthusiasts

©1991 by The Taunton Press, Inc.
All rights reserved

First printing: February 1991
International Standard Book Number: 0-942391-93-4
Printed in the United States of America

A FINE WOODWORKING Book

FINE WOODWORKING® is a trademark of The Taunton Press, Inc.,
registered in the U.S. Patent and Trademark Office.

The Taunton Press, Inc.
63 South Main Street
Box 5506
Newtown, Connecticut 06470-5506

Library of Congress Cataloging-in-Publication Data

The Best of Fine woodworking. Traditional furniture projects :
    25 articles / selected by the editors of Fine woodworking magazine.
        p. cm.
      "A Fine woodworking book"—T.p. verso.
      Includes index.
      ISBN 0-942391-93-4
      1. Furniture making.   I. Fine woodworking.
    II. Title: Traditional furniture projects.
    TT194.B46 1991
    684.1'042—dc20   90-24706
                                                              CIP

The Best Of Fine WoodWorking

Traditional Furniture
Projects

Contents

Introduction

When I was first learning woodworking, I was so concerned with the popular modern look that I couldn't accept anything older or more ornate than the Shakers. One of the best craftsmen I knew, however, warned me that I was making a mistake. The "modern" look that I wanted, he said, was so boring that it was an insult to the complexities of the human mind. Though I still don't agree with him 100%, over the years I have come to understand what he was trying to tell me about traditional furniture.

There is a wonder of design, proportion and just plain great technique in the work of the craftsmen who have preceded us. This collection of 25 articles includes some of the best traditional pieces published in *Fine Woodworking* magazine. Some rely heavily on traditional hand-tool techniques; others are built mostly with modern power tools to the exacting standards of 18th-century cabinetmakers. Most of the designs are based on originals now in museums or prominent private collections. All offer a technical challenge and intellectual treat for modern makers.

—Dick Burrows, editor

The "Best of *Fine Woodworking*" series spans issues 46 through 80 of *Fine Woodworking* magazine, originally published between mid-1984 and the end of 1989. There is no duplication between these books and the popular *"Fine Woodworking* on..." series. A footnote with each article gives the date of first publication; product availability, suppliers' addresses and prices may have changed since then.

Measuring Antiques
Educated guesses fill in the gaps

by Dick Burrows

In colonial times, furniture making was both a highly refined art and a farmhouse necessity. In the larger coastal cities craftsmen, trained in rigid European apprenticeships, produced stunning pieces for the wealthy and status-conscious. Meanwhile, numerous country craftsmen were turning native lumber into practical, yet elegant, family furnishings. Ironically, the best examples of both styles have become classics, creating a seemingly insatiable demand for historical and construction notes on vintage pieces.

Since few cabinetmakers managed to preserve their construction drawings or to take notes, you usually must rely on the furniture itself to show how the old guys did it. Museums and private collections abound with fine 17th- to 19th-century pieces, and are, in effect, living libraries of plans. Carlyle Lynch, cabinetmaker and retired teacher, has devoted years to measuring furniture at places like Old Sturbridge Village in Massachusetts, Old Salem and the Museum of Early Southern Decorative Arts (MESDA) in North Carolina. Although I've never been an aficionado of the old ways, I found Lynch's enthusiasm for period furniture infectious.

While he insists that there are no magic tricks to measuring furniture, there's more to it than poking around with a ruler. Before you can do it right, you need to learn how boards were surfaced, how joints were cut and how furniture was built in the

days when hand tools were the *only* tools. Otherwise, you'll never grasp what's hidden by veneers, moldings and thick layers of yellowed finishes.

Surprisingly, if your skills at reassuring nervous owners are as good as Lynch's, you can examine many pieces. As you trace the delicate carvings with your fingertips and examine centuries-old joints for telltale marking lines and tool marks, the maker and his art come alive. For me, that was the best part of working with Lynch when he measured Duncan Phyfe's personal tool box (the results are shown in the drawing on page 10) at the New York Historical Society and two pieces at MESDA. Before you begin work, make sure the owners of the piece clearly understand what you want to do and how you plan to do it. Some old pieces may be too fragile to be moved or handled much. One owner might let you remove and trace an escutcheon, while another will ask you to leave for just suggesting you want to remove any hardware.

To avoid missing any vital details, Lynch works systematically. He starts with overall dimensions, measuring each major component in turn—sides, top, back, front—then works down to each joint, curve and angle, carving, molding and turning. He sketches each piece, measures it, then marks the measurements on his sketch. Then he remeasures it. By measuring everything twice, you ensure accuracy and the odds are you won't overlook an important detail twice.

When we measured the toolbox used by Phyfe when he was the darling of trendy New York in the early 19th century, Lynch began with a general appraisal of the large, dovetailed pine chest. The chest is painted brown and is as drab as Phyfe's furniture is elegant, although the box's interior is a woodworker's delight of chisels with pewter ferrules, finely set planes and exquisitely shaped saw handles. After removing some of the tools and the chest's sliding inner cabinet, Lynch made one rough, box-like sketch showing the front and side view and another showing the top view. He prefers to make freehand perspective drawings to record his measurements, but any sketch will do as long as you can decipher your notes and match the right measurements to the right part. Lynch strives to be accurate to within $\frac{1}{32}$ in.

He began measuring on the right side. Holding a zig-zag carpenter's rule on the outside of the chest, he measured the depth and height of the end. Then he determined how the side was fastened to the top, bottom, front and back, and noted these details on his sketch. Since the box corners are dovetailed, he measured the pins to find the thickness of the back and front pieces. By inserting the rule inside the chest along the same end, he obtained the inside dimension of the end and verified that it, plus the width of the front and back pieces, equaled the outside

Analyzing antiques is part detective work, some guesswork and much careful measurement. Lynch finds a 6-in. sliding rule good for measuring small pieces like drawers and as a caliper to gauge thicknesses. The 16-drawer mahogany case he's examining is one of the jewels hidden in Duncan Phyfe's tool chest.

From *Fine Woodworking* magazine (July 1985) 53:52-55

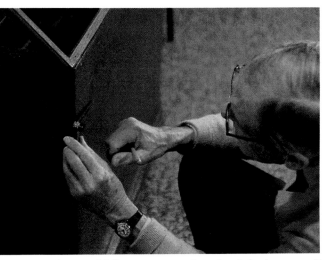

Lynch prefers a folding carpenter's rule, left, because it won't snap back as a steel tape might. Holding his bevel gauge handle parallel to the chest corner, he angles its tongue to match the dovetails, above. He records the angle with a protractor. For something as irregular as this tavern table leg, he uses a simple pen holder to trace contours. The Plexiglas edge of the wooden upright is set directly over the angled pen. As you run the plastic along the piece, the pen records the contour on paper on the instrument's base.

dimension. He also measured the interior height of the box and located the chest bottom on his drawing. Then he made notes of the size, shape and location of hinges, pulls and handles. All the joints were visible and easily identified, but larger carcases can be more complex.

Lynch takes most of his measurements with his carpenter's rule (photo above, left) or a small 6-in. wood-and-brass sliding rule. Both easily extend across or into a carcase, and they can't snap back and scratch a piece the way a metal tape measure can. Metal tapes are handy, however, if you have to flex a rule into a very tight corner. In addition to the two rules, his measuring kit, which is compact enough to fit into a regular briefcase, includes a flashlight and an angled mirror (much like an oversized dentist's mirror) for peering into dark corners; several soft pencils; 10-in. dividers and several sizes of calipers; metal contour gauge; a Plexiglas contour tracer (photo above, right); plumb bob for measuring chair angles; a clipboard with note paper and tracing paper; bevel gauge and protractor; small screwdriver; a thin, flexible palette knife for probing inside joints; and a large sheet of cardboard (mat board or backing board) to protect a piece if you want to turn it on its side.

When he was a beginner, Lynch also brought a detailed checklist of crucial measurements. He would prepare the list at home, based on his cabinetmaking work and studies of period furniture, then fill it in step-by-step when he saw the piece. Now he's experienced enough to rely on a mental checklist, but the written version is good training for neophytes.

Forgetting a significant dimension can be a problem if the piece is miles from your home, or is sold to owners who don't want a stranger poking through their furniture. Sometimes Lynch can entice an owner to check a dimension or refresh his memory about certain details, but a better memory check comes from his camera. He always photographs the overall piece and its details with 1000 ASA daylight color film.

Whenever possible, he also backs up his measurements by tracing details or making a rubbing of distinctive features, like dovetails. For example, you can use your clipboard to hold paper

upside down over the top of a carcase and trace the corner. Or, you could put the board under a leg and trace the shape of a ball-and-claw foot. Mark the measurements on each tracing.

To make a rubbing, put a piece of paper over the object, then use the side of a soft lead pencil to rub over the paper (soft pencils are better than pens for all your work—a pen might smudge or leave a permanent stain). Rubbings are ideal backgrounds for sketching-in details or recording measurements. On the Phyfe chest, Lynch made rubbings of the dovetails, then gauged the angles of the pins and tails with his bevel gauge and protractor. A bevel gauge is good for measuring most angles, but for something like a sloping chair back, he uses a plumb bob. You can, for example, plot the angle of the back by dropping the plumb line from the highest center point of the back, then measuring the distances between the bob's vertical line and the back of the seat rail.

To record the shape of the tool chest's hand-forged handles, Lynch cut two long notches into a sheet of paper so it would slide over the handles and lie flat on the metal backing plate, then made another rubbing. Next, he sketched in the details of the handle and added measurements. Sometimes he unscrews smaller hinges, escutcheons and other hardware, then traces them, but that's not always permitted.

After measuring the back, front, bottom and top in the same meticulous way he did the sides, he concentrated on the chest's special features, like the saw rack fastened to the inside of the lid and the removable set of drawers that fits inside the chest. Since the saw case couldn't be removed from the lid, he had to probe with the saw blades and a bevel gauge tongue to determine the construction of the case. He inserted the probe as far as he could, then measured the penetration. By comparing this measurement with the outside dimensions, he figured the thickness of the walls and the location of interior partitions.

Until we had examined the mahogany drawers in the small cabinet, we had underestimated Phyfe's pride. In most of the chest, the dovetails are fairly large and evenly spaced, but Phyfe had glued 3 in. of solid mahogany to the pine, and dovetails there were tiny and close together. We guessed initially that Phyfe used the mahogany to strengthen the hinges, then cut fine dovetails in the stronger hardwood and larger ones in the weaker pine.

After examining the case's 16 solid mahogany drawers with their turned ivory pulls, we changed our minds. The drawers had delicate dovetails, with pins tapering to less than $\frac{1}{16}$ in. Even on something as mundane as a tool box, Phyfe apparently couldn't resist showing off his skill and added the dovetails for a decorative effect. Of course, that's just a guess, but guessing is part of the fun—it's almost a game that the original makers encourage. Those old guys prided themselves on having all kinds of tricks, many of them unknown to us, and it often seems as if they intentionally left false trails to befuddle those who followed.

While Lynch measures each piece in the same way that he did the tool chest, large carcases are more difficult because of their complex joints, moldings, veneer and decorative carvings. When we measured a Chippendale four-drawer chest at MESDA, for example, we couldn't figure out how the top was attached to the base. We suspected the sides were slip dovetailed to the top, a common technique in Charleston, S.C., where this piece was built, but we couldn't verify it. The joint was invisible, stopped before reaching the top's front edge and hidden at the rear by the case back. Lynch tried to insert a thin knife into the joint, hoping to feel a tenon, nail or dovetail, but the joint was too tight. We couldn't find any sign of a telltale pencil, knife or marking-gauge line that might indicate the kind of joint the mak-

er cut. In cases like this, the owners of the piece may be valuable resources, if they have ever repaired the piece or obtained letters or order forms pertaining to it. We learned that the top had been repaired and a sliding dovetail noted. If you can't find any clues from the owners, you can check other contemporary pieces and come up with an educated guess.

The chest held another mystery. On the dust shelf under the top drawer we found a dovetail groove—its only purpose seemed to be to confuse us. Again, we put ourselves in the old cabinet-maker's boots. In the days before electric thickness planers, we probably wouldn't throw out a surfaced piece either, just because of a miscut groove in a part that wouldn't show. But you wonder if that's the real explanation.

Lynch used several sizes of calipers to measure the width of molding and the thickness of the sides. Since the stiles made it impossible to measure the sides directly, he put his folded carpenter's rule behind the stile against the side and used large calipers to measure both the side and ruler. After measuring the caliper opening, he subtracted the width of the rule to get the thickness of the piece. He used 10-in. dividers to straddle small corner blocks where his ruler wouldn't fit, then measured the distance between points. To record molding profiles, he used a finger-type contour gauge, which looks like a band holding hundreds of tiny, sliding metal strips. When the gauge is gently pushed straight down over the molding cross section, the con-

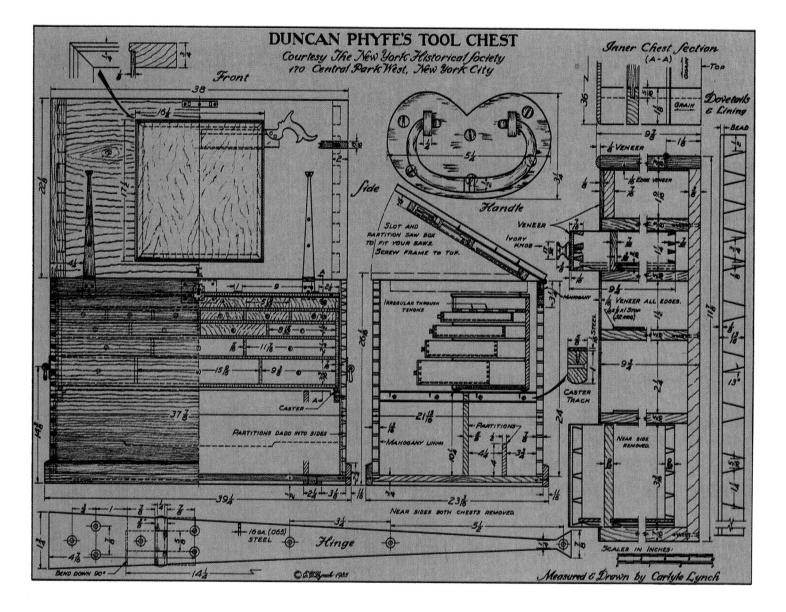

Compiling a materials list

by Jeff O'Hearn

One of the best ways to begin most cabinetry jobs is to invest a little time in studying your construction drawings and compiling a materials list. By sizing each part before you begin work, you'll save time and lumber because you'll be able to cut everything at once. Preparing these lists improves your mind's eye, too—you'll become more adept at dissecting furniture, analyzing joinery and visualizing assembly procedures.

Even though materials lists are fussy, time-consuming work, I've always found they are worth the trouble unless the work is curvilinear or involves many angles in its layout. Your best bet here is to make a full-size drawing on the floor to verify the dimensions, then build directly from the drawing.

For rectilinear work a clearly drawn elevation or front view is a good starting point for developing materials lists, but the most important drawings are the sections drawings, which are imaginery slices through the elevation. You can do most of your figuring with two section drawings—a vertical section showing the front and back faces, and a horizontal section showing what the object looks like from above or below. Drawings of complex pieces may have separate sections wherever the overall profile of the interior parts change.

Organize your materials list in a chart like the one shown above, right. Start anywhere, choose a part, give it a name and call it number one. Is it a vertical or horizontal part? Your vertical section drawing will 'cut through' a part which is on a horizontal plane, and vice versa. For example, you can see the bottom panel of a cabinet in a vertical section. Generally, dimensions are listed in the order thickness/width/length. It's up to you whether you call the depth of the bottom panel the length or the width on your chart,

No.	Pcs.	Part	T	W	L	Material	Machining
1	1	Drawer bottom	$3/16$	$8^{29}/_{32}$	$15^{3}/_{16}$	Mahogany	$3/32$-in. by $3/32$-in. rabbet with bevel at 3 edges.
2	2	Drawer sides	$9/16$	$3^{1}/_{8}$	$9^{1}/_{16}$	Mahogany	Blind dovetails $1/8$-in. from front. Through dovetails at back. Dado for 1.
3	1	Drawer front	$3/8$	$3^{1}/_{8}$	$15^{9}/_{16}$	Mahogany	Blind dovetails at both ends. Mahogany veneer, $1/16$-in. thick. Dovetail for 1.
4	1	Drawer back	$9/32$	$2^{15}/_{16}$	$15^{9}/_{16}$	Mahogany	Through dovetails at both ends.

since the width of the part and the width of the cabinet may be different directions, but there are rules of thumb. If the part is wood or has a face veneer, the length is always in the intended direction of the grain. For a plastic-laminated or painted panel, the length is the larger dimension.

To determine the length of part number one, first visualize the plane of the part, subtract the thicknesses or widths of adjacent parts from the appropriate overall dimension, then add the distance that any joinery extends into the adjacent parts. For example, in the Phyfe tool chest, facing page, the drawer bottoms in the inner cabinet section are shown extending under the drawer backs, and, with a $3/32$-in. tongue, into the $7/16$-in. thick drawer fronts. The drawers are $9^{1}/_{4}$ in. deep, so the width of all the drawer bottoms is $9^{1}/_{4}$ in. minus the $7/16$-in. thickness of the drawer front and its veneer facing plus $3/32$ in. for the tongue. This gives you a total width of $8^{29}/_{32}$ in.

The drawer bottoms similarly fit into both drawer sides, so the length of the middle bottom (largest) drawer is $15^{9}/_{16}$ minus the thickness of the two drawer sides (2 in. by $9/32$ in.) plus the tongues extending into the sides (2 in. by $3/32$ in.). The total works out to $15^{3}/_{16}$ in. In the

machining column, note any joints and edge moldings. The notes should help to clarify the differences between the material list dimensions and the part's final fitting sizes.

Continue with the tool chest's bottom middle drawer and check each of the dimensions, remembering that the process is little more than examining all of the drawings information, and then subtracting thickness and adding joinery distances from the largest relevant dimension.

Proceed in this fashion with each part. When I think that I sized every part, I go back to the drawing and label each part with the number I've assigned to it on the materials list. To distinguish the labels from actual measurements, I circle each one and draw an arrow to the part indicated. If the same part appears in several sections of the drawing, I label it each time. Finally, I go over the drawing again to make sure each part has a circled-number label.

One last tip: Go back through the completed list with someone else. It's easy to make an error or two. □

Jeff O'Hearn is a project engineer for Art Woodworking in Cincinnati and makes sculpture in his basement workshop.

tour of the molding will push the metal strips up different distances. When the gauge completely engulfs the molding, the metal strips will mirror the molding shape.

To record carvings, like the shell on the leg of a Queen Anne dressing table, we used a rubber-based impression material called Coe Flex (Coe Laboratories, Inc., Chicago, Ill. 60658), which is available from many dental supply houses. The material and its catalyst come in toothpaste-type tubes. Mix the two together according to the package directions and trowel the frosting-like stuff over the carving. After it dries (time depends on temperature and humidity), you can peel it off and end up with a mask-like replica of the carving, which can be used to cast a plaster-of-paris model. Exact reproduction is important—no two carv-

ings are alike so you want to preserve each piece's individuality.

Measuring the Phyfe chest took Lynch about five hours. No matter how meticulously he has analyzed the piece, questions linger. "The main problem is: Should I draw it as it is now or as I suspect the maker would have liked it to be if he were working under ideal conditions? I record it as it is, but tell what I think might make it better. Sometimes, though, you can't tell what joinery is involved. You just have to take an educated guess." □

Carlyle Lynch, a designer, cabinetmaker and retired teacher, lives in Broadway, Va. His drawings appear regularly in Fine Woodworking *and are available from Garrett Wade, Lee Valley Tools Ltd. and Woodcraft Supply.*

Building a Chest of Drawers

Joinery and design considerations

by Christian Becksvoort

Anyone who has worked with wood knows that building a piece of furniture involves a series of decisions, from choice of wood, to design and construction details, to selecting the final finish. Even if you build identical pieces over a period of years, you'll probably find yourself making small changes each time—perfecting the proportions, or perhaps just exploring different joineries. In this article, I'll discuss the range of decisions and processes involved in designing and building a chest of drawers, as well as presenting some of the methods that I employ.

One of the first things to consider in designing a chest—and perhaps the most subjective part of design—is the chest's overall appearance. You should style the piece to suit your tastes or to fit into the decor of the room the chest will inhabit. Since I live near one of the last two Shaker communities and have restored several original Shaker pieces, my designs show the strong influence of their simple, unadorned style. I prefer my furniture to

By manipulating the design, construction, and materials, a chest of drawers can be built for any purpose or to fit into any decor. The trim lines of the author's cherrywood chest, left, display the usual austerity of the Shaker style. Inside the chest, below left, web frames support the drawers and add rigidity to the carcase. A dust panel fitted into the bottom frame keeps the chest clean inside. The finished back, below right, is built like a door and permanently fixed to the edges of the carcase, allowing the chest of drawers to be freestanding.

From *Fine Woodworking* magazine (January 1988) 68:36-40

have clean, functional lines that are more at home in a wide spectrum of settings than avant-garde or strictly traditional forms. One nice thing about Shaker-based designs is that you can begin with a basic carcase, then manipulate details like tops, moldings and bases for different effects. Moreover, Shaker construction techniques are sound and durable, yet not so involved that a novice can't employ them.

I begin a chest design by considering what will be stored in it, since the number and size of drawers will determine the chest's overall size. Bulky items, like clothes, will require deep drawers, while smaller items will do well in a larger number of shallow drawers. Casepieces vary widely in their approach to drawer storage. Most chests, however, have drawers of graduated depth, with the deepest drawers at the bottom, the shallowest at the top. This serves to anchor the case visually and keeps the heaviest objects in the lower drawers. Instead of a single shallow drawer at the top of the case, Shaker cabinetmakers often used a pair of drawers, separated by a vertical divider.

Storage capacity and where the chest will be—freestanding, against a wall, at the foot of a bed—will dictate the overall size of the case and its dimensions. Proper proportions are important to the success of a chest design. If you aren't confident about what dimensions to use, measure a piece similar to the one you want to build or find a successful design in a book and go from there. One worthwhile option is to rely on the standard dimensions for furnishings in *Architectural Graphic Standards* by Ramsey and Sleeper (John Wiley & Sons, Inc., 605 Third Ave., New York, N.Y. 10158). The volume costs more than $100, but most larger libraries have a copy. If you need the size of an average dresser, school chair, or even a tuba, it's all there in 750 invaluable pages. Another useful source for design standards is *Human Factors Design Handbook* by Wesley E. Woodson (McGraw-Hill, Inc., 1221 Ave. of the Americas, New York, N.Y. 10020).

When design standards don't suggest useful solutions, you'll have to dimension the piece. Sketching on note pads is a good way to do this. If you are more comfortable with scale or even full-size drawings, by all means use them. They often help uncover tricky details you might otherwise overlook. As a general rule, square shapes don't work well visually for chests—they appear monolithic and squat. However, a chest with a relatively squarish front—that is as wide as it is tall—can still look fine, as long as its depth is less than about a third of its height. Rectangular shapes, for both the chest's front and side views, are far more pleasing than squares. And rectangles based on the golden mean are an excellent starting place. The golden mean is the oldest and most widely understood proportioning method and can be expressed as a simple ratio: 5 to 8. Thus, a golden rectangle is one whose short side measures 1.0 to the long side's 1.6.

In instances where a chest's frontal dimensions aren't fixed by spacial constraints, it makes sense to build proportions around drawer depth. Generally, a drawer for clothes should be 16 in. to 20 in. deep and about 10 in. to 12 in. high. A deeper drawer has two drawbacks: you have to take an awkward step back to open it fully; and the carcase will have to be unpleasingly deep to accommodate the drawers. Very shallow drawers, say less than 14 in., are also a problem. It's too easy to accidentally pull them entirely out of the case, dumping the contents on the floor. Unless there's a concrete reason to do so, such as having to store large sheets of paper flat, I don't alter basic drawer dimensions much.

A case can be as wide as it needs to be, but drawers themselves shouldn't be much wider than 40 in.; otherwise they tend to twist in the opening and bind. Wide cases can have two side-by-side drawers with a vertical divider between them.

In casework, as in any furniture, the basic construction of the carcase affects both the look and the function of the piece. As is the case in designing anything, there are many paths leading to the same point. Your choice of joinery for instance, will depend on your level of skill or the amount of time you want to spend. Material selection also plays a role in joinery methods. Although you may choose to use flat, dimensionally stable plywood, the following discussion of joinery will focus on solid-wood methods, which I prefer. Once its movement is understood and allowed for, the advantages of solid-wood joinery and grain selection far outweigh the drawbacks, in my opinion.

All of the Shaker casework, and virtually all of the 19th-century furniture I've worked with, is constructed in one of two ways, with solid-wood carcase sides or by solid-wood panels let into frames. I use both methods, but I'll focus here on what I call slab-sided construction. (For more on frame and panel Shaker construction, see pages 70-76.) Figure 1 shows the basic anatomy of a solid-wood chest of drawers. The construction is really quite simple, and once you've decided on the design of your chest, you have only to select the joinery appropriate to the material and details you wish to employ.

Although the Post-Modern design movement has revived interest in the use of architectural details and moldings on furniture, I prefer relatively unadorned designs. Still, a simple carcase lends itself to a variety of subtle details. To a large extent, these details will determine the kind of joinery you use to assemble the carcase.

I prefer to join the top with dovetails, because they are strong and decorative. But they aren't absolutely necessary and there are several other options, as shown in figure 1A. The easiest, perhaps, is the butt joint. When it's screwed and plugged or doweled, it's more than strong enough to properly join the case together. The rabbet joint is slightly more work, and if planned correctly, it can be screwed from the side. A splined-miter joint, although strong, is tricky to cut if the panels are even slightly warped. Another more contemporary-looking top joint is what I call a bookcase top, where the carcase sides extend beyond the top, which is let into the sides with a dado, a rabbet and groove, or if you're ambitious, a sliding dovetail.

Moldings can define edges and corners, crown or "set off" tops, break up monotonous surfaces, or cover up dowel and screw holes (see figure 1B). Further, even a simple cove molding can define the top of the case, without giving it the look of a period piece. A molding carried around the top edge of the carcase is another design option. Obviously, this introduces cross-grain construction—the carcase side will shrink and swell, eventually loosening the molding. I've yet to see an old chest that hasn't succumbed to this problem. So if you choose to use a molding, you'll have to live with it. I glue the miter and about the first 1½ in. of the moldings, and nail the rest with brads or finish nails. The nails allow some wood movement. Another way of having a molded top without worrying about it falling off is to build an applied top. Attach the top anyway you choose, such as with blind dowels or tenons. In any case, there's no cross-grain problem since the top moves in the same direction as the carcase sides.

Deciding on the base presents another series of choices and figure 1C illustrates some options. A dovetailed case can sit directly on the floor, with or without a molding at the bottom edge. This is neat, since you don't have to dust under the case, but it can look heavy and the chest won't sit flat on an uneven

Fig. 1: Chest-of-drawers design options

A. Joinery options

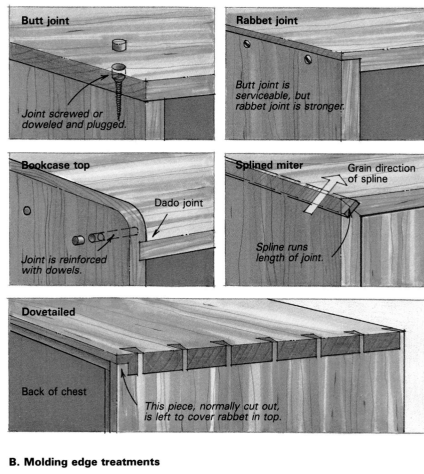

Butt joint

Joint screwed or doweled and plugged.

Rabbet joint

Butt joint is serviceable, but rabbet joint is stronger.

Bookcase top

Joint is reinforced with dowels.

Dado joint

Splined miter

Grain direction of spline

Spline runs length of joint.

Dovetailed

Back of chest

This piece, normally cut out, is left to cover rabbet in top.

B. Molding edge treatments

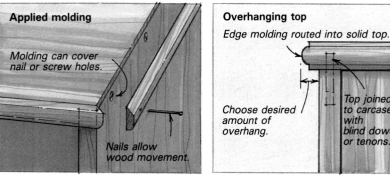

Applied molding

Molding can cover nail or screw holes.

Nails allow wood movement.

Overhanging top

Edge molding routed into solid top.

Choose desired amount of overhang.

Top joined to carcase with blind dowels or tenons.

C. Base options

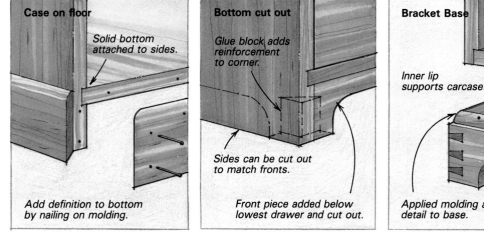

Case on floor

Solid bottom attached to sides.

Add definition to bottom by nailing on molding.

Bottom cut out

Glue block adds reinforcement to corner.

Sides can be cut out to match fronts.

Front piece added below lowest drawer and cut out.

Bracket Base

Inner lip supports carcase.

Applied molding adds detail to base.

Plinth

Carcase overhangs plinth.

Blocks attached to bottom help locate case on plinth.

Simple frame construction

D. Drawer-mounting options

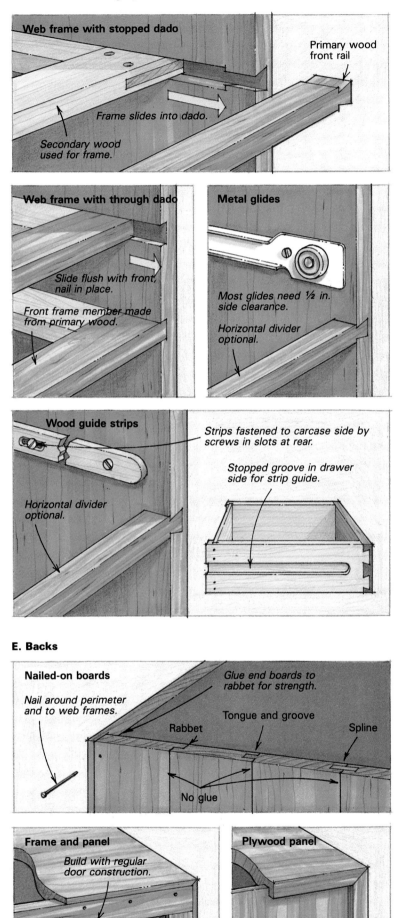

Web frame with stopped dado

Primary wood front rail

Frame slides into dado.

Secondary wood used for frame.

Web frame with through dado

Slide flush with front, nail in place.

Front frame member made from primary wood.

Metal glides

Most glides need ½ in. side clearance.

Horizontal divider optional.

Wood guide strips

Strips fastened to carcase side by screws in slots at rear.

Stopped groove in drawer side for strip guide.

Horizontal divider optional.

E. Backs

Nailed-on boards

Nail around perimeter and to web frames.

Glue end boards to rabbet for strength.

Tongue and groove

Rabbet

Spline

No glue

Frame and panel

Build with regular door construction.

Nail at edges.

Plywood panel

Thin plywood captured in dado in all four sides.

floor. To add visual lightness, you can raise the case a few inches off the floor using any of several methods. One easy-to-make raised base is the plinth, which is simply a frame slightly smaller than the footprint of the case bottom and 3 in. to 5 in. high. The plinth is a good contemporary treatment that would probably go nicely with a bookcase top. Another way is to shape cutouts at the front and/or sides of the chest. In this case, a web frame or solid bottom of the carcase will have to be joined to the sides using one of the joints suitable for a bookcase top. Besides giving the chest some visual lightness, shaped feet also raise the bottom drawer so it won't drag on the floor upon opening. The most involved base treatment I use is the traditional bracket base. Bracket feet suffer from one major drawback—the back feet are bracketed only on one side, and pulling the chest across the floor can easily break them off.

I start building a chest by cutting and gluing up panels for the top and sides (and bottom, depending on the base). Once the glued-up sides and top panels are dry, I rip them to width. To cut the carcase sides to length, I usually clamp them together and cut both at once on the radial-arm saw. These cuts must be absolutely square. Checking for squareness along each step of the way is essential as minor errors early in the construction process tend to accumulate and cause real headaches later.

Lay out the interior of the carcase by clamping the two sides together so that all the edges are flush, and mark the positions of the drawers across the front edges. To figure vertical drawer spacing, first calculate the available drawer space—the total inside measurement of the carcase minus reveal at the top, width of the drawer rails and any applied moldings. Now divide this by the number of drawers to get an average drawer height. If you want the drawers to be evenly graduated from top to bottom, say in 1-in. increments, and you have an uneven number of drawers, figure the middle drawer will be the average height; each drawer above it will be 1 in. smaller than the one below it; and each drawer below it will be 1 in. larger than the one above it. If you have an even number of drawers, add ½ in. to the average drawer height for the drawer just below center and 1 in. to each drawer below it; subtract ½ in. from the average for the drawer just above center and 1 in. from every drawer above it.

Before assembling the basic carcase, you must decide how the drawers will be supported and what they will ride on (figure 1D). Then, prepare the inside of the case accordingly. Very early or primitive chests often had solid-board dividers or bottoms between drawers. Later, light wooden web frames let into the carcase were developed. These support each drawer and add stiffness to the carcase without excess weight. Another all-wood method involves mounting guide strips inside the case that ride in grooves cut into the drawer sides. This works well on banks of small drawers when you don't want to lose drawer height to all those web frames. But the drawer sides must be ⅜ in. or thicker to accept the groove.

For fully extending drawers, such as file cabinets, you'll probably want to use metal drawer glides. These come in many styles and sizes (available from Grant Hardware Co., High Street, West Nyack, N.Y. 10994-0600 or Accuride, 12311 S. Shoemaker Ave., Santa Fe Springs, Calif. 90670). They're strong and easy to mount, but most require ½-in. clearance between the carcase and drawer, so drawer fronts must be wider than the drawers to cover the gap.

If you choose to use web frames (the method I prefer), you'll need to cut the dadoes before assembly. You can use a dado blade on the table or radial-arm saw, but if the sides have a slight

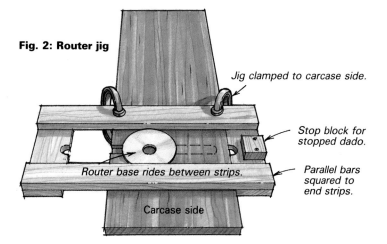

Fig. 2: Router jig

Jig clamped to carcase side.

Stop block for stopped dado.

Router base rides between strips.

Parallel bars squared to end strips.

Carcase side

warp and won't lay flat, cut them by hand or with a router to ensure a consistent depth. For the router method, I made a jig with two parallel bars, spaced the width of the router base and about 30 in. long (see figure 2). The jig is clamped up square to the carcase side and a ¾-in. bit ploughs a groove for the web frame at each location. The dado cuts can either be all the way across or stopped ½ in. to ¾ in. shy of the front edge to allow the fitting of a drawer rail front strip, which I prefer.

Web frames can be four-piece assemblies, but on wider chests, a fifth center member adds stiffness to the carcase. Frames, as well as other interior parts, can be made of a secondary wood, such as poplar or pine. Measure the depth of the frame inside the carcase to the front edge, or to the stopped dado if you add the dovetailed primary-wood drawer rail across the front, as detailed in figure 1D. I mortise and tenon the joints, then glue and pin the frames for strength. Set the case on its back and cut, dovetail, and glue these into place. I prefer half-blind dovetails for a cleaner look on the side of the case, although through dovetails are acceptable and easier to cut. An easier option is to run through-dadoes across the sides and use primary wood for the front members of the frames.

High-style period pieces that have web frames are often fitted with dust panels, which are thin panels let into grooves in the web frames. The purpose of these dust panels is twofold: to keep clothing from getting tangled in adjacent drawers and to provide a barrier against dust. Some makers still use these dust panels, but I find them unnecessary. If I use a web frame, I do, however, install a dust panel for the carcase bottom.

Before the carcase is assembled, you need to decide on the kind of back it will have (figure 1E). Traditional chest backs consist of individual boards (secondary wood is fine) joined together, let into a rabbet and nailed in place. A spline joint is perhaps the best way to join the individual boards since it's easy to make and locks the boards against misalignment in both planes. Under no circumstances should the back boards be glued to each other—the whole idea is to let the boards move. Each board is simply nailed to the top, all web frames and bottom, and the nails are set. Freestanding pieces can have a frame-and-panel back built like a cabinet door out of primary wood and fit into the back rabbet. Panels can be flush, recessed or raised. A frame-and-panel back not only looks much better, but gives the case tremendous strength against racking.

Some notes on assembly—After all the dadoes are in the right places and of equal depth and web frames are identical in length, and square, the case should be dry clamped and tested for square. This is vital. If it's out of square, the drawers will be a pain to fit. Now's the time to find out. Check for square by measuring diagonally from the top left to the bottom right corner and vice versa: The readings should be identical. If not, shift or clamp the "longer" dimension until they are. Sight across all the web frames to check for a warped case. This is seldom a problem, unless the top panel is severely warped.

To install the frames, turn the case back side up and slide each frame into its pair of dadoes. Drive and set a few finishing nails (6d if you're using ¾-in. stock) at a steep angle through the frame into the case. Check the angle carefully, lest the nails come out the other side of the frame or, worse yet, out the side of the case. Even though the frame grain runs perpendicular to the case side, wood movement is no problem, since the nails allow for adequate movement. Purists who disdain the use of nails might use a sliding-dovetail joint instead. I have no problem with nails since they're found in almost all the traditional furniture I've examined.

I won't go into detail about drawer construction here; for that, I suggest you refer to *FWW on Things to Make*, pp. 20-24. However, I'd like to add a few of my own thoughts. First, I fit my drawer sides directly to the opening, making them about ⅜ in. shorter than the case depth. I cut the two sides and front first, then run grooves ¼ in. to ½ in. above the bottom edge to allow room for half a dovetail below the groove. Then I plane 1⁄32 in. from the bottom edge of the drawer front to keep it from dragging on the drawer rail. I lay out the dovetails on the sides with half dovetails, top and bottom, and as many full dovetails as necessary in between. Avoid cutting one directly on the groove for the drawer bottom—that will leave a hole in the front. When the joints are cut, glued and assembled, measure the diagonals to check for square. After sanding, the bottom can be fitted. Make sure the grain runs side-to-side; if it runs front-to-back, any expansion of the bottom forces out the sides, weakens the joints and binds the drawer.

One trick sometimes found on old pieces is to let the bottom act as a drawer stop. The bottom extends ⅜ in. to ½ in. beyond the drawer, so it hits the case back. When the drawer is fitted, the bottom is trimmed until the front is flush. Seasonal moisture changes that cause the case sides to expand and contract will also make the drawer bottom expand and contract, and, in theory at least, the drawer fronts remain flush. Some makers install stops on the web frames that hit the inside top or bottom edges of each drawer, keeping it flush with the case front despite carcase expansion and contraction.

A final word on finishing: I like to belt sand with 120-grit and 150-grit, then vibrate to 220-grit and 320-grit, followed by hand-sanding with 320-grit and 600-grit. On some surfaces, I finish-scrape using my secret weapon: single-edge razor blades (available in boxes of 100 from most paint or hardware stores). Those who don't care for the ritual of sharpening scrapers will find these blades a real boon. They're tremendously sharp and stay that way long enough to do one or two sides. They can then be tossed out or saved as glue scrapers. Although I use an oil finish, the finish you use is not as important as *how* you finish. All exposed surfaces, top and bottom, inside and out, must be finished, because uneven moisture absorption causes uneven wood movement and warping. Many antiques were not finished inside, yet they were seldom built in the Northeast and shipped to the Southwest, nor were they exposed to the forced-air heating common in modern homes. ☐

Christian Becksvoort is a professional furnituremaker. He lives in New Gloucester, Maine.

Holding the Notes

Building an adjustable music stand

by Lance Patterson

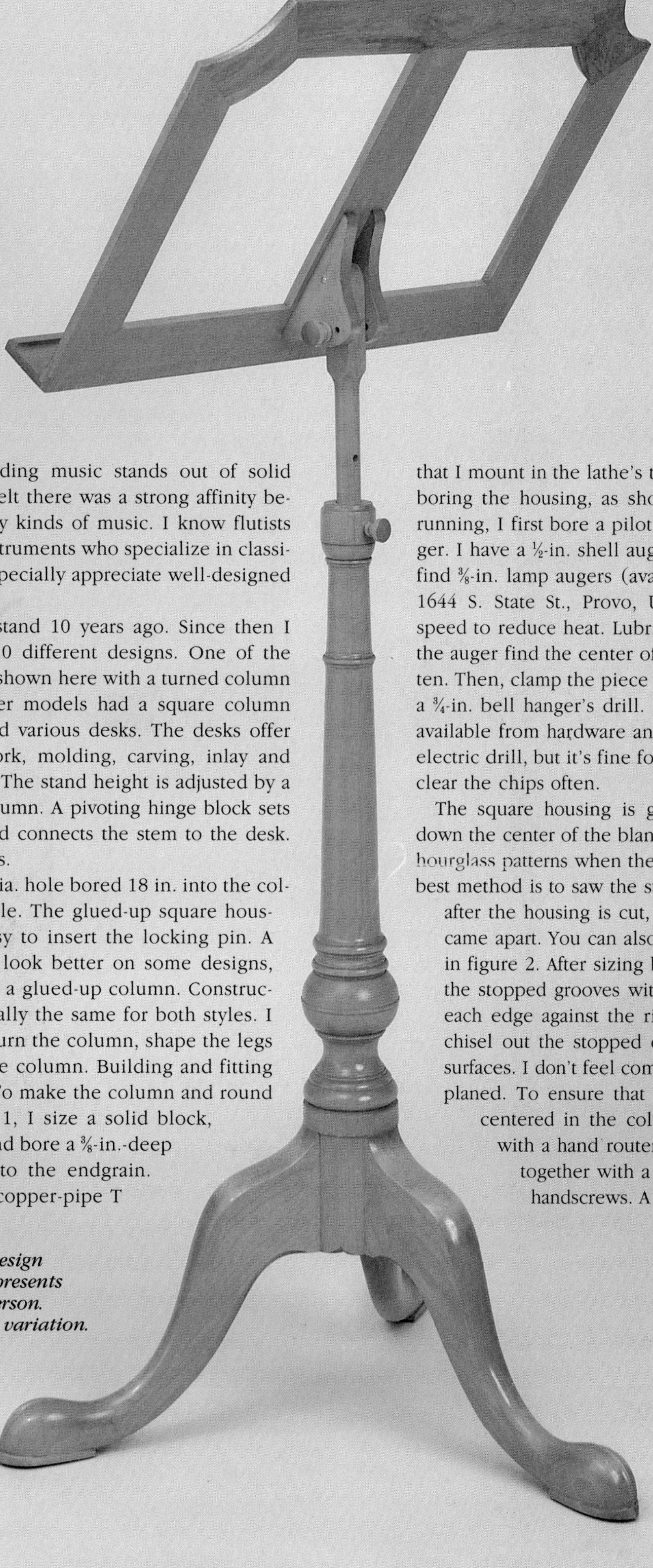

I like the idea of building music stands out of solid wood. I have always felt there was a strong affinity between wood and many kinds of music. I know flutists and players of stringed instruments who specialize in classical and chamber music especially appreciate well-designed solid-wood stands.

I built my first music stand 10 years ago. Since then I have built 23 stands in 10 different designs. One of the most popular is the stand shown here with a turned column and dovetailed legs. Other models had a square column with cross-lapped legs and various desks. The desks offer many possibilities—fretwork, molding, carving, inlay and the use of figured woods. The stand height is adjusted by a stem that slides in the column. A pivoting hinge block sets the work surface angle and connects the stem to the desk. Pegs lock both adjustments.

The housing is a ¾-in.-dia. hole bored 18 in. into the column, or a ¾-in.-square hole. The glued-up square housing and stem make it easy to insert the locking pin. A round housing and stem look better on some designs, though, and don't require a glued-up column. Construction procedures are basically the same for both styles. I cut or bore the housing, turn the column, shape the legs and dovetail them into the column. Building and fitting the desk is the last step. To make the column and round housing shown in figure 1, I size a solid block, 24½ in. by 3 in. by 3 in., and bore a ⅜-in.-deep ¾-in.-dia. seating hole into the endgrain. The seating hole fits the copper-pipe T

Music stands offer many design possibilities. This stand represents one design by author Patterson. The plan on p. 19 shows a variation.

that I mount in the lathe's tool rest as a hollow tailstock for boring the housing, as shown in figure 1. With the lathe running, I first bore a pilot hole with a hand-held shell auger. I have a ½-in. shell auger, but you may only be able to find ⅜-in. lamp augers (available from Craft Supplies USA, 1644 S. State St., Provo, Utah 84601). Use a fairly slow speed to reduce heat. Lubricate the wood with paraffin, let the auger find the center of rotation and clear the chips often. Then, clamp the piece in a vise and ream the hole with a ¾-in. bell hanger's drill. Electricians use the 18-in. drill, available from hardware and industrial supply stores, in an electric drill, but it's fine for reaming in a hand brace if you clear the chips often.

The square housing is glued up. The joint should run down the center of the blank to avoid creating elliptical and hourglass patterns when the bulbous shapes are turned. The best method is to saw the stock down the middle and then, after the housing is cut, glue it back together the way it came apart. You can also slip-match the pieces as shown in figure 2. After sizing both halves of the column, I cut the stopped grooves with a dado set and tablesaw. Run each edge against the rip fence to center the cut, then chisel out the stopped ends. Now, plane the glue-joint surfaces. I don't feel comfortable unless the joint is hand-planed. To ensure that the two grooves form a square centered in the column, I true and equalize them with a hand router plane before gluing the halves together with a careful amount of glue and five handscrews. A scrap of square stock fit into the

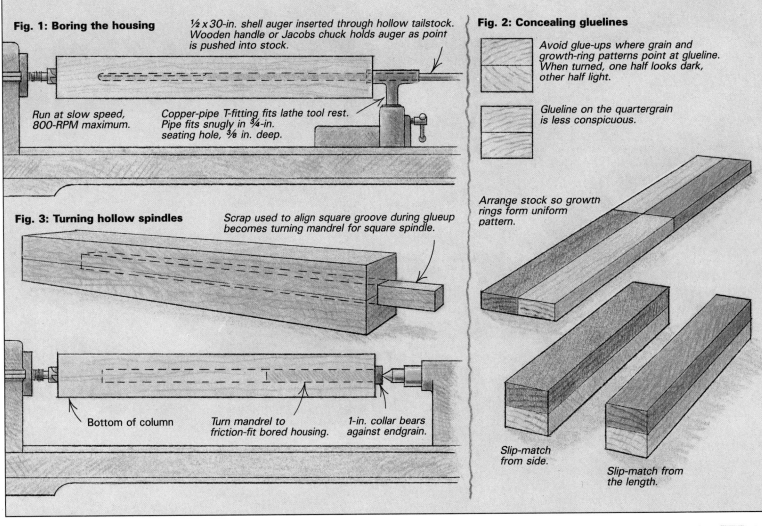

Fig. 1: Boring the housing

½ x 30-in. shell auger inserted through hollow tailstock. Wooden handle or Jacobs chuck holds auger as point is pushed into stock.

Run at slow speed, 800-RPM maximum.

Copper-pipe T-fitting fits lathe tool rest. Pipe fits snugly in ¾-in. seating hole, ⅝ in. deep.

Fig. 2: Concealing gluelines

Avoid glue-ups where grain and growth-ring patterns point at glueline. When turned, one half looks dark, other half light.

Glueline on the quartergrain is less conspicuous.

Arrange stock so growth rings form uniform pattern.

Slip-match from side.

Slip-match from the length.

Fig. 3: Turning hollow spindles

Scrap used to align square groove during glueup becomes turning mandrel for square spindle.

Bottom of column

Turn mandrel to friction-fit bored housing.

1-in. collar bears against endgrain.

The dovetails on the legs are cut entirely by hand. Lay out the shoulders with a marking gauge, then clamp the leg on its side and rough-saw the shoulder, above, staying ¹⁄₁₆ in. from the line. The wood strip clipped to the saw acts as a depth stop. Next, cut

the dovetail slope with a sharp chisel running against a 6-1 angled block, center. Chisel away the waste in two or three steps until you can pare right off the block. Finally, shoot the shoulder to the gauge line with a small plane, right.

housing aligns the pieces during glueup. The scrap piece is also good for wiping glue from the housing.

The centered hole means the blanks must be mounted on a mandrel to be turned. For the bored housing, I turn an 8-in. wooden plug to fit the hole as shown. I plug the square housing with the alignment scrap from the glueup, wedging it to eliminate slop. I cut the other end of the blank to length and turn the column. The cylinder where the legs join the column must be perfectly straight. Check it with a straightedge. If the walls are either hollow or bulbous, the shoulders of the leg joints won't fit well. Also, note how the cylinder profile steps out ³⁄₃₂ in. This step, which is almost always present on traditional work, hides

any discrepancies at the top of the leg-to-column joint.

To shape the legs, cut a ⅛-in.-thick plywood pattern of their side profile, including the dovetail. For strength, the grain should run the length of the leg. I fair the legs with a #49 or #50 patternmakers' rasp (available from Jamestown Distributors, 28 Narragansett Ave., P.O. Box 348, Providence, R.I. 02835). If you clamp the legs together with a large C-clamp that can be swung out of the way, you can reach all the edges. The endgrain at the foot and joint are squared with a smooth plane.

The housed dovetail on this stand can easily be cut, as shown in the picture series, with only handtools—dividers, marking gauge, chisels, dovetail saw, carving gouge, a 6-1 chisel block

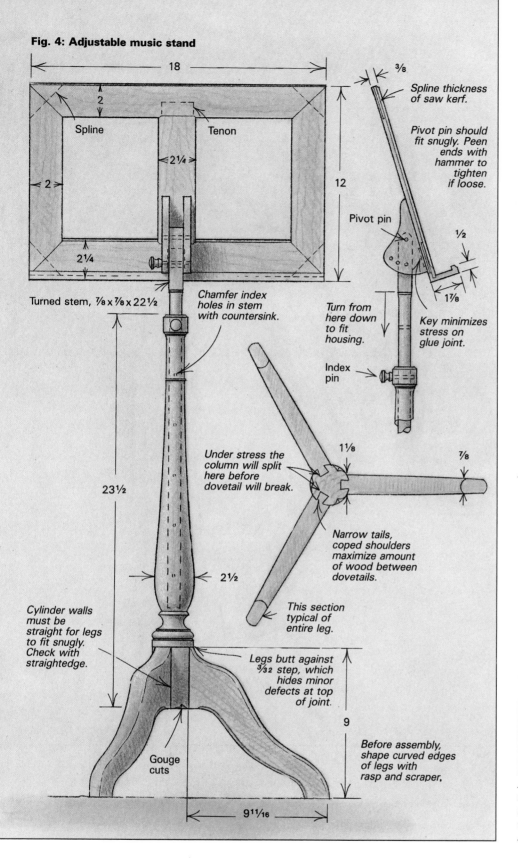

Fig. 4: Adjustable music stand

18

2

2

Spline

Tenon

2¼

2¼

2¼

12

Turned stem, ⅞ x ⅞ x 22½

Chamfer index holes in stem with countersink.

⅜

Spline thickness of saw kerf.

Pivot pin should fit snugly. Peen ends with hammer to tighten if loose.

Pivot pin

Turn from here down to fit housing.

Key minimizes stress on glue joint.

½

1⅛

Index pin

23½

Under stress the column will split here before dovetail will break.

1⅛

⅞

Narrow tails, coped shoulders maximize amount of wood between dovetails.

This section typical of entire leg.

2½

Cylinder walls must be straight for legs to fit snugly. Check with straightedge.

Legs butt against ³⁄₃₂ step, which hides minor defects at top of joint.

9

Gouge cuts

Before assembly, shape curved edges of legs with rasp and scraper.

9¹¹⁄₁₆

Coping the shoulders requires careful paring. Line up a pattern of the column base with the top and bottom shoulders of the dovetail and trace the curve, top. Carve to the line with a carving gouge.

After sawing and coping the shoulder at the top of the dovetail, hold the leg against the cylinder, align the centerline of the leg with that of the housing and trace the tail. Shaped blocks secure column in vise.

and a shoulder plane. Cut the tails first and trace them to lay out the housings. Saw ¹⁄₁₆-in. on the waste side of the lines, then cut the slope of the tail by paring with a chisel guided by an angled block. Plane to the line and repeat the process on the other side.

For small cylinders, it's always better to cope the legs rather than make flats on the cylinder, since this leaves more wood between the tails and makes for a stronger stand. To cope the shoulder you'll need a file-folder cardboard template that's the same diameter as the base of the column. Make a mark every 120° to indicate leg locations. Line up the cardboard circle with

the shoulders at the top and bottom of the leg and trace the curve. Pare to the line with a carving gouge (or an in-cannel firmer gouge). Finally, saw and cope the shoulder at the top of the dovetails. Don't worry if you cut too deeply on the insides of the shoulder since these aren't important glue surfaces and the step will hide them. If you really mess up, set your marking gauge a bit deeper, re-mark the shoulders and try again. I usually plane the straight taper on the legs right after cutting the tail. Use a marking gauge to set the finished thickness of the foot and plane to the lines. To hold the leg, cut a hole the shape of the leg

After remounting the column on the lathe, finish laying out the joint with a post scribe. The scribe slides on the lathe bed and draws housing lines parallel to the centerline of the column.

Use a backsaw to cut just inside the layout lines of the dovetail housing, left, then pare to the lines with a sharp chisel. The waste will come out in long strips. Once the leg goes in an inch or so, use the first part of the joint to guide the chisel to the full length of the housing, right.

If necessary, you can secure one leg in a bench vise and use a clamp as shown to pull the shoulders tight on the tails.

into ¼-in.- to ½-in.-thick plywood and clamp the sheet to a bench.

Before laying out the dovetail housings, remember that it's important, aesthetically, that the growth-ring patterns of the column be symmetrical to the front legs, and thus centered on the back leg, as shown in the plan. Use your circular pattern to mark out the centers of the housings, and draw straight lines on the endgrain from these marks to the spur center mark. To mark out the dovetails, hold the tail you just cut on the leg against the bottom of the cylinder, align the leg's centerline with the housing centerline and trace the tail with a sharp pencil. Letter each leg and housing, so you can match them up later. To extend these marks, the borders of the housing, down the column to the step, put the piece back on the lathe and set up a post scribe. The scribe rides on the lathe bed, holding a pencil horizontally, so the housing will be parallel to the column's centerline and the legs will fit properly.

When you cut the housing, saw as far as you can, just leaving the layout lines. Chisel out the waste. There's no need for drilling here, since the wood comes out in long pieces and the main glue surfaces are the sides (the depth is less important). To fit the joint, pare to the pencil lines and try the leg. You can see where you need to pare by how the shoulders fit. The leg should go in all the way with just hand pressure.

If the joint is loose at the top, shim the housing with a piece of veneer. A rag stuffed in the housing provides enough pressure to clamp the shim while the glue is drying. The shim gives you a second chance and will not affect the strength of the joint. Use as many clamps as you need to pull the joint tight at glueup. Finally, fair the top of the legs to the column with rasp and cabinet scraper, and cut the decorative chamfers on the bottom of the column by tapping a carving gouge into the end of the column at about 45° to the cylinder sides. Aim toward the center point, or where it would be if extended out from the endgrain.

The desk on this music stand is a rectangular frame with one vertical muntin, to which the ledge and hinge-block are joined. On this desk the frame is mitered and splined, and the muntin is mortised and tenoned into it. You could also use a half-lap joint for the muntin and half-lap miter at the corners. Join the muntin to the top and bottom rails first, since the muntin determines the length of the stiles. The shoulders of the joints are cut-in to miter the cove molding that runs around all the front edges. This means you have to cut the molding on the inside edges of the rails and stiles and on the muntin first, in order to determine the size of the miter and depth of the shoulders. I use chisel blocks clamped to the stock to help cut the miters and rail shoulders. I chop the mortises with a proper ⅛-in. mortise chisel. The corner miters are cut next. I use a shooting board, always clamping each piece to the board. I glue the muntin in, then fit the stiles. After the frame is glued up, the splines are added and the cove molded on the outside front edges. The lower back edge of the frame is rabbeted on the tablesaw to form a tongue that will fit in a groove in the desk's ledge as shown.

The hinge block is next. I start with 1¾-in. stock and cut the ¾-in.-wide by 2-in.-deep groove in the middle of the block with a dado head. For safety, I use wood at least 12 in. long, dadoing two blocks at a time. The stock for the stem is thicknessed to fit the dado groove. Then the lower 19 in. of the stem is planed or turned, depending on the housing you're using, to fit into the column. I drill the ³⁄₁₆-in. pivot-pin hole and the indexing hole in the top end of the stem about 1½ in. apart. These holes will be guides for drilling the hinge block, to ensure that the indexing holes line up.

Draw a line on one face of the hinge-block blank showing the

To ensure that the stem and hinge are properly aligned, use the ³⁄₁₆-in.-dia. hole bored in the stem as a guide for drilling the hinge blank. A screw or pin inserted through the hinge and the stem holds the pieces together while the holes are bored.

depth of the groove. Trace a side-view pattern on this face, lining up on the groove depth line. Also mark the pivot point, then drill the pivot-pin hole on a drill press. A piece of scrap wood fit tightly in the groove helps prevent splintering as the drill goes through. To drill the indexing holes in the hinge block, the stem is lined up against the outside face of the hinge blank, and the pivot pin or a screw is inserted while the holes are drilled through the stem index hole into the hinge block.

I finish the hinge block by bandsawing the side profile, plan- ing the joint and fairing the bandsaw marks from the curves with a rasp and cabinet scraper. To mechanically protect the joint be- tween the back of the desk and the hinge block, I chisel recesses into both pieces for a small wooden key, 1⅛ in. long by 1 in. wide by ¼ in. high, and glue the block and key to the desk.

The pivot pin is a plain ³⁄₁₆-in.-dia. brass rod, but I add a wood- en knob to the brass for the index pin. I run a ¼-in. by 20 die on the pin for about ½ in. to cut light threads in the metal. Then, with a little epoxy added, I screw the pin into a ³⁄₁₆-in.-dia. hole in the wood knob blank. I then turn the knob with the pin mounted in a Jacobs chuck on the lathe.

A V-block is needed for drilling the column and stem for the height adjustment. I clamp the V-block to the table with the V centered under the bit. The column should be clamped with the back leg vertical while you're drilling the ³⁄₁₆-in. hole at the top of the column. The hole doesn't need to go all the way through, but it should go into the other side a little.

To ensure an accurate alignment on the height adjustment, the stem is drilled inside its housing. I put a piece of rod or a ³⁄₁₆-in. chainsaw file through the pivot-pin hole, to help line up the front of the stem with the front of the pedestal. (The chain- saw file is useful if any holes need to be relieved later for the index pins to slide easily.) I drill the first hole with the stem all the way in. After drilling the first hole, I put a pencil mark on the stem at the point where it leaves the housing. Then I mark

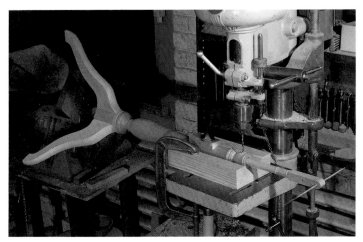

The stem is bored after being inserted into the housing, which is clamped in a V-block on the drill-press table. The chainsaw file in the pivot-pin hole aligns holes with the front of the pedestal.

every 3 in. down the stem from this mark. I drill another hole every time the alignment marks reach the top of the housing. The orientation should be checked each time by sighting the rod through the pivot-pin hole.

There is nothing special about the finishing. I often use shellac and/or an oil finish. These music stands are a good meeting place for the creativity of the musician and the cabinetmaker. The artful musician's medium is sound, using instruments to produce sounds that can, as if by magic, attract and move the emotions and spirit of those who hear them. Artful cabinetmakers use wood and tools to build functional forms that attract our eyes and hands, and stir up good and positive feelings about humanity. □

Lance Patterson is a cabinetmaker and shop instructor at the North Bennet Street School in Boston, Mass.

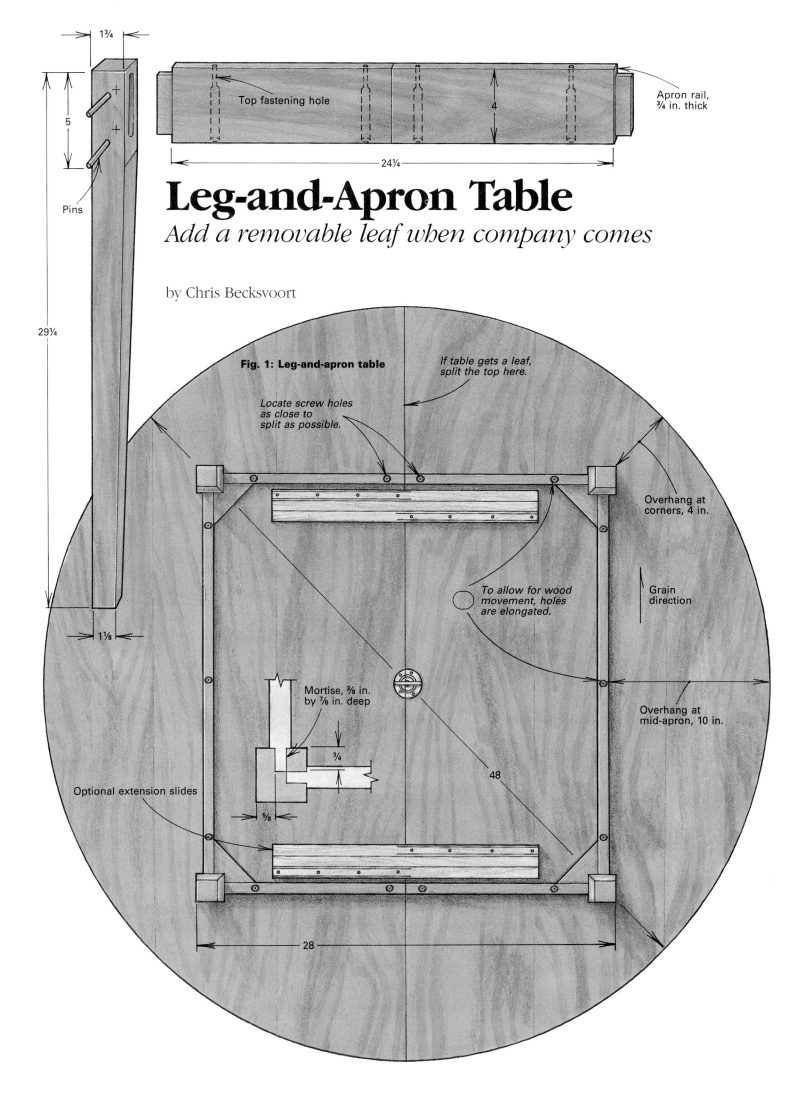

1¾

5

Pins

29¼

1⅛

Top fastening hole

4

Apron rail,
¾ in. thick

24¼

Leg-and-Apron Table
Add a removable leaf when company comes

by Chris Becksvoort

Fig. 1: Leg-and-apron table

*If table gets a leaf,
split the top here.*

*Locate screw holes
as close to
split as possible.*

Overhang at
corners, 4 in.

*To allow for wood
movement, holes
are elongated.*

Grain
direction

Overhang at
mid-apron, 10 in.

Mortise, ⅜ in.
by ⅞ in. deep

¾

48

Optional extension slides

⅝

28

I designed this round table to solve a space problem in a tiny apartment my wife and I once shared. Our dining room was a niche surrounded by three walls, leaving far too little space for a rectangular table. A round tabletop on a square leg-and-apron base promised the most usable surface area in the least floor space. I've since built about 30 of these tables, some with up to three removable leaves that expand the top to accommodate more people. Over the years, I've refined the details a little, but the table remains a straightforward piece you can build with minimal tools in a couple days.

The tabletop is 48 in. in diameter, which will seat four comfortably or six in a pinch if you don't wish to add a leaf. You can scale the top and base up or down slightly, but wholesale departure from the dimensions given isn't advisable. The plans call for a 24-in. space between the legs—plenty of room for knees and legs. For a smaller top, you could move the legs a little closer together, but if you scale the top up and widen the leg stance accordingly, spacing greater than about 26 in. will look awkward. Leg spacing is complicated by the fact that a round top overhangs a square base unevenly. As a result, when the apron is viewed from straight on, the table appears to be all overhang; when viewed diagonally, it appears to have too little overhang. By experimenting with a mock-up, I arrived at a visual compromise represented by the dimensions in figure 1. If you need a larger table, I suggest you add one or two leaves instead of gluing up a bigger single-piece top.

Getting started—There are any number of ways to build a leg-and-apron table, but for expediency, I follow a definite order of events, regardless of the method. First of all, I glue up one or more tabletops several days before beginning construction. When I do my weekly errands in Portland, I drop off the tops at a local millwork house where they're sanded to 150 grit on an abrasive planer. This machine sanding is well worth the $20 or so it costs: The tops emerge perfectly flat and ready to finish after a final sanding to 220 grit.

Some woodworkers argue that it's best to glue up a tabletop so the boards' growth rings are either all up or all down, reasoning that any cupping will be easier to restrain if it occurs in the same direction. Others alternate the growth rings, claiming it's better to have several small warps than one big one. Frankly, I don't accept either point of view. I'm most interested in a nice-looking top, so I orient the boards for best color and grain match and let the growth rings fall where they may. So far, I've had no problems with warping. Whether the table will have a leaf or not, I glue up the top in two sections that can fit through the mill's 36-in. capacity sander. For a top without a leaf, I glue the two sections together before marking the circle with a trammel and bandsawing it. Leafed tabletops are clamped for marking, then bandsawn as two halves.

I begin construction of the base by making the legs. Over the years, I've experimented with various sizes and tapers and have finally decided there's no good argument for making the legs thicker than the minimum dimensions needed to support the table. Even the thinnest legs will support vertical loads imposed on a table, so the chief design concern is balancing the legs' visual weight with their ability to resist wobble. On the table illustrated here, the legs taper from 1¾ in. to 1⅛ in. This proportion looks just right with a 48-in.-dia. top, ¾ in. thick, and it results in a rigid base. For visual balance, a thicker or larger top might look nice with a heavier leg, but I think the table would look awkward with a 2-in.-thick leg.

To save the trouble of crosscutting them individually, I rip all the legs from a single 1¾-in.-thick board cut to the exact

With a 48-in. round top on a square, leg-and-apron base, the author's table will accommodate four people. Built with three removable leaves, there's room for eight to 10 people.

Fig. 2: Tablesaw taper jig

Top of leg goes here.

Begin with scrap longer than leg.

Screw acts as stop for minor adjustments.

Position marked-out leg as shown, trace outline on scrap, then bandsaw the angle.

Feed this edge against fence.

Start of taper intersects jig here.

Trace outline.

Marked-out leg

Feed.

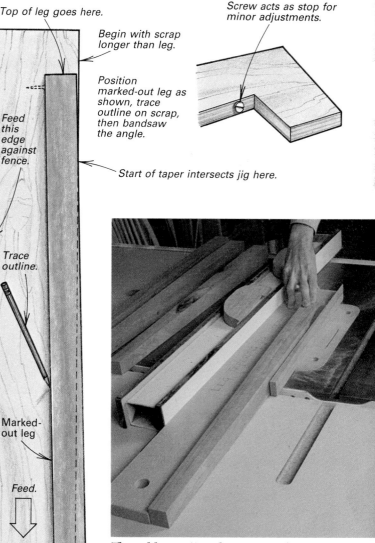

The tablesaw jig, above, provides a reliable way to taper the legs. Tapers are cut only on the legs' two inside surfaces.

For tenoning with a single setup, above, the tablesaw's cutting depth is set to the shoulder depth, the fence (or a stop block) to the shoulder length. With the stock held firmly against the miter gauge, multiple passes form the cheek.

Glue blocks, above, glued and screwed at the bottom edge of the apron bolster the joint against damage from an accidental kick. The author's trademark, a penny let into the leg, dates the piece for posterity. Pulled home with clamps, the tenons, below, are pinned with ¼-in. dowels.

Wooden extension slides convert an ordinary table into one that expands. To install the slides, the top is attached to the base and the slides are screwed to the underside of the top. Then the base is removed so the apron rails can be tablesawn, above, using a miter gauge. A scrap taped to the apron acts as a shim, preventing binding during the cut. A brass latch, below, locks the leaves together.

length of the legs. Each leg is then tapered on the tablesaw with the jig shown in figure 2. If you prefer, you can mark the taper on the leg and bandsaw to the line, or you can taper them with several passes on a jointer. Keep in mind, though, the tapers are cut only on the legs' two inside surfaces. Position the legs to expose the nicest figure and color on the two outside surfaces. Also, note that the taper starts about 5 in. below the top of the leg, leaving a flat for the apron to bear against.

The apron—As with the legs, the table apron's width is a trade-off between ergonomics and aesthetics. A 4-in. apron is wide enough to provide substantial tenon shoulders, but not so wide that you bang your knees on it. The few tables I've made with 3-in. aprons look fine, but aprons 5 in. or larger give the table a low-slung, bottom-heavy look. In leg-and-apron tables, the aprons are usually joined to the legs by a mortise and tenon. On older tables, you'll often see a haunched tenon. Even though a haunch will help keep the apron from twisting, I don't think it's worth the extra time required to cut it. Also, the apron is screwed to the tabletop near the corners, which are further braced against twisting with stout glue blocks. Besides, the apron twisting doesn't threaten the joint as much as a swift kick to the end of the leg does. The glue blocks, positioned at the bottom edge of the apron and screwed into the leg, are good insurance against such a broken joint.

The detail in figure 1 shows the joint dimensions. I cut the mortises on a slot mortiser equipped with a fence and a series of stops. This means I have to mark out only one of the legs, then use it to set the fence and stops for cutting the rest of the pieces. If you plan to chop the mortises with a mortise chisel, or by some other method that's not jigable, you'll need to mark each joint individually. In either case, take care to cut the mortise in the right place, that is, on the sides with the tapers. And, don't forget to offset the mortises toward the outside of the leg, as shown in figure 1. Mortises ⅞ in. deep will just meet inside a 1¾-in.-thick leg, and there's really no need to make them any deeper. If you've cut mortises with a router or slot mortiser, you'll need to either square the mortise with a chisel or round the tenon. I've found that rounding the tenon with a knife is a quick, rather pleasant job.

Cutting short tenons—Tenons are easy and quick to cut on the tablesaw. To set up for tenoning, I take a long scrap cut from the stock used for aprons and center it over one of the leg mortises. With a knife, I mark the mortise width on my scrap, then set the tablesaw's depth of cut just shy of the knife marks. Next, I position the fence (or a stop block clamped to it) so it's as far from the *inside* edge of the blade as the shoulder is long, in this case, ¾ in. Allowing for a ⅛-in. kerf, this produces a ⅞-in.-long tenon. The shoulders are cut first by firmly holding the scrap in the miter gauge and feeding its squared end against the fence or stop block. To form the cheeks of the tenons, I nibble away the waste in multiple passes, starting at the squared end and working toward the shoulder cut. With both cheeks wasted, I try the fit. If the tenon's too loose, I reduce the depth of cut and try again with another scrap. If it's too tight, I increase the depth until the fit is just right. Because increasing the depth removes material from both sides, make minute adjustments and try the fit as you go.

Assembly—With all the parts cut out, the base goes together in about 10 minutes. I first bore holes in the aprons for the top mounting screws and sand everything to 220 grit. I don't usually dry-assemble a simple piece like this table, but I do check that all the tenons fit snugly into their mortises and that the shoulders seat correctly. At final assembly, I pull the tenons home with clamps and bore ¼-in.-dia. holes through the joint into which 1¼-in. hardwood dowels are driven, pinning the tenon. The dowels are later pared flush with the leg surface. You can turn your own dowels or buy them in hardwood species from Midwest Dowel Works, 4631 Hutchinson Road, Cincinatti, Ohio, 45248. At assembly, check two critical things: Make sure the aprons go into the correct mortises, or the holes you bored for the top will be upside down; check the base for square by measuring diagonally across the inside edges of the legs. If everything looks right, I make up glue blocks, then screw and glue them at the corners.

All that remains is to screw the top to the base. Before I do this, however, I elongate the screw holes with a rasp to give the screws room to move as the tabletop shrinks and swells with the seasons. When drilling the mounting holes, it's a good idea to use a depth stop on the bit. Nothing is more embarrassing—or harder to repair—than an accidental hole through a tabletop.

Adding a leaf—If the table is to get a leaf, I screw the two separate tabletop sections to the base, just as I would a single-piece top. Then, after the table extension mechanism is installed on the

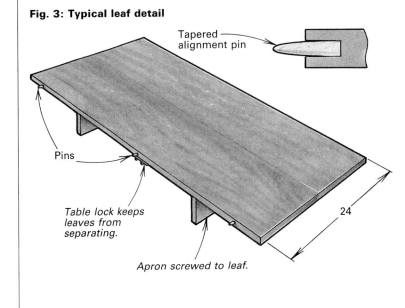

Fig. 3: Typical leaf detail

Tapered alignment pin

Pins

Table lock keeps leaves from separating.

Apron screwed to leaf.

24

underside of the top, I remove the base and simply crosscut the aprons on the tablesaw, using a scrapwood shim under the apron so it won't pinch the sawblade. Once the base is reinstalled, the kerf space remaining between the two halves of the apron allows for wood movement. You can make your own extension slides for the table, or you can buy one of the many commercial models available. I prefer a commercially made wooden slide made by Walter of Wabash and available from the Woodworkers' Store (see sources of supply). For a single leaf, 24 in. wide, use a slide with a 26-in. opening. Two leaves will require a 50-in. opening slide, but the table will then expand to a racetrack shape 8 ft. long, with room for eight or 10 people. The table could accommodate up to three leaves, providing seating for 10 to 12 people, but I wouldn't recommend making it any bigger without a center leg to support the additional leaves.

The leaves should be about 24 in. wide and their length should equal the diameter of the top. To keep the apron from warping and to hide the extension mechanism, fasten short sections of apron rail to the underside of the leaves. To align the leaves, table pins made from tapered dowels should be let into the edges of each leaf. Pin spacing isn't critical, but a 4-ft. leaf should have at least three table pins. To keep the leaves from separating, install table latches under the top and position them so each leaf can be latched to its neighbor.

A final sanding followed by the finish of your choice completes the table. I normally use Watco oil, but if the top will see hard, daily use, lacquer or varnish would be more appropriate because of its durability.   □

Christian Becksvoort is a professional furnituremaker and author in New Gloucester, Maine.

Sources of supply

Table slides, tapered alignment pins and table locks are available from The Woodworkers' Store, 21801 Industrial Blvd., Rogers, MN 55374, (612) 428-4101.

Table locks and slides are available from Garrett Wade, 161 Ave. of the Americas, New York, NY 10013, (800) 221-2942 or (212) 807-1757 (in NY), and in Canada from Lee Valley Tools Ltd., P.O. Box 6295, Station J, Ottawa, Ont. K2A1T4, (613) 596-0350.

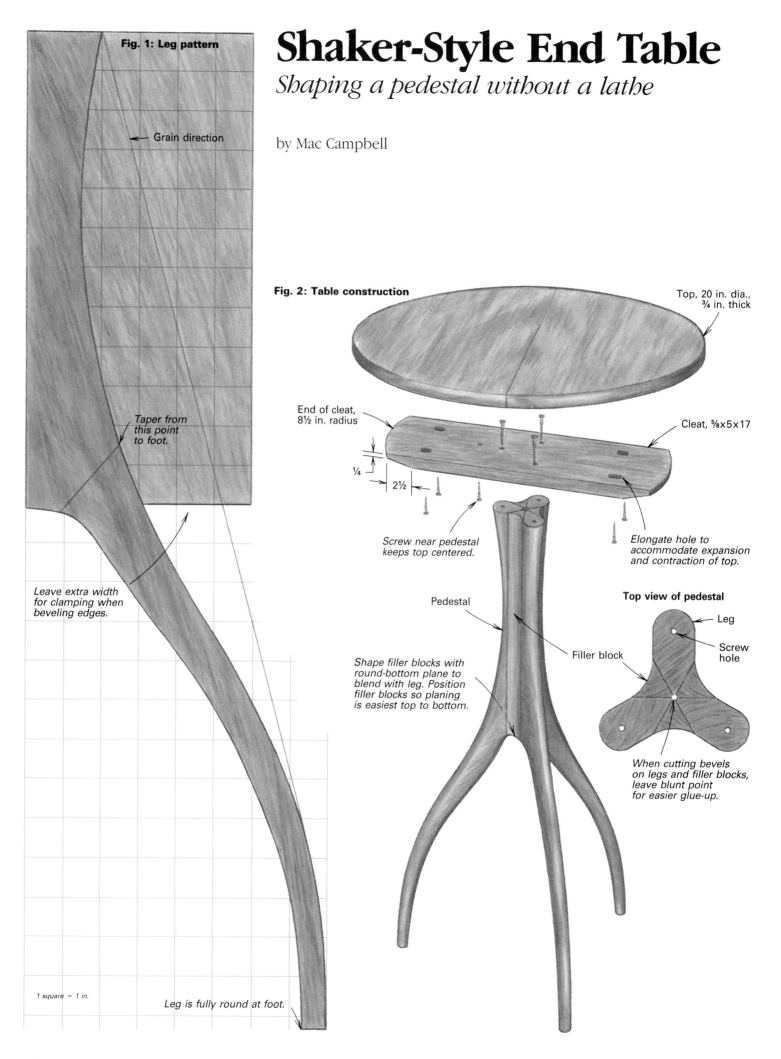

Shaker-Style End Table

Shaping a pedestal without a lathe

by Mac Campbell

Fig. 1: Leg pattern

← Grain direction

Taper from this point to foot.

Leave extra width for clamping when beveling edges.

1 square = 1 in.

Leg is fully round at foot.

Fig. 2: Table construction

Top, 20 in. dia., ¾ in. thick

End of cleat, 8½ in. radius

Cleat, ⅝ x 5 x 17

¼

2½

Screw near pedestal keeps top centered.

Elongate hole to accommodate expansion and contraction of top.

Pedestal

Shape filler blocks with round-bottom plane to blend with leg. Position filler blocks so planing is easiest top to bottom.

Filler block

Top view of pedestal

Leg

Screw hole

When cutting bevels on legs and filler blocks, leave blunt point for easier glue-up.

To my taste, the Shakers developed the finest pedestal tables. I'm particularly fond of the cherry table made at Hancock, Mass., Shaker Village around 1830. The transition along the leg, up through the pedestal, is remarkably smooth. Still, there is a transition, and I've never been comfortable with the visual disruption it creates. Ideally, I think, the lines of the table should flow from the floor to the tabletop in a single, smooth, unbroken sweep. When a client asked me to design a contemporary pedestal table based on the Shaker theme, I jumped at the opportunity to "get it right."

My solution was to form each leg as an extension of the pedestal itself. Where the Shaker stand has a turned pedestal with legs joined at the bottom, my pedestal takes its shape from the way the three legs join together continuously along the vertical centerline of the table. And unlike the Shakers, I don't have to turn any parts to build it. Instead, I add filler blocks in the angled space between adjacent legs and then shape them to smooth the transition from leg to leg. The table shown in the photo below is the result. It is mahogany, but walnut or cherry are equally suited to the style.

In building the table, I first make a template for the legs. I mark out 1-in.-thick stock for the three legs and rough them out on the bandsaw. I also prepare stock for the filler blocks. Then, I carefully rip-cut a 30° angle along both edges of each leg and of each filler block where they will be joined together along the table's vertical centerline. After tapering the legs on a jointer and further refining their shape with rasps and files, I glue up the legs and the filler blocks, using specially made fixtures, to form the pedestal. A cleat is screwed to the top of the pedestal and screws, in turn, are run up through the cleat to secure the top. After sanding the table, I apply French polish or oil.

Making the leg/pedestal template – The basic information you'll need to make the full-size leg template and to construct the rest of

the table is shown in the drawings on the facing page and below. Plywood and Masonite are good materials for patterns, but I prefer to use ⅛-in.-thick Lucite. Because Lucite is transparent, I can lay out the work with an eye toward the best grain orientation and avoid defects in the wood. Cut out the pattern on a bandsaw, then smooth the pattern edges to eliminate flat spots and to ensure fair curves. Rasps, files and sandpaper work best for this. Smoothing the pattern at this point is far easier than correcting mistakes on each of the three legs later on.

The grain patterns of the filler blocks and legs should match closely; you want the visual "fit" of the shaped pieces to be as good as the physical fit. When roughing out the 1-in.-thick stock for the legs and filler blocks, leave the pieces wide enough to extend a few inches above the fence on your tablesaw, so you'll have room to clamp the pieces when you make the 30° ripcuts along the mating edges. Mark out the leg with the template, orienting the grain parallel to the leg's long dimension for maximum strength. As you bandsaw each leg, cut away from the pattern (as shown in figure 3 below) to leave extra width opposite the leg's inside edge; this edge must be straight and square to run against the saw table. Save the waste from these bandsaw cuts because it'll be used later when making the clamping jigs and cauls needed to assemble the pedestal. Finally, joint the inside edge of each leg and one edge of each filler block. Final shaping of the legs and filler blocks isn't done until after you bevel the edges, as shown in figure 4 on the following page.

Fitting the legs and filler blocks – The legs project radially from the vertical centerline of the pedestal, separated from each other by 120°. For a good fit, the mating edges of the legs and filler blocks must be cut accurately, so it pays to be meticulous in setting up your saw to make these 30° cuts. You will be making a total of

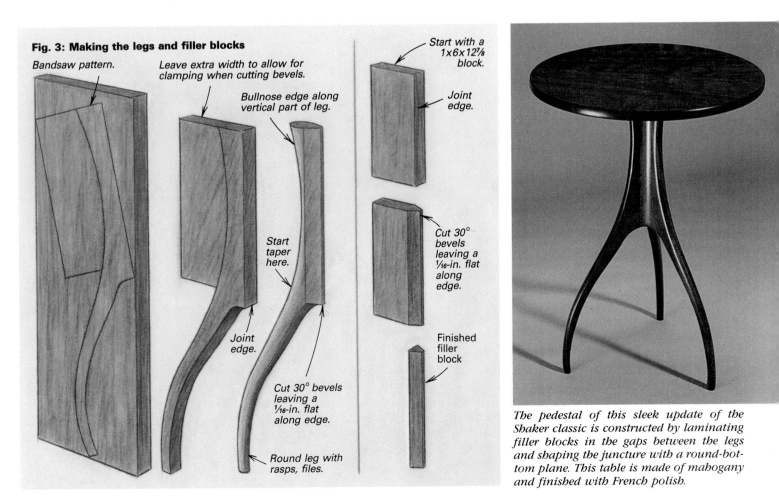

Fig. 3: Making the legs and filler blocks

Bandsaw pattern.

Leave extra width to allow for clamping when cutting bevels.

Bullnose edge along vertical part of leg.

Start taper here.

Joint edge.

Cut 30° bevels leaving a ¹⁄₁₆-in. flat along edge.

Round leg with rasps, files.

Start with a 1x6x12⅞ block.

Joint edge.

Cut 30° bevels leaving a ¹⁄₁₆-in. flat along edge.

Finished filler block

The pedestal of this sleek update of the Shaker classic is constructed by laminating filler blocks in the gaps between the legs and shaping the juncture with a round-bottom plane. This table is made of mahogany and finished with French polish.

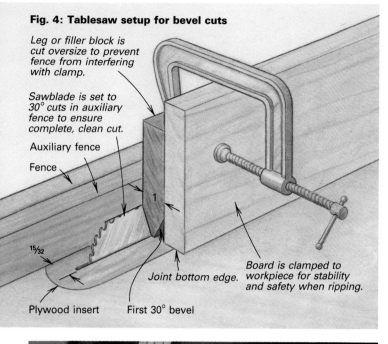

Fig. 4: Tablesaw setup for bevel cuts

Leg or filler block is cut oversize to prevent fence from interfering with clamp.

Sawblade is set to 30° cuts in auxiliary fence to ensure complete, clean cut.

Auxiliary fence

Fence

1

15/32

Plywood insert   First 30° bevel   Joint bottom edge.

Board is clamped to workpiece for stability and safety when ripping.

The author freehands penciled guidelines along the leg's edge before shaping with planes, rasps and files.

12, 30° ripcuts: two cuts along the mating edges of each leg and each filler block. The error from each cut accumulates, so after the parts are assembled, the total error can be appreciable.

These cuts, like any made on a tablesaw, can be dangerous, so be extra careful. It's a good idea to make a plywood insert for the blade slot so the work will be fully supported at all times. Lower the blade below the level of the table (use a smaller-diameter blade if necessary, to get sufficient clearance) and fit the insert snugly into the blade slot. Set the blade to 30° (from the vertical), turn on the saw and raise the blade slowly so it can cut its own clearance slot. I continue to raise the blade until it just cuts into the auxiliary fence. This ensures that the ripcut will extend cleanly through the legs and filler blocks. Be careful to stand away from the back of the saw while making these cuts, as the waste piece, pinched between the blade and fence, may be kicked back by the blade at the end of the cut.

Here's how I set the blade to eliminate any perceptible error: Square up a length of 1-in.-wide scrapwood to about ½ in. thickness. With the ½-in. edge down, I make a crosscut with the blade set at 30°. Then I flip the piece 180° (the other ½-in. edge will now be down) and make another crosscut to produce an equilateral triangle. When I have six triangles, I fit them together on a flat surface with sawn surfaces butted to form a hexagon. Any error in the tilt of the blade is evident when I try to fit the last triangle. If necessary, I adjust the blade a bit and cut six more triangles, repeating the process until all the joints in the hexagon are snug.

After setting the blade angle, I adjust the fence so the blade

will begin its cut a hair less than halfway into the thickness of the legs and filler blocks, as shown in figure 4 at left. The small flat that will be left after both angled cuts have been made will allow for a little play in aligning the pieces when they are glued up. Figure 4 also shows how I clamp the workpiece to a scrapboard (its bottom edge jointed) for making these angled ripcuts. In addition to keeping your hands well clear of the blade, the scrapboard increases accuracy, because the jointed edge of the scrap piece bears on the saw table and minimizes the tendency for the workpiece to wobble during the cut. Remember to stand off to the side, away from the back of the saw.

Finish the job by bandsawing off the extra width you had left for clamping the legs. Also, reset the tablesaw blade to its vertical position and rip-cut the filler blocks along the edge formed by the intersection of the bevel and the flat side of each piece. Now the cross section of each filler block is an equilateral triangle measuring 1 in. on each side, but with one of the corners slightly flattened. For easy shaping later, determine the grain orientation of the surface opposite the flattened corner by making a light pass with a handplane. The direction of easiest planing—no tendency for the wood to tear—for each filler block should be oriented from top to bottom when you assemble them to the legs; mark each block accordingly.

Shaping the legs—Before gluing up the legs and filler blocks, I use rasps, files, flat Surforms and a spokeshave to refine the leg profiles and to eliminate any remaining bandsaw marks and irregularities. At this stage, the goal is to produce a nice flowing line rather than velvety smoothness, so don't worry about sanding yet. Take time to fair the profiles nicely: Shaping will be more difficult after you've assembled the legs and added the filler blocks. Now is also the best time to finish shaping the legs' cross sections. The legs should be bullnose shaped along the vertical part of the pedestal, then taper gradually to the foot, where they are fully rounded. I shape the legs in two steps: First, I taper the sides of the lower portion of the legs; second, I form the cross-sectional contour of the legs.

The taper begins at the bottom of the pedestal, where the legs flare away from the center of the table, and continues to the foot, where ⅛ in. is removed from each side of each leg. You can make this taper with a handplane, but I find it is easier and faster to do it on the jointer. Adjust the infeed table so it is ⅛ in. lower than the outfeed and clamp a stop block securely to the infeed table 14½ in. from the leading edge of the outfeed table. For safety, I use push boards to move the legs over the cutterhead. Both sides of each leg get tapered.

Contouring the cross section of the legs is strictly handwork, but it's not particularly difficult. I first shape the lower, tapered portion of each leg. The goal here is to gradually soften the shape, ending with the foot fully rounded. As a guide, pencil in three lines lengthwise along each edge and side of the leg, dividing each surface into quarters. Make these lines freehand, running your fingers along the leg's edge to guide and steady your hand as you draw each line. All of the shaping is done with files and rasps: First, chamfer the corners between the outermost lines on each side and edge; then round these newly formed corners, working between the middle of the chamfer and the centerlines on each side and edge. The upper half of the leg is simpler: Here you just need to soften the edges a bit. You can do this with files and rasps or by routing with a ½-in. quarter-round bit, but I prefer to do all the shaping by hand to avoid the harsh uniformity of a machined surface. Finish the shaping by hand-sanding the legs with 150-grit.

These three photos show the fixture and clamping arrangements used for assembling two legs with a filler block (left); two filler blocks with a leg (center); and the final pedestal glue-up (right). A scrap piece, left over from the bandsawing of the legs, is used as a caul.

Gluing up the pedestal—Assembling the legs and filler blocks to form the pedestal is a little tricky because there are so many pieces. To make glue-up easier, I do the job in three stages: First, gluing two legs to a filler block; then gluing two filler blocks to the third leg; and finally, gluing these two assemblies together (see the photos above). Two simple clamping fixtures make the job go smoothly. First I place two legs on a 12-in.-sq. piece of ¾-in.-thick plywood, inside edge to inside edge (separated by about ¹⁄₁₆ in.) and resting on the 30° angled surface. Double-face tape acts like a third hand to hold the legs temporarily in place. Then I fit a filler block between the legs and adjust the position of the legs until the four angled surfaces mate cleanly along their length. Butting three blocks of scrap along the outside edge of each leg and screwing the blocks to the plywood prevents the legs from slipping laterally when gluing pressure is applied to the filler block. The pressure on the filler block will also tend to squeeze the legs up and out of the jig, so it's a good idea to hold the legs down with a piece of scrapwood spanning the legs and screwed to the middle, butting edge blocks. Waxed paper under the legs prevents glue squeeze-out from sticking to the plywood and a clamp at each end of the fixture insures uniform pressure is applied to the filler block.

Follow a similar procedure to fashion a fixture for gluing up the two filler blocks to the third leg. Position the blocks edge to edge (the edges with the flat tips) on the plywood, separated by about ¹⁄₁₆ in. Fit the third leg between the filler blocks and make any necessary adjustments as before. Screwing scrap pieces to the plywood along the outside edges of each filler block prevents sideways slippage. I use waxed paper again to eliminate problems with glue squeeze-out, and clamp the leg in position. Scrap pieces, left over from bandsawing the legs, are placed under the clamp and distribute the gluing pressure evenly.

When these subassemblies have dried, I then joint their mating faces—just enough to produce a good, flat gluing surface. To prevent the pieces from sliding out of alignment during glue-up, I use two ½-in.-long dowels (³⁄₁₆ in. in diameter) inserted into the face of the surfaces being glued; small brads (with the heads nipped off) will work as well. Again, cauls, fashioned from scrap pieces I saved when the legs were bandsawn, help position the gluing clamps and distribute the pressure.

All that remains to complete the pedestal is to shape the filler blocks, adjust the pedestal so it will be plumb to the floor and true up its top. I do most of the shaping on the filler blocks with a shopmade round-bottom plane, but you can also do the job with a carving chisel, scraper and sandpaper. I aim for a shape that is pleasing to the eye and smooth to the touch. After the shaping is completed, place the table base on a large, flat surface and use a framing square, held against the outside surface of each filler block, to see if the pedestal is plumb. If the pedestal touches the square at its top end but there is a gap at the bottom between it and the filler block, you'll need to trim a bit off the bottom of the leg directly opposite that filler block. Work from filler block to filler block, trimming the appropriate leg a little bit at a time, until the square contacts each filler block along its entire length.

When the pedestal is plumb, place a large, flat piece of plywood on the pedestal's top and measure the distance from the plywood to the floor. Trim the top of the pedestal gradually until the distance to the floor is the same all around. A small auto-body grinder with a medium-grit disc does the trimming quickly.

Finishing up—The rest of the table is straightforward. Make the cleat from ⁵⁄₈-in.-thick stock, form the beveled ends with a handplane and round all of its exposed edges. The cleat supports the table's top and holds it in position with four screws. Cut elongated holes, ³⁄₁₆ in. wide by ⁵⁄₈ in. long, in the cleat for these screws, to allow for seasonal expansion and contraction of the top; a fifth screw, near the pedestal, keeps it centered. The grain of the cleat will be oriented perpendicular to the grain of the top, so the elongated holes should be cut parallel to the cleat's long dimension. Position the cleat on the top of the pedestal and drill a ³⁄₁₆-in.-dia. pilot hole through the cleat into the top of each leg for three 2-in. #8 screws.

In keeping with the simple lines of the piece, the table's top is circular and bandsawn to 20 in. in diameter from ¾-in.-thick stock. Use a file and sandpaper to gently round the edges. Position the cleat on the underside of the top and use the elongated holes to mark the location for the screws. Drill pilot holes for the four screws that will fasten the top to the cleat.

Before assembling the table, sand it and apply the finish. I French-polished the table shown on page 27; a traditional oil finish would also work well. This table has a distinctly modern look, but its relation to the Shaker classic is evident. The blend of modern and traditional styles is one of my primary goals as a furniture designer. □

Mac Campbell operates Custom Woodworking in Harvey Station, N.B., Canada, specializing in furniture design and construction.

Making a Hepplewhite Card Table

Recapturing an essential delicacy

by Eugene E. Landon

A reproduction of subtle Hepplewhite elegance.

In the restoration and repair of antiques, I sometimes make faithful reproductions of the best that enter my shop. Recently, I had the chance to work on an 18th-century card table, and I copied it for my own home. Unlike today's card tables, most of which are so ugly that they hide in closets during the day, these antique tables have nothing to be ashamed of—they fold in half, so that they can double as handsome hall or end tables. Judging from the many antique gaming tables that have survived, gambling must have been one of early America's passions. The craze lasted from at least the Queen Anne period through the Federal, and table styles ranged from simple country designs to some of the most elaborate and sophisticated of the time. Depending on the period, you can find extensive carving and inlay. Some pieces have dishes carved into the tops for chips, and recesses carved at the corners for candle stands.

The design reproduced here, called a D-shaped card table because of the profile of its top, is a pure, conservative example of the Hepplewhite period, circa 1790. It relies on pristine lines, subtle inlay and figured mahogany veneer to elevate it above the ordinary. Its top and legs are solid mahogany, the hinged rail is walnut, and the rest is white pine. The front rail is veneered with fancy crotch grain, and the sides and curved parts are straight-grain veneer. Similar tables might have been made anywhere along the Atlantic seaboard from Boston to Charleston, but I suspect that this one came from Philadelphia. The family it belongs to has a long Philadelphia history, and the table's secondary woods are just right for that city. Farther north, you would expect maple or cherry instead of walnut; farther south, you'd see some yellow pine.

When it came into my shop, the table stood tremulously, on the verge of falling into pieces. A delicate design to begin with, over the years its cross-grain construction had taken a toll—wood movement in the brick-stacked curved rails had broken loose about half the veneer, and all the glue blocks at the top of the legs had loosened. Somebody had tried to repair them with nails, but the legs require a glue joint at these blocks for strength and were, consequently, very shaky. Even the glue between the stacked bricks had failed—with every change in humidity, each layer had strained at 90° to the next.

With so much glue failure, I had no option but to dismantle the table down to its last piece and then rebuild it completely. Such an experience is a rare privilege for any cabinet-

Gene Landon, of Montoursville, Penn., writes about "Making the Chippendale Chair" on pages 102-109.

maker. It gave me the opportunity to make a reproduction that duplicated the table exactly, even to the hidden toothing-plane marks left by the original cabinetmaker nearly two hundred years ago.

You might ask what steps I took to counteract the cross-grain joinery that had caused the problems in the original table. For my table, none. The drawing on p. 32 shows a stabler way to stack bricks, however. In this method, the bricks are not at 90°, but are laid up to form a gradual curve around the corner, so that both ends are entirely long grain, and so that the grain in all the layers runs in the same direction. You could employ this method in your copy, but if you do, you won't be making a true reproduction. I've never seen an 18th-century American table made this way, although some French bureaus of the same period have this construction. You would be making merely a modern adaptation of an 18th-century design, and in my opinion you would be making a mistake. The table's fugitive delicacy is essential to its nature; my advice is, don't try to change it. In my mind, the real reward in creating this table is that perhaps in two hundred years someone like me will come along, take my gracefully aged copy entirely apart, and get as much enjoyment from the job as I did.

For the same reason, I use hide glue in my work. A modern glue may seem to have some "advantages," such as a stronger bond and more moisture resistance, but these qualities, in the long run, may not be real advantages at all, especially in period construction. Wood movement will inevitably open any joint, and a hide-glued joint is fairly easy to disassemble, repair and reglue. Not so with some of the modern glues. With these, instead of finding failure limited to within a joint, you'll often find the part itself failing—a split leg instead of just a loose tenon, for example.

If reconstructed faithfully, the table will require many skills of the 18th-century cabinetmaker. Take a look at the interesting joinery shown in the back corner detail on the facing page. There are, in effect, two back rails, one inside the other. The outer rail is hinged so that one leg can pivot out to support the unfolded tabletop. The inner rail is permanently joined to the rest of the understructure. The back legs are mortised and tenoned to the hinged rail. Sawing the tenons on this rail will be one of the last steps in the construction—the shoulders determine how far apart the back legs are and how well they fit the frame. The stationary part of the hinged rail is glued and screwed to the inner rail, and the moving arm is relieved on its top surface so as not to scrape the underside of the table-

D-shaped Hepplewhite card table

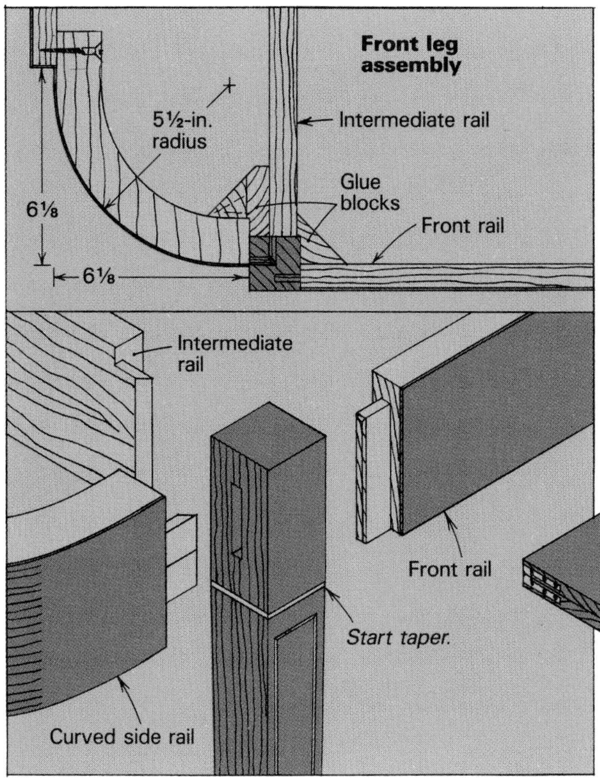
Front leg assembly
5½-in. radius
Intermediate rail
Glue blocks
Front rail
6⅛
6⅛
Intermediate rail
Front rail
Start taper.
Curved side rail

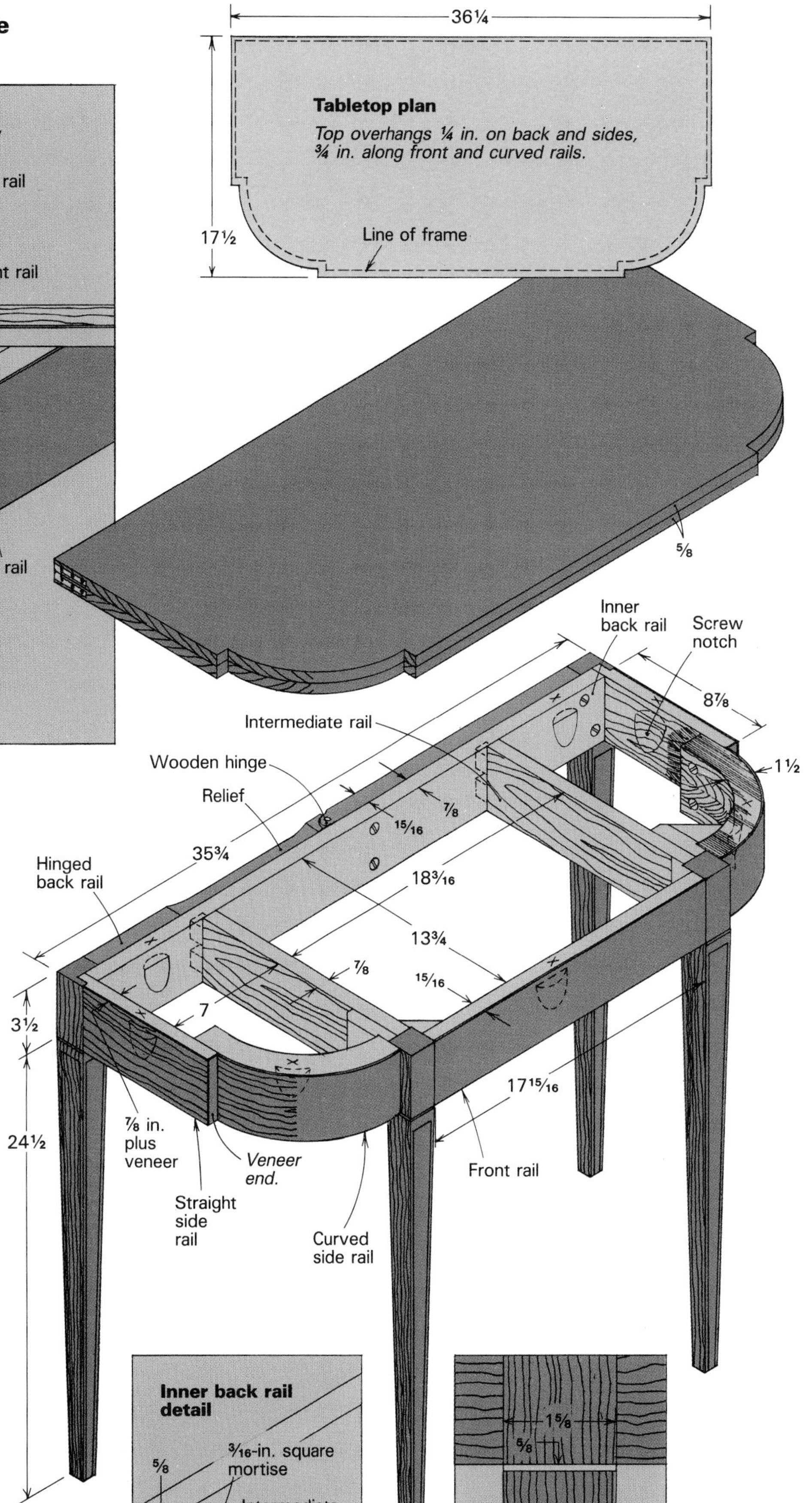
36¼
Tabletop plan
Top overhangs ¼ in. on back and sides, ¾ in. along front and curved rails.
17½
Line of frame
⅝
Inner back rail
Screw notch
8⅞
1½
Intermediate rail
Wooden hinge
Relief
⅞
15⁄16
35¾
18³⁄16
Hinged back rail
13¾
⅞
15⁄16
7
3½
24½
17¹⁵⁄16
⅞ in. plus veneer
Veneer end.
Front rail
Straight side rail
Curved side rail

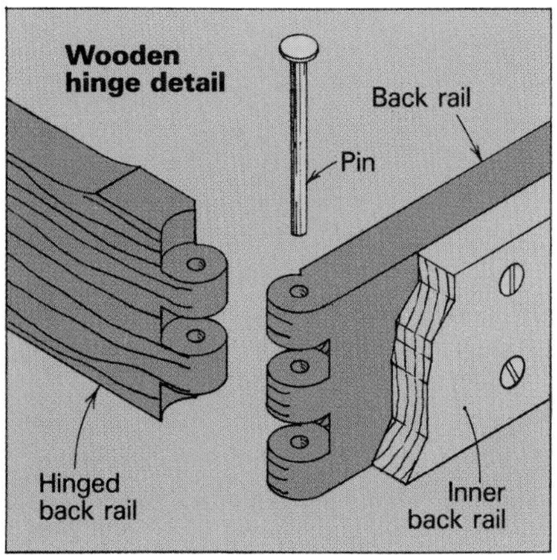
Wooden hinge detail
Back rail
Pin
Hinged back rail
Inner back rail

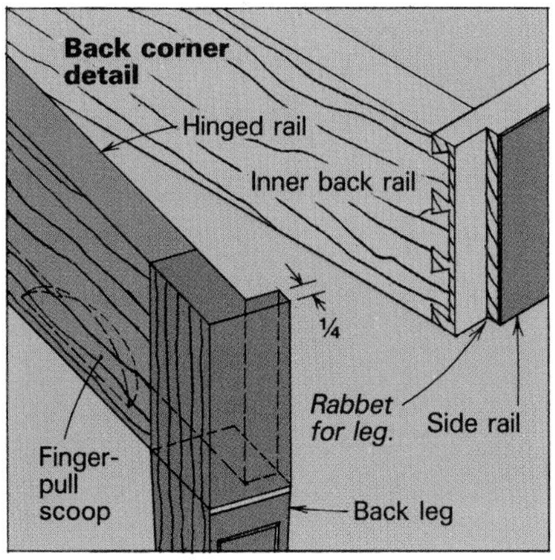
Back corner detail
Hinged rail
Inner back rail
¼
Rabbet for leg.
Side rail
Finger-pull scoop
Back leg

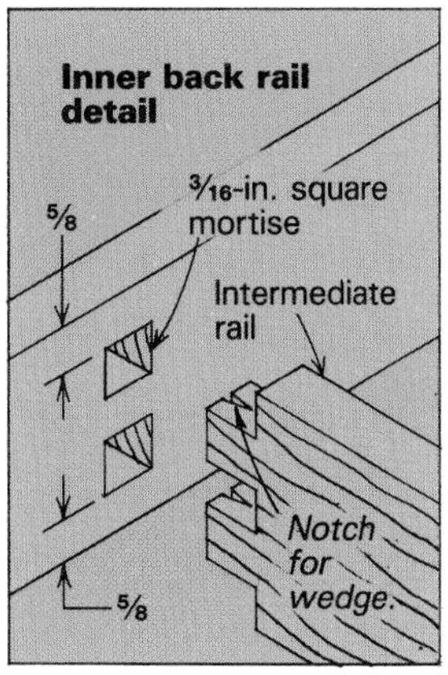
Inner back rail detail
⅝
³⁄16-in. square mortise
Intermediate rail
Notch for wedge.
⅝

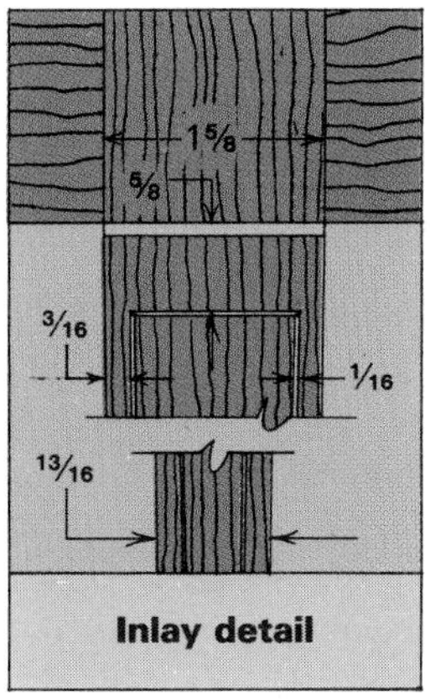
1⅝
⅝
³⁄16
¹⁄16
¹³⁄16
Inlay detail

Drawing: Louis M. Bassler

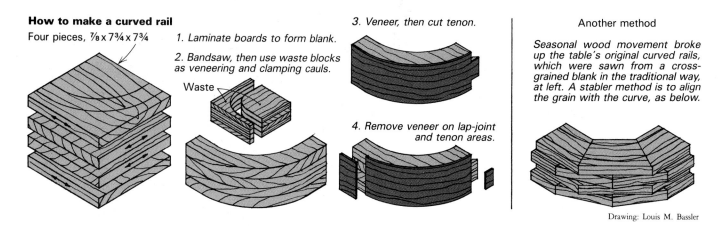

How to make a curved rail

Four pieces, ⅞ x 7¾ x 7¾.

1. Laminate boards to form blank.

2. Bandsaw, then use waste blocks as veneering and clamping cauls.

Waste

3. Veneer, then cut tenon.

4. Remove veneer on lap-joint and tenon areas.

Another method

Seasonal wood movement broke up the table's original curved rails, which were sawn from a cross-grained blank in the traditional way, at left. A stabler method is to align the grain with the curve, as below.

Drawing: Louis M. Bassler

top. The cabinetmaker attached the inner rail to the side rails with half-blind dovetails.

Two intermediate rails extend back from the front legs and are through-tenoned to the inner back rail. These add rigidity to the frame, but, more important, they provide a bearing surface for the rubbed-on glue blocks, which are essential for strength in the front legs.

To make the table, first bandsaw the tapers on the legs and plane them smooth. Mahogany often tears out unexpectedly when being planed. There was a little tearout on the original table, in fact, and the maker had carefully oriented the best sides of the legs forward to hide it.

The leg inlay is ⅛-in. wide maple strips, sawn and hand-planed to a little less than 1/16-in. thickness, mitered at the corners and then glued edge-down into narrow grooves. In 1790, the cabinetmaker probably had a special grooving tool, for he would have done a lot of inlaying. It was like a mortising gauge with sharp cutters. When run along the side of the leg, it cut the two sides of the groove, and a built-in chisel removed the waste. You can still buy such inlay cutters from many tool suppliers, but I make the equivalent from two razor blades clamped together with a metal washer as a spacer. The blades are so thin that they tend to follow the grain of the wood instead of cutting straight. So I first cut one edge of the groove with a sharp marking gauge, then I use that line and a straightedge to stabilize the razor blades when I cut the groove. It's best to make several shallow passes to achieve the full depth of about 1/16 in. Then clear the waste with a very narrow chisel. Note in the drawing on p. 31 that some surfaces are left plain, and that the additional inlay strip across the top of each leg is a little wider than the rest. After chiseling the waste, apply glue to the groove, not to the inlay, and be sure that the strip is higher than the surface of the leg so it can be pared and smoothed flush after the glue has dried.

The front rail must be perfectly flush with the front face of the legs, so veneer the rail before you mark out and cut the tenons. This not only makes it easier to get a clean shoulder cut through the veneer, but it also allows you to mark both the mortise and the tenon using a single gauge setting. Lay out the tenon-shoulder cuts with a knife, saw the shoulders, then relief-cut them slightly with a chisel to ensure snug surface joints. As was standard 18th-century practice, the backs of the rails in this table are not veneered. Mark out and cut the intermediate rails now, too.

Next glue up the brick stacks for the curved side rails in four layers, as shown above. The grain in the two center layers runs in the same direction, which allows the tenon to be long grain. At the other end of the rail, the top and bottom layers

provide long grain for the lap joint. Bandsaw the shape and save the waste pieces from each side. They will later come in handy as clamping blocks when gluing up the frame, and right now you can use them as cauls for veneering. Shape the outside of the waste so you can clamp it to the workpiece, then dry-clamp with the veneer in place to test the fit. The bandsaw kerf is probably about the right width to accommodate the veneer thickness and allow even pressure. If not, pad the gap with layers of newspaper or with a thin rubber sheet.

After veneering, make the tenon's front shoulder by simply knifing through the veneer and splitting it off the tenon. This shoulder obviously doesn't provide any strength, but it does cover the edge of the mortise and conceal any irregularities. The original table's mortise was so cleanly cut that even today's 1/28-in. veneer was sufficiently thick to do the job.

The veneer at the lap joint will also be cut away, because if it's left in the joint, it's just another glueline that can eventually fail. But don't cut away this veneer until you're ready to glue up the frame—the precise position of the cut depends on how much the straight and curved rails overlap.

Make the straight side rails, and veneer their outer faces and front ends. Cut the inner back rail and chop the through mortises in it, two for each intermediate rail. Cut the dovetails, saw the rabbets for the back legs and notch the legs to fit.

Gluing up is best done in stages. On a flat surface, clamp up the two front legs to the front rail, and add the intermediate rails and the inner back rail, wedging the through tenons. Check for squareness and allow this subassembly to dry. Next glue and screw the lap joint between the straight and curved side rails, and add them to the main frame. Then rub the glue blocks into place.

Now make the wooden hinge, as explained on the facing page. Carefully fit the back legs to the back rail, paring the shoulders on the tenons until the legs fit tight in their rabbets. Then attach the assembly with glue and screws.

On your table, determine the profile of the top pieces according to the outline of the frame. The original top was screwed on and hinged as shown. Hinges are available from Horton Brasses, Nooks Hill Rd., Cromwell, Conn. 06416.

The original table had a French-polish finish, which I was able to refresh with a few more thin coats of rubbed shellac. I tried to duplicate the effect on my reproduction, but it will require some time to achieve the old table's glowing patina.

Many old gaming tables have warped tops from standing closed too long—moisture can't escape easily from between the folded leaves. So give your table a chance to stretch its legs and spread its wings once in a while. Besides, it's a good excuse to invite the neighbors over for a game of cards. □

An 18th-century wooden hinge

A few years ago, a collector showed me a Pembroke table for which he'd just paid $6,000. At that price, it was a steal—a relatively rare design in excellent condition, easily worth several times the price. I'd done some restoration for him previously, at a handsome fee. But in this case he wanted me merely to authenticate the table's age, for it didn't need any work. I suspect that he also wanted to gloat a little over his good fortune.

Well, the drawer was old. But several other things made me suspicious. The drawer runners, for instance, were hardly worn. When I showed him this, the owner said that maybe nobody had ever used the drawer much. When I pointed out that the finish was too good to be original and too bad to be a restoration—unless somebody was trying to fake it—he hemmed and hawed and said it looked all right to him. When I saw that the cross-grain glue blocks were all still tight, I knew that somebody had been working on the table recently, and had gone to considerable trouble to dirty things up afterward. The collector began to sweat a little.

But the final proof was the wooden hinge for the back leg. It was nothing an 18th-century cabinetmaker had ever laid a hand to. A good hinge shows no gaps anywhere, and this one didn't even stop at 90°! The man who had faked that table obviously had never seen an 18th-century hinge, had never studied the old scribe marks to see how to lay one out, had never taken one apart to see how it was made. The table was a steal all right. I doubt that it was as old as I am, and I'm no antique.

To his credit, instead of asking me to right the wrongs, the collector quickly disassociated himself from the table, selling it "as is" at the next auction. It brought $3,000, which is about what you would expect for an outwardly handsome reproduction with an old drawer in it. The collector wasn't entirely happy with the way things turned out, but at least he'd learned something. He wouldn't jump so quickly at future bargains, and he'd know an 18th-century hinge the next time he saw one.

Ironically, such a hinge isn't at all difficult to make, not if you follow the method used in the old days. The drawings at right show how it's done, step by step. I'll caution you about only one thing: When you pick up your chisel to round the knuckles, first shave some hair off the back of your hand for luck. If your chisel won't shave, step over to your sharpening stones. —*E.L.*

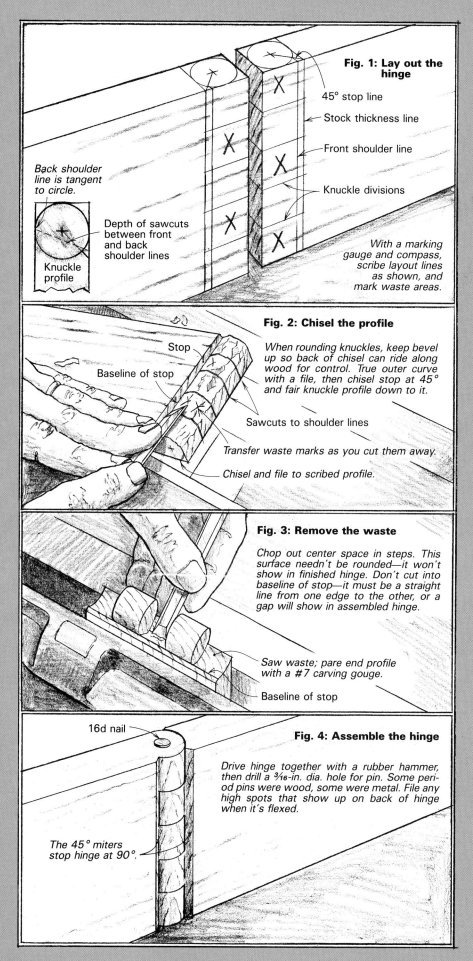

Fig. 1: Lay out the hinge

45° stop line

Stock thickness line

Front shoulder line

Knuckle divisions

Back shoulder line is tangent to circle.

Depth of sawcuts between front and back shoulder lines

Knuckle profile

With a marking gauge and compass, scribe layout lines as shown, and mark waste areas.

Fig. 2: Chisel the profile

Stop

Baseline of stop

When rounding knuckles, keep bevel up so back of chisel can ride along wood for control. True outer curve with a file, then chisel stop at 45° and fair knuckle profile down to it.

Sawcuts to shoulder lines

Transfer waste marks as you cut them away.

Chisel and file to scribed profile.

Fig. 3: Remove the waste

Chop out center space in steps. This surface needn't be rounded—it won't show in finished hinge. Don't cut into baseline of stop—it must be a straight line from one edge to the other, or a gap will show in assembled hinge.

Saw waste; pare end profile with a #7 carving gouge.

Baseline of stop

Fig. 4: Assemble the hinge

16d nail

Drive hinge together with a rubber hammer, then drill a 3/16-in. dia. hole for pin. Some period pins were wood, some were metal. File any high spots that show up on back of hinge when it's flexed.

The 45° miters stop hinge at 90°.

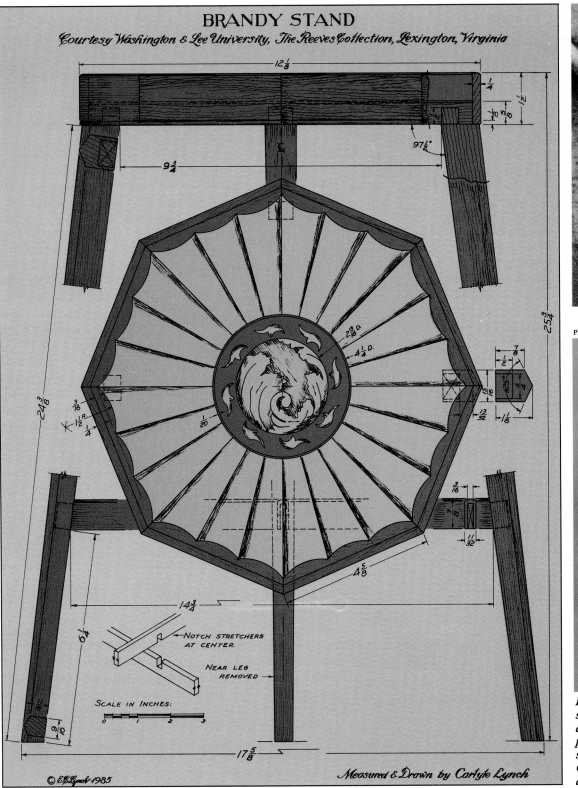

BRANDY STAND

Courtesy Washington & Lee University, The Reeves Collection, Lexington, Virginia

NOTCH STRETCHERS AT CENTER.

NEAR LEG REMOVED

SCALE IN INCHES:
0 1 2 3

© E.E. Lynch 1985

Measured & Drawn by Carlyle Lynch

Photo below: Roy Early; other photos: Carlyle Lynch

Lynch's delicate brandy stand, above, is a reproduction of an original pair, probably used as urn stands, from The Reeves Collection at Washington and Lee University.

Brandy Stand

A lightweight table with a marquetry top

by Carlyle Lynch

From *Fine Woodworking* magazine (September 1987) 66:82-84

The cherry block is grooved and excavated, left, for the inlay. With the block attached to a faceplate, above, a shoulder is cut on the face to the final diameter of the pattern before a thin disc is cut off. The text below describes a safe tablesaw method, in which the block is left square, not turned round.

Some years ago, Washington and Lee University in Lexington, Va., was given a collection of antique Chinese export porcelain of such beauty and value that a museum was built to display it. This bequest included several pieces of furniture, among them a pair of small mahogany stands with marquetry tops. The exact age of the stands has not been determined, but similar ones, identified as urn stands, appear in George Hepplewhite's 1794 classic, *The Cabinet-Maker & Upholsterer's Guide.*

I was eager to tackle a marquetry project, and the curator at the university museum graciously gave me permission to measure the original stands and make the drawing you see on the facing page. Since the stand is a good height to place by an easy chair to rest one's late-afternoon pick-me-up upon, I think it's appropriate to call it a "brandy stand." The maple, mahogany and greenish-color wood (possibly yellow-poplar heartwood) marquetry on the originals is handsome, but you may prefer to create your own design or substitute other woods. Use your imagination to make a pair of these old and unusual stands, given a new name to suit a new use.

Construction notes—Begin with the stand's top, which consists of a substrate covered by the marquetry design. Since solid wood could shrink and swell, damaging the marquetry, I used dimensionally stable ¾-in. birch plywood with the good side facing down, where it will show. Start by cutting out an octagon from a 10¾-in. square of the plywood. Use a fine-tooth handsaw and cut close to your lines. Now, draw a 4⁹⁄₃₂-in.-dia. circle on the center of the top's top and carry all of the octagon's diagonals through it. These lines will be helpful in aligning the marquetry pieces later. You also need to decide if the mortises for the legs on the underside of the top will be straight or angled. Mark and chop out these mortises before you begin to veneer.

I can't tell how thick the veneer is on the original stands, but it's probably thicker than the commercial veneer available today. I cut all my own ³⁄₃₂-in.-thick veneer on a tablesaw with a fine-tooth plywood blade projecting through a close-fitting throat plate. You'll need to resaw enough stock (I used maple) to get four 3½-in. squares for the pattern in the center disc, as well as the 24 fan leaves and eight small arabesque figures that surround the center design. Also cut eight (or more, for mistakes) 4½-in.-long strips of cherry veneer for the scalloped border. Make them ½ in. wide to allow for trimming after they're glued in place.

The decorative marquetry that forms the center of the disc on my stand is made from the four maple veneer squares with the grain running in different directions and with some of the edges hot-sand-scorched to give the design a three-dimensional quality. To cut the central design, use the patch-pad marquetry method (see *FWW on Marquetry and Veneer,* pp. 32—33). Draw a 2¹³⁄₁₆-in. circle on one square and trace the pattern on it. Now, stack the four squares so their grain runs in different directions like a pinwheel, and use a fine-bladed fret or jewelers' saw to cut through all four layers at once. Hold the blade perfectly vertical throughout. Split the line when sawing the curvaceous center portion, but saw to the outside of the line marking the circle. Cut out the rest of the maple and cherry marquetry pieces, and lay them aside for the time being.

For the background of the center scene and the arabesque border, bandsaw a 5-in. square of 4/4 stock (cherry is a closed-grain wood that cuts clean for inlays). Use short screws to fasten the block to a faceplate and mount it on the lathe. Face the piece flat and smooth, and cut a ³⁄₃₂-in.-deep by 2¹³⁄₁₆-in.-dia. recess in it for the center design (see photo, above left). Next, use a narrow chisel (I ground one to size from a file tang) to cut a 4¼-in.-dia. groove ¹⁄₁₆ in. deep by ¹⁄₂₀ in. wide for a line of holly inlay (available from Dover Inlay, 234 E. 2nd St., P.O. Box 134, Mineola, N.Y. 11501). After removing the faceplate from the lathe, mark the position of the block on it (so it can be remounted in the same position later) and unscrew the block.

Now, arrange the small arabesque pieces in place and draw around each piece with a needle-sharp pencil. Use a carving gouge and a ⅛-in. chisel to excavate a recess ³⁄₃₂ in. deep for each arabesque. Then, loosely assemble the four parts of the center design and trim their outer edges to fit into the recess that was cut on the lathe.

In a saucepan on a hot plate, heat a couple of cups of clean white sand (sandbox sand from a building-supply store is fine) and use it to scorch some of the edges of the marquetry pieces, shown on the drawing as shading. This may distort some of the delicate center pieces but, when cool, most of the distortion will disappear as the pieces regain their lost moisture.

When all of the inlays have been fitted, spread yellow glue in the recesses and press the marquetry pieces in place. Press one end of a 14-in. strip of the narrow holly inlay into the circular groove cut earlier with the file tang. Use the face of a hammer to

Drawings: Carlyle Lynch

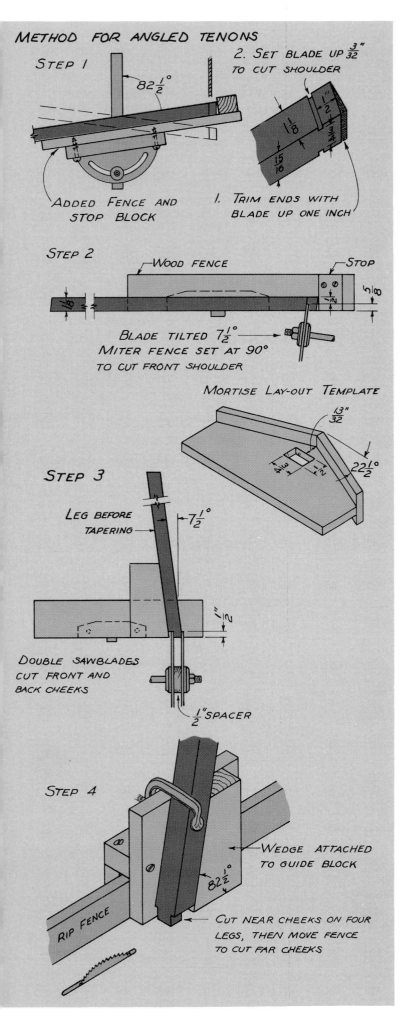

METHOD FOR ANGLED TENONS

STEP 1

82½°

ADDED FENCE AND STOP BLOCK

2. SET BLADE UP 3/32" TO CUT SHOULDER

1. TRIM ENDS WITH BLADE UP ONE INCH

STEP 2

WOOD FENCE — STOP

BLADE TILTED 7½° — MITER FENCE SET AT 90° TO CUT FRONT SHOULDER

MORTISE LAY-OUT TEMPLATE

13"/32

22½°

STEP 3

LEG BEFORE TAPERING — 7½°

DOUBLE SAWBLADES CUT FRONT AND BACK CHEEKS

½" SPACER

STEP 4

WEDGE ATTACHED TO GUIDE BLOCK

82½°

RIP FENCE

CUT NEAR CHEEKS ON FOUR LEGS, THEN MOVE FENCE TO CUT FAR CHEEKS

press the holly into the groove. Work your way around the circumference, and trim the strip to length with a sharp knife.

Now, place a scrap of wood over the freshly glued veneer and clamp the surface evenly. Before the glue dries, remove the clamps, wipe off excess glue and reclamp the piece with wax paper positioned between the marquetry and the clamping block.

Once the glue is dry, reattach the block in its original position on the faceplate and mount it on the lathe. With a parting tool, cut a ¼-in.-deep shoulder ⅟₁₆ in. outside the holly inlay, and turn the *top third* of the block's thickness to 4½ in. in diameter—to avoid ripping out the holly. (Note: This method leaves two-thirds of the block square, and makes the next step—sawing off the inlaid disc—safer and easier than working with a block that has been turned in its entirety, as shown in the top right photo on p. 35.) Now, cut a ³⁄₃₂-in.-thick wafer from the face of the block by passing it through a tablesaw set to cut the disc off on the left side of a fine-tooth blade. Make the cut in four passes, rotating the block 90° each time.

After gluing the marquetry disc to the center of the plywood top, you're ready to trim the edges of the fan leaves to fit the center disc on one end and the scalloped border pattern on the other. To aid this part of the fitting job and make smooth, accurate concave curves, I made two sanding drums from cylinders turned on the lathe: one with a 2¼-in. radius for the center curves, another with a 1½-in. radius for the border curves.

Next, fit each of the eight sets of three fan leaves in the spaces between the diagonal lines drawn earlier. Be sure to number the leaves in order to avoid a mix-up. When the leaves are all trimmed and fitted, lightly scorch their clockwise edges (see shaded areas of drawing on p. 34) with hot sand. Take care not to overdo the scorching—any charring will result in unwanted ridges when the top is leveled. After gluing the leaves and scalloped border in place, trim the edges of the overhanging border strips with a small handplane, and use a hand scraper to level the marquetry.

The eight pieces that form the top's raised rim are cut from a single 40-in. length of stock that has a small bead along its bottom edge (cut with a scratch stock) and a rounded-over top edge. Miter the ends of each piece to 22½° and fit, glue (no nails) and band-clamp them to the plywood top, as well as to each other.

Once the top is completed, construct and assemble the legs and stretchers. Since the legs on my stand are splayed, they join the top at an angle, presenting the dilemma of cutting angled mortises and straight tenons, or vice versa. It's easy enough to cut angled mortises by hand, but I chose to cut angled tenons instead, using the tablesaw jigs shown at left. In either case, the methods illustrated are handy for cutting the angled shoulders.

Before tapering the legs, lay out and cut the mortises for the stretchers and the tenons on the ends of the legs. To lay out the legs, measure from the back side—the one side that will remain untapered. I tapered the legs neatly on the tablesaw using a notched-board tapering jig. Then, I drew a centerline down each leg's front side and planed two 125° chamfers, checking my work with a T-bevel. Although tedious, this made nice-looking legs.

The tenons on the stretchers are cut in the same manner as the ones on the legs, only thinner. Join them with a 90° lap joint where they meet in the center before rounding their top edges.

You can finish the stands any way you like, but the tops should certainly have an alcohol-proof finish—after all, somebody might accidentally knock over a snifter of Courvoisier. □

Carlyle Lynch is a retired designer, cabinetmaker and teacher. He lives in Broadway, Va. More of his drawings are available from Garrett Wade and Woodcraft Supply.

A 17th-Century Chest

Scooping curves with a scrub plane

by Peter Schuerch

This 17th-century travelers' chest looks coopered, but it's actually carved from three planks. Handforged hardware, above, accents the chest's dovetails, adding to its French flavor. You can antique commercial hardware by hammering it, then blackening it with linseed oil ignited with a propane torch.

When I began woodworking, I never guessed it would lead me back to Samuel de Champlain's search for the Northwest Passage in the 1600s. But for the last several summers I've played the role of Charles Boivin, master carpenter, at the restored mission of Saint Marie de Gannentaha, near Syracuse, N.Y. Champlain's voyages led to the founding of this French mission, the first European settlement in upstate New York, which was rebuilt in 1932 as a living museum where costumed workers portray historical characters.

My job was to build 17th-century furnishings, like the dovetailed travelers' chest shown here, "by hand." The light chest is compact enough to tuck under a person's arm, yet sufficiently sturdy to be bounced around in a canoe or small boat. Although the chest appears to be coopered like a barrel, it's actually a square box that is carved to look round.

I based my design on illustrations in Jean Pallardy's book, *The Early Furniture of French Canada*. Building the chest with handtools is pleasant, but you might prefer power tools for some operations. I hollowed out the three 2½-in.-thick planks for the sides and lid with a scrub plane, for example, but you could remove most of the waste with a tablesaw, then clean up the surface with a handplane. Begin by cutting all the stock slightly larger than the dimensions shown in the drawing, and lay out all the parts. Select straight-grained, easily worked lumber. I used American chestnut, but pine or butternut also work well. Small knots are okay, but can be hard to plane.

Lay out the ends with a compass, then use the same compass settings to draw patterns for the sides and top. Make sure you locate the compass at the same centerpoint on each face of each end—you'll need accurate lines on both faces later when you cut

17th-century round chest

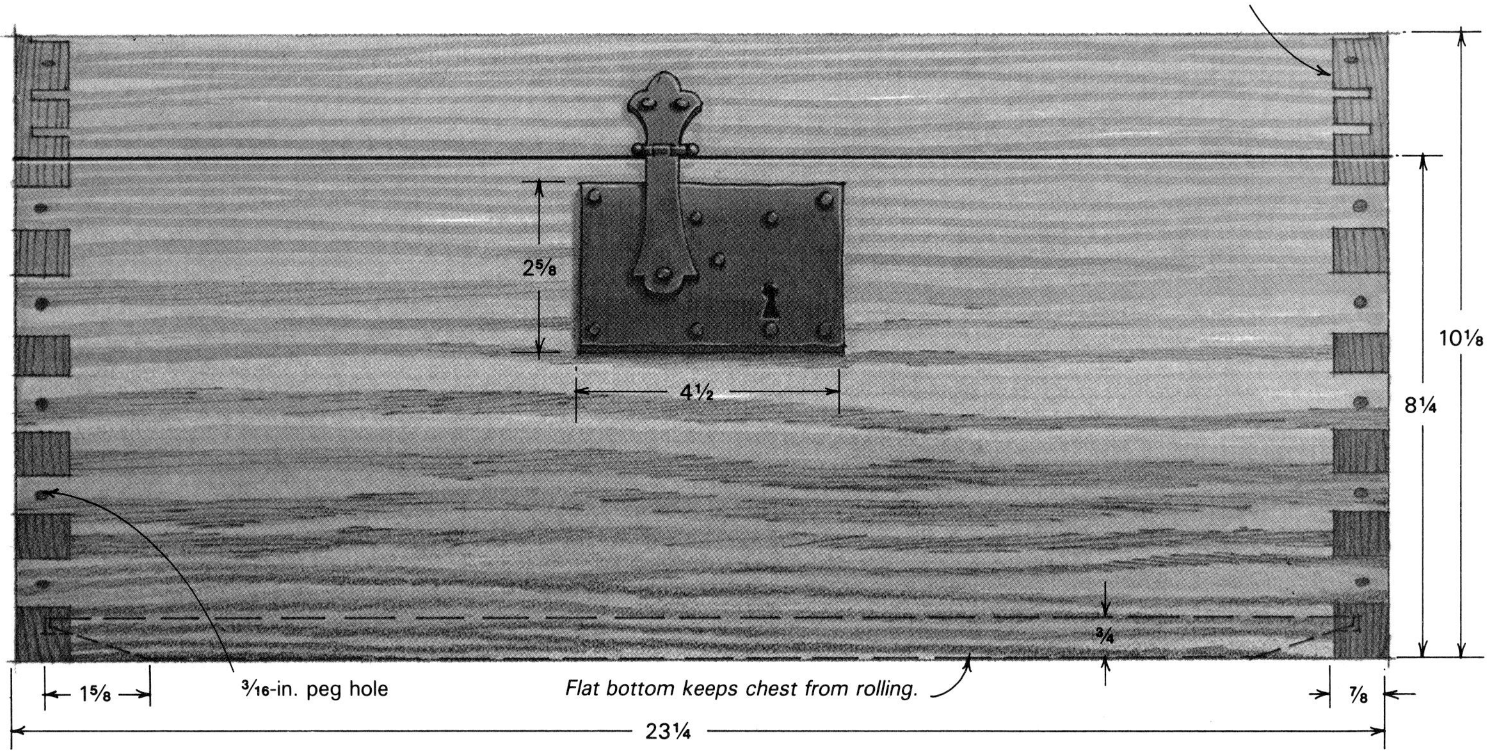
Half-blind dovetails join lid to end.
2⅝
4½
10⅛
8¼
¾
1⅝
³⁄₁₆-in. peg hole
Flat bottom keeps chest from rolling.
⅞
23¼

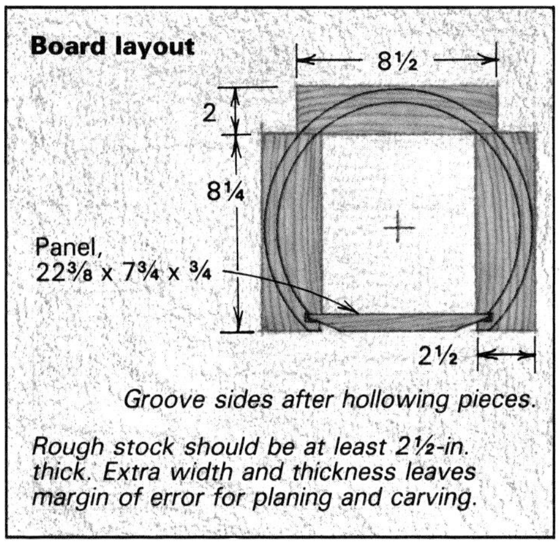
Board layout
8½
2
8¼
Panel,
22⅜ x 7¾ x ¾
2½
Groove sides after hollowing pieces.
Rough stock should be at least 2½-in. thick. Extra width and thickness leaves margin of error for planing and carving.

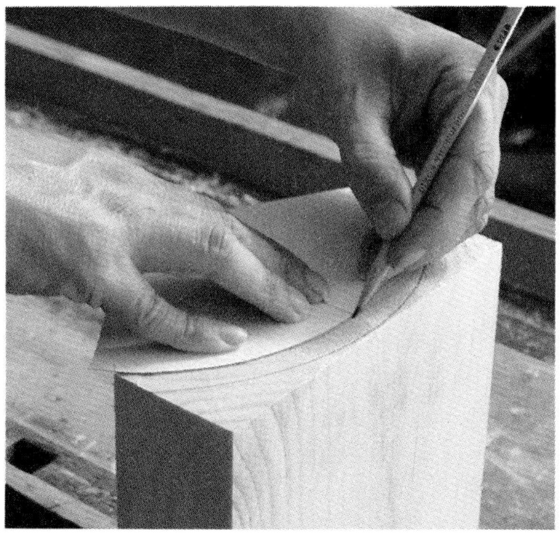

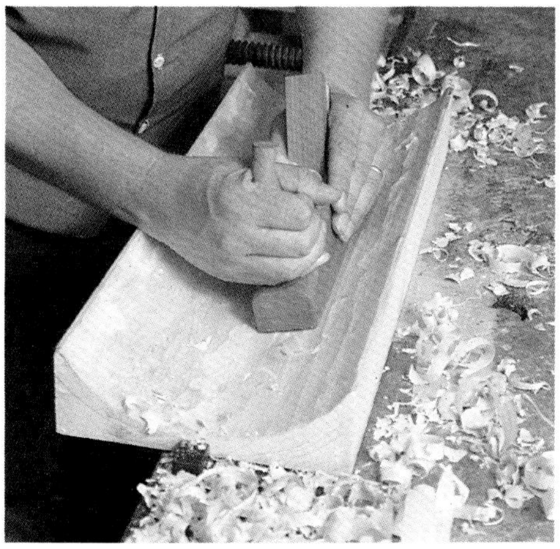

To set the curvature of the sides and top, trace wedge-shaped patterns, above center, for the chest's outer radius and its inner radius on each piece. Then, hollow each piece with a scrub plane, above right. Plane along the full length of the board. After removing most of the outside waste with the scrub plane, switch to a jack plane, bottom left, and plane right down to the line. Then lay out the dovetails in three steps. Sketch in the tails on the circular ends with a bevel square set for 80°, bottom center. Use any arrangement of tails that looks good—accuracy isn't that important. Next, hold a side board against each end and scribe the pin locations onto the side. After using the bevel gauge to mark the pins on the end grain, bottom right, saw and chop the pins. Then, hold the side against the end and scribe accurate tails from the completed pins. Cutting the tails completes the job. Scrap bandsawn to fit the chest's inner radius steadies the side during layout and makes a good cutting board for chopping the pins.

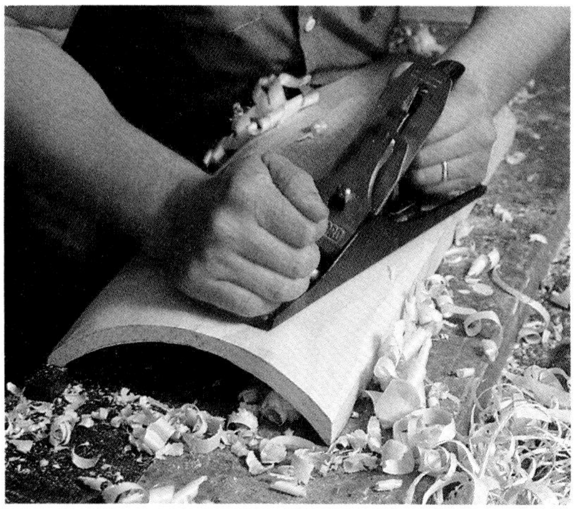

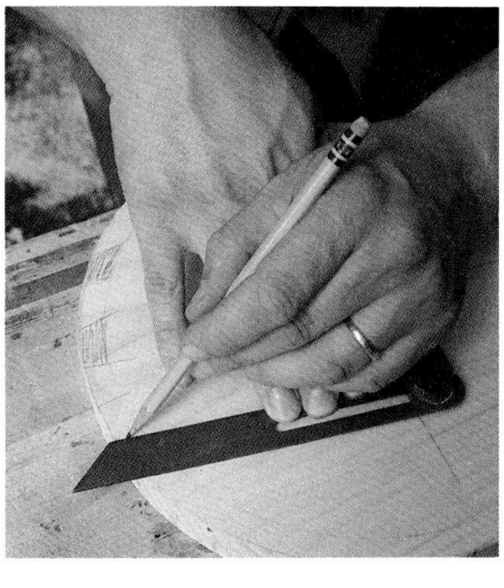

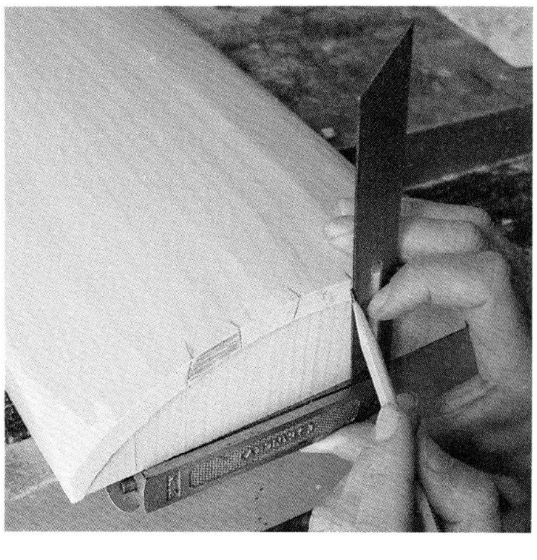

Drawings: Joel Katzowitz

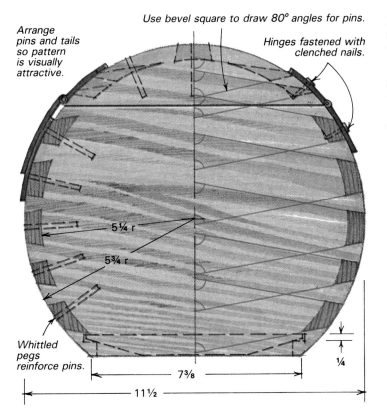

Arrange pins and tails so pattern is visually attractive.

Use bevel square to draw 80° angles for pins.

Hinges fastened with clenched nails.

5¼ r

5¾ r

Whittled pegs reinforce pins.

7⅜

11½

¼

the dovetails. To locate the centerpoints, square up the ends and mark a centerpoint on one face. Place a try square on the edge of the stock and draw a line to the centerpoint, then use the square to carry the line across the edge and down the other face. Repeat the process with the square on the adjacent edge. The two lines intersect at the centerpoint.

Set your compass for the chest's 5¾-in. outer radius and scribe circles on both sides of each end. Before resetting the compass, draw the same radius on a piece of cardboard and cut a 120° wedge-shaped pattern. Repeat the whole procedure, including making the pattern, for the 5¼-in. inner radius. Next, hold the 5¾-in. pattern on the end grain of a side board, with the top of the curve about 1/16 in. below the edge. Mark the pattern where it intersects the bottom edge, and trace it onto the end grain. Turn the board end-for-end and repeat the tracing, using the guide marks on the pattern to align it so both curves are in the same plane. Do the same thing with the 5¼-in. radius, aligning the pattern ½ in. inside, and concentric to, the outside radius. Trace the patterns on the other side piece and the top. Saw the round ends with a bowsaw or bandsaw.

I first scooped out the inside radius with a scrub plane, which has a round-nose plane iron that cuts through wood like a gouge. Cabinetmakers traditionally pushed the plane across the grain when they wanted to reduce a board's thickness, but the tool works fine with the grain. The depth of cut depends on how hard you like to push the plane and how easily your plane clogs. Experiment with different settings. I found that mine worked best when I set the iron for a 1/16-in. cut. When you near the scribed curve, retract the iron until it cuts a curve that matches the inner radius. You will be taking thinner shavings, but the plane sole will guide the iron to cut a curve matching the one scribed on the end grain.

To remove the waste with a tablesaw, set the blade to cut to within ⅛-in. of the curve in the center of the board. After cutting the centerline, move the fence about a saw kerf closer to the blade and make another cut. Without changing the fence, flip the

piece end-for-end and make the same cut on the other side of the centerline. Repeat the cuts, lowering the blade as needed, until you hollow the side. Clean up with a scrub plane.

After hollowing the insides, turn the boards over, butt each against a bench stop and use your scrub plane to remove most of the outside waste. When you get near the line, switch from the scrub plane to a jack plane, and plane right down to the mark. With a fine-tooth backsaw, crosscut all three boards about ⅛ in. longer than the chest's finished dimension. Use a marking gauge shouldered on the end grain to draw the cut-off lines.

I mark out the through dovetails on the ends in three steps. First, pencil the tails on the outer face, but don't cut them. Instead, hold the hollowed-out pieces between the two radii scribed on the end and use your penciled-in tails to mark the pins on the sides and lid. After cutting the pins, go back to the end, hold the side in the same place as before and re-mark the tails to fit the cut pins. I mark out the joint from each end's central axis, using a bevel square set for an 80° angle, which seems to make a strong joint. The major factor in deciding the number of pins and tails is appearance, as long as the pins and tails are large enough to be strong. I recommend you start with the arrangement shown in the plan, then modify the pins until you like the look.

The dovetails on the lid and sides are sawn and chopped in the conventional manner (*FWW on Boxes, Carcases, and Drawers*, pp. 14-18), except you'll need a curved chopping block that fits under the hollowed sides to support the wood while you're chopping the pins. When chiseling the ends, you can maintain the shoulder curve of the smaller radius at the shoulder by making numerous narrow paring cuts with a 1/16-in. or ⅛-in. chisel.

After cutting the joints, draw a line defining the semi-circular lid end, as shown, and carefully separate the lid section from the rest of the end with a thin-blade saw. I use a beveled panel for the bottom. It's easy to fit the ends of the panel into the hollowed sides, and you still have a good, flat surface to keep the chest from rolling on the floor. I grooved the sides with a plow plane, and the ends with a scratch stock. I clamped each hollowed side to my bench, then balanced the plane and cut the groove by eye. I didn't groove the sides before hollowing them because it would have made the carving more difficult to align.

Now put the chest parts together halfway to make sure everything fits—you don't want to loosen the joints with trial fittings. If everything fits, put one end on your bench, tap in the pins of the sides, slide in the bottom and tap down the second end. Assemble the top the same way. Next, drill ³/16-in. holes through the pins and about 1¼ in. into the ends. Split out small sticks and whittle one end to make a 1¼-in. peg to fit the hole. Drive in the peg, saw it off, and whittle another.

After assembling the lid, you may have to plane around the lid and base to level the pieces. Don't take off too much, or you'll spoil the fit between the lid and sides. Finally, clean up the exterior with a block plane to make everything smooth and flowing. I attached the handmade hinges, which add to the French flavor of the chest, with nails, clenched over on the inside. For the lock, you could probably substitute a regular keyhole lock, then cover it with a curved plate or just hammer a commercial hasp to match the curve of the chest. The outside of the chest is coated with linseed oil, but the inside is unfinished—even 17th-century travelers didn't want oil bleeding onto their clothes. □

Peter Schuerch designs furniture and works for Warren Platner Associates, an architectural firm in New Haven, Conn.

Hepplewhite Chest of Drawers
Delicate inlay fans life into a traditional piece

by Carlyle Lynch

An aura of mystery cloaks this beautiful chest: where was it made and by whom? Adding to its charm is the delicate string inlay and fan, shown full-size at top of page.

At an antiques show, a small mahogany Hepplewhite chest with a delicate fan inlay beckoned me. The owners let me measure and draw it, but we haven't been able to learn much more about this beautiful unsigned piece, except that it came from an old home in Fauquier County, the heart of Virginia's horse country.

The owners presume that the chest was made nearby in the old port city of Alexandria. Overland transport of heavy lumber was so difficult two hundred years ago that most mahogany furniture was built in coastal areas. The chest's secondary wood is white pine, but that's no clue to its origin, since cabinetmakers in both New England and Virginia used white pine extensively as a secondary wood, and northerners shipped a great deal of mahogany furniture to wealthy southern farmers. If the secondary wood were yellow pine, you could reliably classify the piece as a southern antique.

The construction techniques shown on p. 42 are typical of those that were used by 18th-century cabinetmakers. On the original chest, ⅛-in. thick mahogany strips hide the rail housings in the solid-mahogany sides, and similar strips face the white-pine drawer rails. The apron and the edge of the solid-pine base also are veneered. A white string inlay highlights the solid-wood top and the drawer fronts. A narrow diamond-pattern inlay band runs around the front and sides just below the level of the chest base. To reproduce the piece, you could use solid wood throughout, except for the apron, where veneer and a marquetry fan are more appropriate.

The original top, a single piece of ⅜-in. mahogany, is so thin that I wonder if the maker resawed a board to get the same beautiful grain for a second chest. The top appears to be glued all around. Because any seasonal wood movement in the thin top is in the same direction as in the sides, the top is still tight and without cracks, nearly two hundred years after it was made.

The fan inlay is a most appealing feature of this chest. Today you can buy a pre-cut veneer fan, patch it into a mahogany veneer sheet and apply the sheet to the apron, as if you were gluing down a marquetry picture. Readers wishing to reproduce the original authentically, however, will probably prefer to make their own ⅛-in. thick veneer, and their own fan, as discussed below. In this method, the apron blank is first veneered with mahogany, then a recess is carved in it to accept the lighter-colored pieces of the fan. Before you start on the inlay, cut the veneered apron to size, but don't scroll-saw it to shape yet. Wait until the inlay has been done. That way you can saw the apron to match the bottom curve of the inlay.

If you cut your own fan, make an exact copy of the inlay from thin cardboard before making one from wood. Start with a piece of cardboard slightly larger than the fan. That way, as you cut out the individual leaves, you'll be making the fan-shaped cutout you'll need later for a fitting template. If you want to make an elliptical fan like the original, you can trace the photo

Photos: top, Richard Aufenger; bottom, author

on the facing page and transfer it to the cardboard. Here I'll make a slightly different, circular inlay. Either way, after you make the template, cut out the eight leaves with a sharp knife.

Next, using a sharp pencil, trace each leaf pattern onto ⅛-in. thick maple. As much as possible, avoid short cross-grain near the narrow ends of the leaves. Saw the leaves out with a jewelers' saw, fine scroll saw or coping saw. Cut on the waste side of the pencil lines, then plane and file the edges down to the lines and fit the pieces into the cardboard template.

Once the leaves fit snugly in the template, they must be individually shaded by scorching in hot sand. When making the fan inlay for this article, I used only about three tablespoons of fine white sand in a small metal plate, but you might find it easier to control the temperature with about an inch of sand in a pan. Put the container on a hot plate set on medium until the sand is hot. Before risking the real leaves, experiment on scrap pieces to determine how long each must be heated. Grip each one with tweezers and dip its edge in the sand. For a start, try about five seconds; you may have to adjust the temperature. On the original, the tone gradually lightens across the leaf, giving the fan a real three-dimensional look. Don't overdo it, or you'll char the pieces.

While the shaded pieces are cooling, use the template to trace the fan shape on a 2-in. wide piece of brown-paper packing tape. The tape should be cut the same size as or slightly smaller than the template; any overhang will just get in your way. Now fit the maple back into the template and tape the leaves together. Lift the inlay out as a unit, sandwich it between two pieces of wood that can be clamped in a vise, and file the fan's back edge to a slight bevel to ensure a tight fit.

Clamp the beveled fan in position on the apron and carefully pencil a line around it. Remove the fan and use a ⅜-in. gouge to carve a recess about 3/32 in. deep within the outline, then flatten the bottom with a hand router plane. Cut the recess shallow enough to leave the fan about 1/32 in. proud of the apron surface. Dry-fit the inlay and pare the recess outline for a snug fit. Next spread yellow glue over the recess bottom, drop the entire inlay as a unit into the indentation, put a smooth piece of wood between the inlay and a clamp, and press the fan into place. Immediately remove the clamp and block, and wipe off excess glue with a damp rag. The inlay should be stuck firmly enough to stay put while you sand off the tape. A little more sanding will create enough dust to fill any small spaces between the leaves. To ensure that the fan is down, cover the inlay with waxed paper, replace the wood block, and reclamp the assembly until dry.

Rabbet the top edge of the apron with a router, saw or shaper to take the 3/16-in. wide diamond inlay band. The apron now requires a narrow, curved groove for the maple stringing, and similar grooves are needed on the top and the drawer fronts. I prefer to cut straight grooves by hand with a homemade scratch stock similar to the one discussed below, but for cutting curved grooves, a small router, such as a Dremel hand tool with its router attachment, is faster.

If you don't want to use a router—and I didn't until recently when I was given a Dremel tool and discovered how handy it can be—all the inlaying can be done with a small homemade scratch stock, as shown at right above. I used it with a pivot for cutting the circular-arc inlay, and clamped a wooden fence to the beam for cutting straight grooves. To make the cutter, use a 100-grit aluminum oxide wheel to grind a piece of hand hacksaw blade. No bevel is needed; the sides should be ground square with the face. To use the tool, hold it firmly near the blade and lean it a little toward the direction you are moving

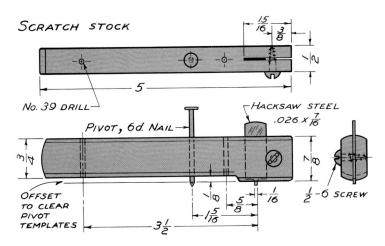

SCRATCH STOCK

it. Use a light scraping pressure, working first in one direction and then in the other.

To cut a 1/16-in. circular inlay groove under the fan, clamp a piece of wood to the apron edge, mark on it the center for the 3½-in. radius arc and punch a small hole there. The hole will anchor the scratch-stock pivot or the Dremel pivot guide. After the groove is cut, soften the string inlay in boiling water so it can be bent around the curve. I recommend that you use commercially available 1/16-in. by 1/16-in. sawn maple inlay—it's easier to bend than the 1/28-in. by 1/16-in. types, which are cut from veneer and tend to flip over on edge when bent. I used maple stringing because it's more readily available than the holly used on the original chest. If you don't want to buy inlay, you could saw your own with a fine-tooth plywood blade. Once the inlay is soft enough to bend, apply a thin coat of yellow glue to the bottom and sides of the groove, and press the inlay in with the face of a hammer. When the glue has dried, sand all the inlay flush with the apron surface.

Next cut the inlay grooves for the top and the drawer fronts. Whether you use a scratch stock or a Dremel tool, cut the straight grooves first. Then by starting the cutter in the groove, you can work around the curves without chipping any corners. To do the curves, I recommend clamping the piece to the workbench and using homemade metal templates, shown below, to protect the wood and to anchor the guide pivot of the Dremel or scratch stock. Set the pivot in the indentation punched in the metal template and place the cutter bit in the end of a straight groove to start. Then pivot the cutter to the end of the next straight groove. When inlaying the top and drawers, apply glue to the groove and press in long, straight pieces wherever possi-

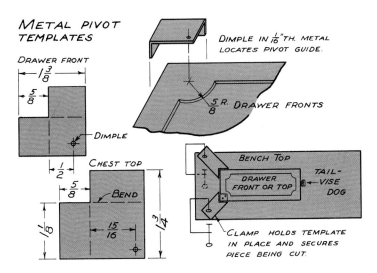

METAL PIVOT TEMPLATES

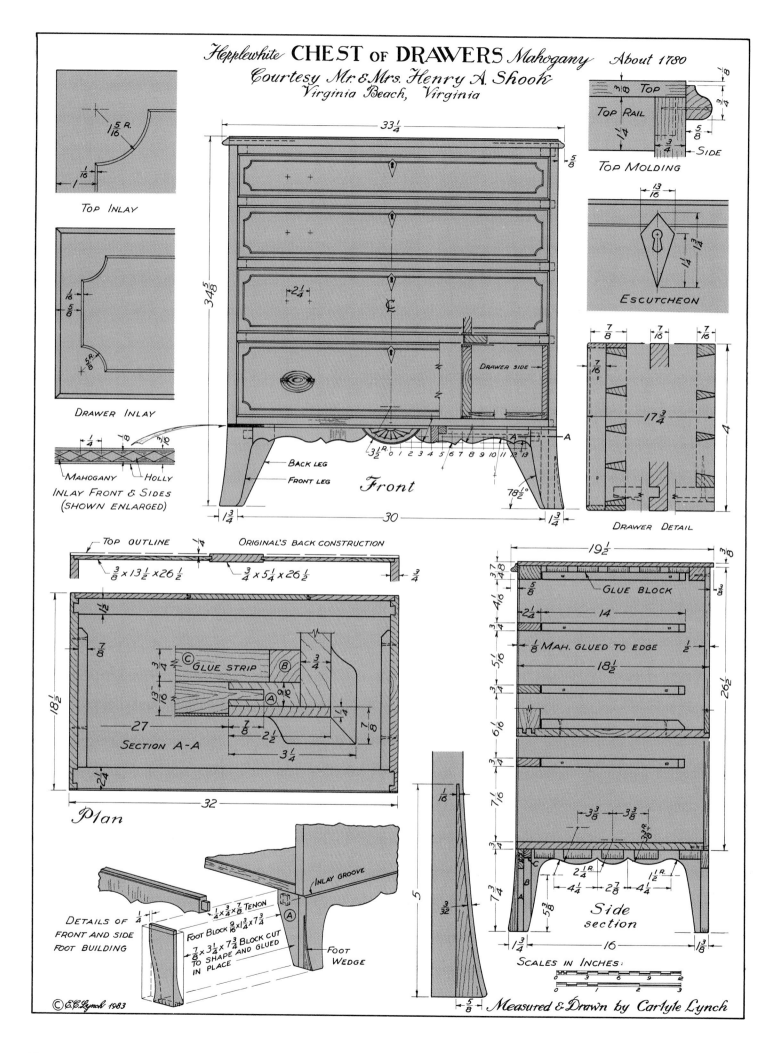

Hepplewhite CHEST OF DRAWERS Mahogany About 1780

Courtesy Mr. & Mrs. Henry A. Shook
Virginia Beach, Virginia

TOP INLAY

DRAWER INLAY

INLAY FRONT & SIDES
(SHOWN ENLARGED)

TOP MOLDING

ESCUTCHEON

DRAWER DETAIL

Front

TOP OUTLINE

ORIGINAL'S BACK CONSTRUCTION

GLUE STRIP

SECTION A-A

Plan

GLUE BLOCK

Mah. glued to edge

Side section

DETAILS OF FRONT AND SIDE FOOT BUILDING

Foot Block
Block cut to shape and glued in place

FOOT WEDGE

INLAY GROOVE

SCALES IN INCHES:

© C.C. Lynch 1983

Measured & Drawn by Carlyle Lynch

ble. To join pieces at the corners, put a piece of tape across the groove where the joint will be and cross the inlay strips over it, so they're held out of the glued groove. Cut a miter through both strips with a sharp knife and remove the tape. The joint will be tight when the pieces are forced into the groove.

Regardless of whether you buy pre-cut inlay or make your own, be careful when applying finishes. Much of the beauty of the original chest is due to the clear, unstained dark mahogany, which is enhanced by the white inlay and brightly polished hardware. The types of mahogany available today, however, usually need to be stained as well as filled in the finishing process, and there's a danger of staining the inlay out of existence. Although it may sound tedious, an easy way to protect the white areas is to take a tiny watercolor brush and apply enough white shellac to seal the inlay before you stain the chest.

If you reproduce the piece from my drawing, note that the top rails are dovetailed into the sides, while blind mortises with twin tenons are used on the lower rails. If you prefer, you can dovetail all the drawer rails. Also, cut a housed dovetail joint so that you can slide the bottom in from the back. Notch the bottom's front corners to hide the joints.

The feet can be made in two ways. Foot pieces with a concave taper can be glued into recesses cut into the sides, then the front of the foot assembly covered with a shaped piece. On the sides, if you want to shape the legs without interrupting the grain pattern, glue flaired wedges into kerfs sawn in the side feet. Since a 10-in. tablesaw can cut only 3-in. deep kerfs, cut the space for the wedges in two steps, beginning with a tablesaw and finishing up with a handsaw. To be safe, make the tablesaw cuts clear across the sides while they're square. Bandsaw the

sides to the scroll pattern to make it easier to handsaw the remaining 2 in. of the 5-in. deep kerf. I find that two handsaws clamped together will make a kerf as wide as that of a 10-in. combination blade. Drive in the glue-coated wedges after soaking the area with hot wet towels for 10 minutes, and clamp.

The drawer fronts listed in the bill of materials are 5/16 in. narrower, top to bottom, than the opening, allowing 1/4 in. for the cock beading and 1/16-in. vertical play. Mahogany is stable in humid conditions, but 3/32-in. to 1/8-in. vertical play may be needed in some regions. It's better to be generous in allowing for vertical play, rather than trying to shave down a cock-beaded drawer. Drawer runners are strips fastened to the sides with two nails each. Don't secure them more firmly than that, or the sides may eventually split from wood movement.

The back shown here is made of tongue-and-grooved vertical boards. The original chest's back has two thin boards that fit into grooves cut in the edges of a thicker, center support. Nails hold the thin boards in rabbets in the chest sides, to the top rail, and to the edge of the bottom. □

Carlyle Lynch, a designer, cabinetmaker and retired teacher, lives in Broadway, Va. Drawings by the author. For more of Lynch's plans, see pp. 34-36, 58-60, and 77-79. Others of his drawings are available from Garrett Wade, Lee Valley Tools Ltd., and Woodcraft Supply. Constantine's (2050 Eastchester Rd., Bronx, N.Y. 10461) stocks fans, escutcheons and inlay borders suitable for the chest shown here. Manhattan Supply Corp. (151 Sunnyside Blvd., Plainview, N.Y. 11803) has 1/16-in. end-mill router bits with 1/8-in. shanks. For more on inlay, see Lynch's article on pp. 34-36.

BILL OF MATERIALS

Amt.	Description	Wood	Dimensions T x W x L
Case:			
1	Top	mahogany	3/8 x 18 7/8 x 32
1	Top molding	mahogany	5/8 x 3/4 x 34
2	Top moldings	mahogany	5/8 x 3/4 x 20
2	Sides	mahogany	3/4 x 18 1/2 x 34 1/4
1	Bottom	pine	3/4 x 18 x 30 1/2 s/s
3	Drawer rails	pine	3/4 x 2 1/4* x 30 1/2 s/s
1	Top rail	pine	1 1/4 x 2 1/4* x 30 1/2 s/s
1	Top back rail	pine	1 1/4 x 1 1/2 x 30 1/2 s/s
6	Drawer runners	pine	3/4 x 7/8 x 14
2	Kickers	pine	3/4 x 7/8 x 14
1	Back (tongue-and-grooved boards)	pine	1/2 x 31 1/4 x 26 1/2
1	Apron	pine	3/4* x 1 7/8 x 27
2	Front feet	mahogany	7/8 x 3 1/4 x 7 3/4
2	Front foot blocks	pine	9/16 x 1 3/4 x 7 3/4
2	Apron and foot glue blocks (makes two pairs)	pine	3/4 x 3/4 x 29
4	End foot wedges	mahogany	5/8 x 2 x 5
2	Back feet	pine	3/4 x 4 3/8 x 7 3/4

Hardware: Eight brass pulls, 2 1/4-in. bore, similar to D-3 or D-5 from Ball and Ball, 463 West Lincoln Hwy., Exton, Pa. 19341; four drawer locks with barrel keys, 7/8-in. selvage to key pin.

Amt.	Description	Wood	Dimensions T x W x L
Drawers:**			
1	Front	mahogany	7/8 x 3 3/4 x 30 7/16
1	Back	pine	7/16 x 3 1/16 x 30 7/16
2	Sides	pine	7/16 x 4 x 17 5/16
1	Front	mahogany	7/8 x 4 3/4 x 30 7/16
1	Back	pine	7/16 x 4 1/16 x 30 7/16
2	Sides	pine	7/16 x 5 x 17 5/16
1	Front	mahogany	7/8 x 5 3/4 x 30 7/16
1	Back	pine	7/16 x 5 1/16 x 30 7/16
2	Sides	pine	7/16 x 6 x 17 5/16
1	Front	mahogany	7/8 x 6 3/4 x 30 7/16
1	Back	pine	7/16 x 6 1/16 x 30 7/16
2	Sides	pine	7/16 x 7 x 17 5/16
4	Bottoms (1/4-in. plywood can also be used)	pine	3/8 x 17 1/4 x 29 3/4
8	Cock beading	mahogany	1/8 x 1 x 30 7/16
2	Cock beading	mahogany	1/8 x 1/2 x 24
Inlay:			
12	String inlay	maple	1/16 x 1/16 x 36
1	Fan inlay (makes eight leaves)	maple	1/8 x 1 1/2 x 5 1/2
4	Escutcheons	maple	1/8 x 13/16 x 1 3/4
3	Base diamond inlay band		3/16 x 1/24 x 36

s/s = shoulder-to-shoulder. Allow 1/2 in. to 1 in. extra length for each tenon or dovetail.
  * Veneered
  ** Dimensions include 1/16-in. vertical allowance for humidity changes.

Spice Boxes
Hidden compartments for special seasonings

by Alex Krutsky

In Colonial times, the spices we take for granted today were rare commodities brought to America at great expense on sailing vessels. The people affluent enough to buy spices would commission local craftsmen to build exquisite little chests of drawers for storing their spices and other valuables. Some spice boxes were scaled-down versions of high chests; others, like the William-and-Mary chest below, were decorated with elaborate inlays.

The spice box was most popular in Europe and the Colonies during the early part of the 1700s, but it continued to be in fashion in Pennsylvania well into the early 1800s. Because of this regional popularity, most of the examples surviving today were probably built in the Chester County area, or as one collector put it, "within a 50-mile radius of the statue of William Penn atop the Philadelphia City Hall." Although I grew up in Pennsylvania, I didn't pay any attention to the local furniture forms until I enrolled at the North Bennet Street School in Boston, where students learn woodworking by building furniture in traditional 18th-century English and American styles. This influence led me back

home to the Chester County Historical Society in 1986.

Lee Ellen Griffith, an antique dealer and guest curator, had put together a show and catalog of 58 spice boxes encompassing the popular styles from William and Mary of the late 1600s to Hepplewhite of the late 1700s. I was already aware of the spice-box form and the line-and-berry inlay, but the variety of work in this show inspired me to further study.

As in most traditional casework, the spice box shown here is dovetailed together, and the interior partitions are inserted into dadoes in the case ends after the carcase has been glued up. A separate frame forms the base, and the ball feet are attached to it with wedged tenons turned on top of the feet. The cornice and base moldings are glued and tacked to the cabinet top and base frame. The line-and-berry inlay patterns of these small chests were often very intricate.

Secret drawers, one of the more intriguing aspects of Pennsylvania spice boxes, reflect the value of the spices. Often the back of the case will slide down to reveal compartments hidden behind shallow interior drawers or behind the cornice molding, as in the box shown here. The sliding partition with a hidden drawer attached to it was also used in some of the early pieces.

Getting started—It's a good idea to begin with a full-scale drawing to determine dimensions and to lay out the joinery and the arrangement of the drawers. It takes about 25 sq. ft. of wood to build this box. I've designated square feet instead of board feet, because if you resaw thicker stock to get the smaller dimension parts, as opposed to planing them, you'll need much less than 25 bd. ft. I made mine with pieces of walnut left over from other projects. I resawed some old walnut table leaves into thin panels wide enough for the interior partitions and drawer parts, and I picked out some highly figured pieces for drawer fronts.

No matter how you get your wood, you'll need about 7 sq. ft. of ½-in.-thick walnut for the carcase, door and drawer fronts, and about 8 sq. ft. of ¼-in.-thick walnut for the partitions and drawer parts. For drawer bottoms and the case back, you'll need 8 sq. ft., ⅜ in. thick. I used aromatic cedar for these parts to add a pleasant surprise when the drawers are opened.

The molding and base frame require about 2 sq. ft. of 1-in.-thick stock, and the feet are turned from a 2x2x12-in. block. You'll also need a piece of rosewood about ¾x¾x12 in. for the drawer pulls and cupboard turn (latch).

Building the carcase—Before beginning the construction of the carcase, I'd like to point out something I learned the hard way about the layout of the door. On my first box, I inset the door between the carcase ends, but the hinge barrels were in the

This William-and-Mary spice box has more drawers than first meet the eye: Two are concealed behind shallow conventional drawers, with one, the dual drawer, attached to a sliding partition. A third secret compartment located behind the cornice molding can be accessed only by moving the back panel.

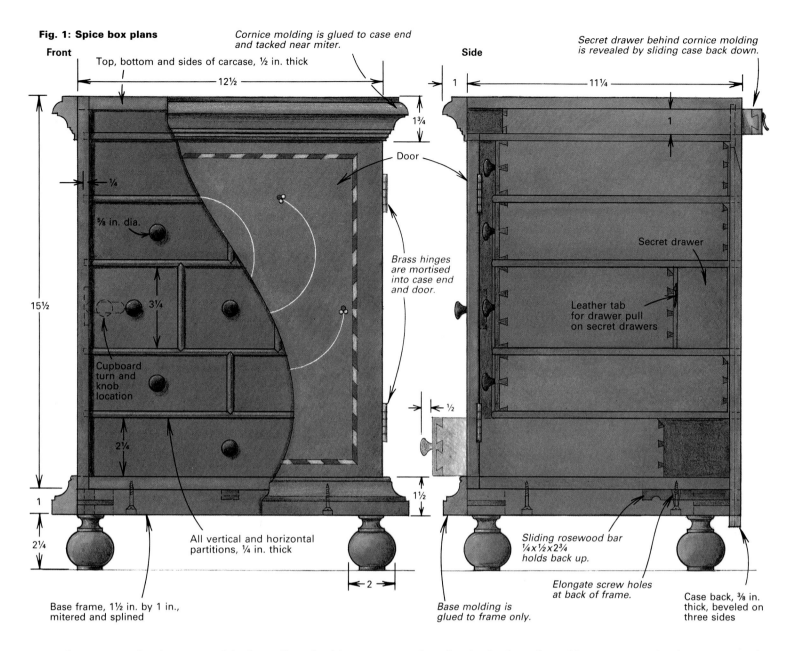

Fig. 1: Spice box plans

Front

Cornice molding is glued to case end and tacked near miter.

Top, bottom and sides of carcase, ½ in. thick

— 12½ —

1¾

Door

¼

⅝ in. dia.

15½

3¼

Cupboard turn and knob location

2¼

1

2¼

All vertical and horizontal partitions, ¼ in. thick

— 2 —

Base frame, 1½ in. by 1 in., mitered and splined

Side

Secret drawer behind cornice molding is revealed by sliding case back down.

1 — 11¼ —

1

Brass hinges are mortised into case end and door.

Secret drawer

Leather tab for drawer pull on secret drawers

½

1½

Sliding rosewood bar ¼ x ½ x 2¾ holds back up.

Elongate screw holes at back of frame.

Base molding is glued to frame only.

Case back, ⅜ in. thick, beveled on three sides

way for opening the drawers, so I had to adjust the hinge mortises and plane down the drawers slightly. On the next box, the one pictured on the facing page, I let the door overlay the carcase on the hinged side. This got the hinges out of the way but created joinery problems on the bottom panel and on the horizontal partition immediately above the door. These pieces need to be "notched" to extend past the carcase on the hinged side, as shown in figure 2 on the next page. The notch for the horizontal partition is simply bandsawn. To notch the bottom panel (the top panel doesn't need to be notched), I rip a strip from its front before the top and bottom are cut to final length. With the strip removed, I crosscut the top and bottom panels the same length and cut the carcase dovetails. Then, before carcase assembly, I glue the strip back in place so it will extend past the half-blind dovetails and come flush with the outside of the cabinet.

Half-blind dovetails are better than through dovetails here, because seasonal swelling of the exposed endgrain of the through tails will eventually force the cornice molding from the case ends. The dovetails are laid out with a half-tail at the back of the top and bottom to conceal the back dado (see figure 2). This was a common practice on period furniture, because the backs were usually rabbeted into the carcase and this half-tail allowed the rabbets to run through on all four carcase pieces.

After the carcase dovetails are cut and fitted, the stopped da-

does for the horizontal partitions are sawn in the carcase ends with a dado blade on the tablesaw. Because this requires pieces to be dropped onto the spinning dado blade, use stop blocks for safety and accuracy. The dadoes are cleaned out to the stop with a small router plane or narrow chisel. These dadoes extend through the back, but stop about 1⅜ in. from the front edge to allow for a shoulder at the front of each horizontal partition, a space for drawer pulls and the thickness of the door. The only exception is the top partition: It gets notched and inserted from the front, to allow for the door overlay on the right side, so the dadoes for it run through from front to back. This exposed joinery will be covered later by the cornice molding (see figure 1 above). After dadoing for the horizontal partitions, I run the dado for the case back in both ends. Then, I bandsaw the notch on the right carcase end to allow the door to overlay it (see figure 2) and clean up this edge with a scraper. I also rip a piece off the back of the bottom panel so the case back can slide past it to reveal the hidden drawer behind the cornice molding. I then glue up the case and clean it up with a handplane or sanding block.

Interior partitions—When the carcase is glued together and cleaned up, you're ready to tackle the interior partitions that form the drawer spaces. I measure the case to get the exact sizes of the partitions, and rip and crosscut them to length and width on the tablesaw. Don't forget: The top partition is wider than the other horizontal partitions. It must be the same width as the case bottom so it can extend over the top of the door, and it should be about ¼ in. longer to allow for the notch on the right end. After crosscutting this partition to length, I bandsaw the notch and set it aside until assembly.

Next, using a scratch stock (see *FWW on Period Furniture*), I slightly round over the front edges of the other partitions. This adds a subtle variation in depth at the plane of the drawer fronts and creates a nice mitered detail where the partitions intersect. I mold the edges before cutting the shoulders or dadoes in the horizontal partitions to avoid rounding over the ends of the partitions where they meet the case or losing the crispness of the miter where the partitions intersect.

To mark the shoulders for the horizontal partitions, I slide them into place and scribe a pencil line on the front edge up against the case ends. I cut a ¼-in. notch from each end (see figure 3 below) with a fine-tooth saw. After cutting all the shoulders, I cut the ⅛-in.-deep dadoes for the vertical partitions. All these dadoes extend through the back edge of the horizontal partitions and stop about ¼ in. from the front edge. I cut the groove for the sliding partition by hand, using a chisel and a 45° angle block as a guide (see figure 3). I use this same angle block to chisel the miter at the front edge of each of the other dadoes, but as I chisel, I alter the angle just enough so the point of this groove is just short of the dado's depth. This lets you lose a little of the partition's height, which is almost unavoidable, when you pare the front edge to fit. Then, I slide the vertical partitions into place, mark the V-shape miter on their front edges, remove them and pare the first ¼ in. of each partition to these lines.

Since squeeze-out could be a problem in the tiny drawer spaces, I use a minimum amount of glue in the dadoes. All the partitions slide in from the cabinet's back, except the top panel, which must be inserted from the front.

Base and moldings—The base is a mitered frame of 1-in. by 1½-in. stock reinforced at the corners with splines. I cut slots for the splines, after the frame is glued together, using a V-block on the tablesaw, and I glue in the splines with their grain perpendicular to the angle of the miters. The frame should be the same depth front to back as the bottom of the cabinet so the back can slide by it. And, the frame should be slightly wider than the carcase so it can be planed perfectly flush with the case ends after it's attached to the bottom.

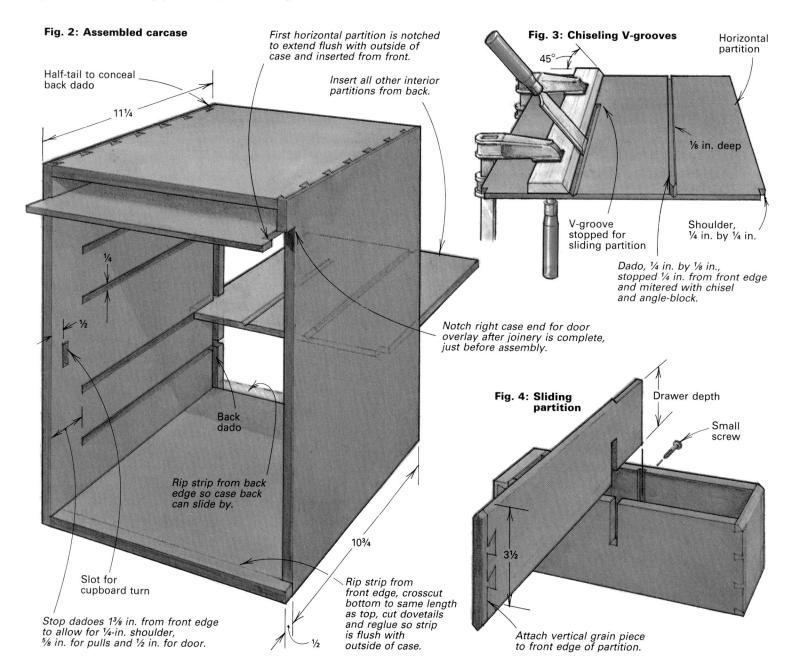

Fig. 2: Assembled carcase

Half-tail to conceal back dado

11¼

First horizontal partition is notched to extend flush with outside of case and inserted from front.

Insert all other interior partitions from back.

¼

½

Back dado

Slot for cupboard turn

Rip strip from back edge so case back can slide by.

Stop dadoes 1⅜ in. from front edge to allow for ¼-in. shoulder, ⅝ in. for pulls and ½ in. for door.

10¾

½

Rip strip from front edge, crosscut bottom to same length as top, cut dovetails and reglue so strip is flush with outside of case.

Notch right case end for door overlay after joinery is complete, just before assembly.

Fig. 3: Chiseling V-grooves

45°

Horizontal partition

⅛ in. deep

V-groove stopped for sliding partition

Shoulder, ¼ in. by ¼ in.

Dado, ¼ in. by ⅛ in., stopped ¼ in. from front edge and mitered with chisel and angle-block.

Fig. 4: Sliding partition

Drawer depth

Small screw

3½

Attach vertical grain piece to front edge of partition.

The feet are turned with tenons that are glued into holes drilled through the base frame. I wedge the tenons to ensure they stay put. For these wedges to be most effective, I enlarge the holes slightly from the top side of the base frame with a round rasp, and then taper them, preserving the original diameter where the tenon is inserted. As I glue each foot in place, I make a slot in the tenon's endgrain, with a chisel on which I've ground a long bevel, and tap in a wedge. Don't get carried away when enlarging the holes: A ⅟₃₂-in. taper and a small wedge will do the job.

The moldings for the cornice and base can be made at this time. When deciding what profile to use, consider the scale of the piece and the fact that one is a cornice molding and one is a base molding. If in doubt, use the profiles in the drawings. I patterned these after moldings on one of the spice boxes I saw at Griffith's Chester County exhibit.

I remove the base frame from the case and glue the base molding to the frame, not to the case, to accommodate wood movement between the molding and case end. Make sure the top of the molding will reach the top of the bottom panel once the frame is screwed back onto the carcase. I glue the top molding to the case front and ends using white glue, because it is the most flexible glue I know of, and I tack the side moldings near the mitered front corner to help ensure that the miter stays tight. I'm wary of gluing the cornice molding cross-grain to the carcase, but doing so helps avoid an open crack between molding and case.

Drawers and door—After I've applied the moldings to the carcase, I rip and crosscut all the drawer components to size and join them with hand-cut dovetails. As you can see in the photo on p. 44, the right side of the hidden drawer on the left, and the left side of the hidden drawer on the right, are beveled along the top edge. Looking closer, you'll see that the conventional drawers have this same bevel on the back. This is because I have a habit of beveling the back of each drawer to make it easier to insert them into the case. With this case, the hidden drawers actually go in sideways.

The sliding partition is attached to the hidden double-drawer with a crosslap and cut to drawer depth where it crosses through the drawer. If you use one of your regular vertical partitions with the grain running up and down, as I did, you will find it pretty fragile, especially where it's notched to lap the drawer side. To remedy this, you can make the partition with the grain running front to back and attach a vertical-grain piece to its front edge, as shown at left in figure 4.

I cut the drawer bottoms and case back from ⅜-in. cedar, with the grain running from side to side. I saw a raised panel bevel on three sides of each bottom and on the back. With the tablesaw blade tilted about 10°, I adjust the fence so I'm left with an edge that fits the grooves. The drawer bottoms extend into a dado in the front and are held in place with a brass screw in the bottom edge of the back. A sliding rosewood bar between the case bottom and base frame holds up the case back.

The door on this piece is so nice, I had to come up with a design for the line-and-berry inlay that would add excitement without obscuring the door's outstanding character and figure. After completing the inlay (see the sidebar at right), a pair of brass hinges are mortised into the door and the case end. The case is finished with Behlen's Super Blonde shellac. ☐

Alex Krutsky is a part-time instructor at the North Bennet Street School and a member of Fort Point Cabinetmakers, a cooperative shop in Boston, Mass. For further reading, see "The Pennsylvania Spice Box" by Lee Ellen Griffith, Chester County Historical Society, West Chester, Pa. 19380; 1986.

Line-and-berry inlay, with its characteristic motif resembling curved branches ending in three round berries, is found in some of its most intricate patterns on spice-box doors.

Line-and-berry inlay

Line-and-berry's circular sweeps of light wood stringing combined with red and white dots (berries) are occasionally accompanied by initials, a date and a herringbone border.

The grooves for the stringing can be made with a Dremel tool fitted with a router-base attachment and templates, but I prefer a pair of trammel points mounted on a wood bar. The cutting tool is a broken drill bit inserted into one of the trammel points. This bit is sized on a grinder to cut a groove as wide as the thickness of the stringing. Using this rig, I scratch a ⅟₁₆-in.-deep groove into the primary wood. On the old work, the centers of the arcs are obvious because of the hole left by the trammel point. To avoid this, I temporarily spot-glue or double-stick-tape a maple scrap at the center points.

The white stringing is holly veneer, tablesawn with a fine-tooth veneer blade into strips slightly more than ⅟₁₆ in. wide. I make a wood table insert that snugly fits the blade, and put a small finish nail at the end of the blade slot to spread the cut veneer. I clamp a wood auxiliary fence to the rip fence, extending just to the arbor. I press the fence tightly against the saw table to keep the veneer from catching under. A featherboard clamped to the auxiliary fence holds down the veneer as it's cut and also covers the blade.

I cut the holly stringing to length with a knife or chisel, spread glue into the grooves with my finger and then lay the stringing into the groove. Using the bevel of a chisel as a burnisher, I seat the stringing, working quickly because the glue causes the stringing to swell. Where the lines intersect, it helps to glue in one string first, and when it has set, scratch through it.

The white "berries" are holly, and the red are aromatic cedar. I make the berries by cutting several plugs in a narrow board that I then resaw to release ⅟₁₆-in.-thick discs. As a rule, I run the stringing first, sand it flush and then drill for the berries with a brad-point bit.

To make the herringbone border, I glue together alternate pieces of light and dark wood, such as ash and cedar, then true up the block on the tablesaw and cut a 45° angle on one end. Running that angled face against the fence, I saw ⅜-in.-wide pieces and then resaw these into ⅟₁₆-in. strips that I inlay into the panel. *A.K.*

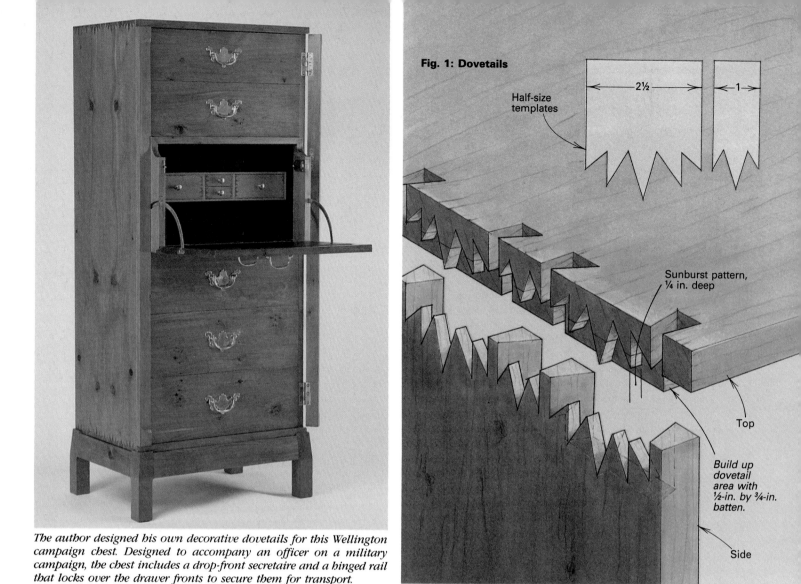

Fig. 1: Dovetails

Half-size templates

2½

1

Sunburst pattern, ¼ in. deep

Top

Build up dovetail area with ½-in. by ¾-in. batten.

Side

The author designed his own decorative dovetails for this Wellington campaign chest. Designed to accompany an officer on a military campaign, the chest includes a drop-front secretaire and a hinged rail that locks over the drawer fronts to secure them for transport.

Campaign Chest
Locking drawers and a drop-front secretaire

by Vernon Harper

For more than 300 years, cabinetmakers on the island of Bermuda have been designing personal decorative dovetail patterns to join the carcases of their chests-on-frames. Because I was living in Bermuda when I built the Wellington campaign chest shown in the photo above, I followed this tradition and designed my own "sunburst" variation for the carcase dovetails. Named after the first Duke of Wellington (the British commander known for defeating Napoleon at Waterloo), Wellington chests are made to be removed from their base frame so they can accompany an officer on a military campaign. A hinged locking rail (on the right side of my chest) overlaps the drawer fronts, holding the drawers closed when the chest is being transported. To maintain symmetry, an

identical dummy rail is glued to the edge of the carcase's other side. In addition to serving as a mobile chest of drawers for an officer's personal possessions, these chests provide a portable office. The secretaire component, concealed behind the false double drawer-front, is the highlight of the piece for me. When the false front is pulled out, it brings with it a separate cabinet, which slides out about 2 in. on one of the U-frame drawer guides. With the secretaire cabinet pulled out, you can reach through scalloped cut-outs on the sides of its face frame, unlatch the false drawer front and pull it down to create a writing surface.

My chest is constructed of native Bermuda cedar. Actually a juniper (*Juniperus Bermudiana*), Bermuda cedar is one of the few trees

Photo: Ann Spurling; drawings: Kathleen Creston

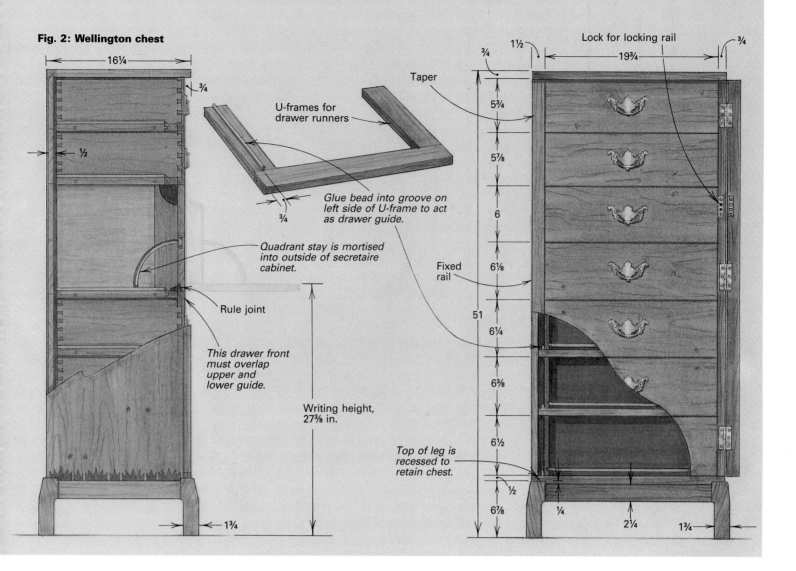

Fig. 2: Wellington chest

16¼

¾

½

U-frames for drawer runners

Glue bead into groove on left side of U-frame to act as drawer guide.

¾

¾

Quadrant stay is mortised into outside of secretaire cabinet.

Rule joint

This drawer front must overlap upper and lower guide.

Writing height, 27⅜ in.

1¾

Lock for locking rail

1½   ¾

¾   19¾

Taper

5¾

5⅞

6

Fixed rail

6⅛

51

6¼

6⅜

6½

Top of leg is recessed to retain chest.

½

6⅞

¼

2¼   1¾

---

able to withstand pounding salt spray and the hurricane gales that frequently batter the island. However, the extensive use of cedar by shipwrights, carpenters and furnituremakers, coupled with several destructive cedar blights, has virtually decimated the island's once-abundant cedar stands. Consequently, the availability of cedar is extremely limited, and milled cedar is very costly—approximately $20 per board foot at present. Cedar is also a difficult wood to work, due to its irregular grain around the knots and its difference in hardness between the earlywood and latewood. As a result, the creation of a large piece of furniture in Bermuda cedar is a true labor of love.

Designing the chest—My principal design consideration was arriving at a comfortable height for the secretaire's writing surface while preserving visually pleasing proportions for the heights of the seven drawer fronts. I decided on 27⅜ in., slightly less than the standard table height of 30 in. I arrived at this height by making the top drawer front 5¾ in. high and increasing the height of each front by ⅛ in., resulting in a 6½-in.-high bottom drawer. The drawers of most chests increase in height from top to bottom, and even this ⅛-in. increase provides a pleasant visual effect.

Once I was satisfied with the design, I made a quarter-scale drawing to establish dimensions. Then, I glued up the chest's individual components: sides, top, bottom and back. Because I acquired the wood myself, I was able to keep the boards together in the same order they were sawn from the log. This made it possible to bookmatch the grain on the chest's sides and top by edge-gluing consecutively sawn boards. Grain isn't a major concern on the bottom,

because only its edges are visible. The solid back panel is glued up from ½-in.-thick boards with their grain running side to side. After cutting the back panel to size, all four edges are beveled on the tablesaw to create a fielded panel that fits into dadoes cut in the carcase.

Dovetailing the carcase—To show off the Bermuda dovetails to maximum advantage, I laid them out with the sunburst on the sides of the chest, as shown in the photo. This meant cutting the tails on the chest's top and bottom and the pins on its sides. To accommodate the size of the dovetails' decorative pattern, I glued a ½-in.-thick, ¾-in.-wide, short-grain batten along the ends of the top and bottom to increase their thickness from ¾ in. to 1¼ in.

To add variety to the overall pattern of the carcase dovetails, I made two templates from plastic laminate in my sunburst design: one with five "rays"; the other with three (see figure 1 on the facing page). I also made a third, smaller three-ray template for use on the four small secretaire drawers. To make the templates, draw the pattern on pieces of laminate, saw them out with a hacksaw and clean up and refine them with a file. Then, glue and pin each template to a small woodblock to act as a reference block when laying out the patterns. The largest sunburst can't extend beyond 1¼ in., because that's the thickness of the built-up ends of the top and bottom. With regular dovetails, you can make adjustments to the depth of the pins by paring the flat shoulders to true or square them up. If this leaves the ends of the pins proud of the surface after assembly, you can just sand the pins flush—not so with Bermuda dovetails. Here, one must preserve the integrity of the original marking-out lines or lose all reference to the fit of the rays. Be-

From *Fine Woodworking* magazine (May 1989) 76:68-71

cause of this need for precision, I use a sharp knife instead of a pencil line when marking from the template. Then, I saw close to the line and carefully trim to the line with a chisel.

Figure 1 on p. 48 shows how the sunburst patterns are incorporated into the cutting of the half-blind pins and tails. I mark out for the sunbursts and the pins on the chest's sides, alternating the five- and three-ray templates to determine spacing. With a marking gauge, I mark the ¼-in. depth of the decorative pattern on the endgrain of both sides and on the interior surfaces of the top and bottom. I then reset the gauge to the 1¼-in. thickness of the top and bottom and mark for the shoulder of the pins on the interior surface of each side. I saw the pins out down to the peaks of the rays and chisel out the waste from behind the ¼-in.-thick patterned area, down to the shoulder's gauge line. I use a small fine-tooth dovetail saw to cut out the sunburst and then chisel into the acute, angled corners with a ³⁄₁₆-in. chisel that I ground and sharpened on the skew specifically for this purpose. I work to the layout lines and use the templates to double-check my accuracy.

When I'm satisfied with the pins, I hold them up to the mating top and bottom ends and carefully mark for the tails on the inside surfaces. I use the templates to lay out the sunbursts on the end-grain of the top and bottom. The tails are sawed out like normal dovetails, and the sunburst patterns are chiseled ¼ in. deep into the endgrain. Make sure all surfaces are crisp and square before assembling the parts, because you can't fit them together and take them apart without a great risk of breaking off the points of the ray patterns. You should assemble the corners only once—during glue-up.

After the carcase is assembled, I install U-shape frames to support, guide and stop the drawers (see figure 2 on the previous page). Because the dummy rail on the left is fixed and does not swing out of the way, the drawers need to be offset to the right so they can slide past this fixed rail. A bead is glued into a groove on the left side of each U-frame, in line with the edge of the rail, to act as a side guide for the drawers. The U-frames are then fastened to the cabinet sides with brass screws in slightly oversize holes, to allow for expansion or contraction of the carcase sides.

The seven drawer fronts are arranged so the grains are book-matched on adjacent drawers. The third and fourth drawer fronts from the top are actually the drop-front desktop of the secretaire. They're edge-glued together and grooved to give the impression of two separate drawers. I made all the drawer parts, sides, backs and bottoms from solid cedar, but would not do so if building the chest again. The wood-to-wood contact between the drawer sides and case seemed to increase the cedar's tendency to weep its sticky resin. Because of this and the softness of the wood, I lined the bottom edge of the drawer sides and the bearing surfaces of the U-frames with strips of plastic laminate. The drawers are joined with dovetails all around: through dovetails in the back and half-blind ones on the fronts of the large drawers. The four small secretaire drawer fronts are Bermuda dovetailed together so the sunburst motif is reiterated on their fronts (see figure 3 above). The drawer bottoms are ⁵⁄₁₆-in.-thick, solid, fielded panels slid into grooves in the drawer sides and front, and pinned in the bottom edge of the back.

Assembling the secretaire – The secretaire cabinet shown in figure 3 is ¾-in. mahogany plywood joined at the corners with splined miter joints. Before cutting the miters, I covered all four interior surfaces with black plastic laminate. The black laminate contributes a pleasing aesthetic to the interior of the secretaire as well as provides a practical finish. The ¼-in. plywood back panel is also covered with laminate and fitted into a rabbet in the back edges of the cabinet sides, top and bottom.

The mitered cedar face frame that covers the plywood front

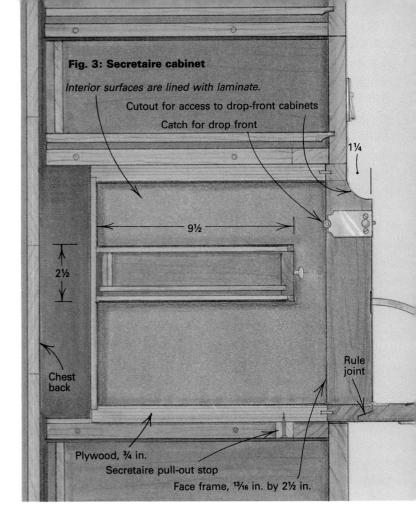

Fig. 3: Secretaire cabinet

Interior surfaces are lined with laminate.

Cutout for access to drop-front cabinets

Catch for drop front

1¼

9½

2½

Chest back

Rule joint

Plywood, ¾ in.

Secretaire pull-out stop

Face frame, ¹³⁄₁₆ in. by 2½ in.

edge of the secretaire is 2½ in. wide by ¹³⁄₁₆ in. thick. Before the frame is glued up, the scalloped cutouts, for access to the drop-front catches, are bandsawn in the side pieces, and the top piece is ripped to the proper width to match the cutouts. The cedar frame is then edge-glued with splines to the secretaire cabinet. After gluing up the frame, I reinforce the miters by handsawing angled kerfs in the outside corners and gluing in pieces of veneer the same thickness as the sawkerfs. I call this "key-veneering," and in spite of the thinness of the veneer, this strengthens the miter joint considerably. A narrow case containing the small interior drawers completes the secretaire cabinet. It's made from ¼-in. plywood; the top and bottom are covered with black laminate; and the front is edge-trimmed with cedar. The case is slipped into the secretaire cabinet and held in place with countersunk screws from the outside of the secretaire into the drawer case. Make sure the screws don't come through and interfere with the drawers.

My design calls for black leather on the writing surface of the drop-front desk. To inset the leather, I chisel a 1-in.-wide chamfered recess in a rectangle approximately 1½ in. from the edge of the drop-front panel. The deepest part of the recess is the same depth as the leather's thickness. The leather is glued in place after the finish is applied to the chest. An angular rule joint is tablesawn on the bottom edge of the drop-front panel and on the bottom edge of the secretaire cabinet. The joint's profile is designed so the bottom edge of the secretaire cabinet is concealed when the drop front is closed.

The drop front is attached to the cedar face frame with flush-mortised table hinges and supported by brass quadrant stays. I rout arcs into each side of the secretaire cabinet for the brass quadrant stays by running the router base against a curved template. Finally, I mortise the latches that secure the drop front into the sides of the face frame and the mating catches into the wood around the leather writing surface.

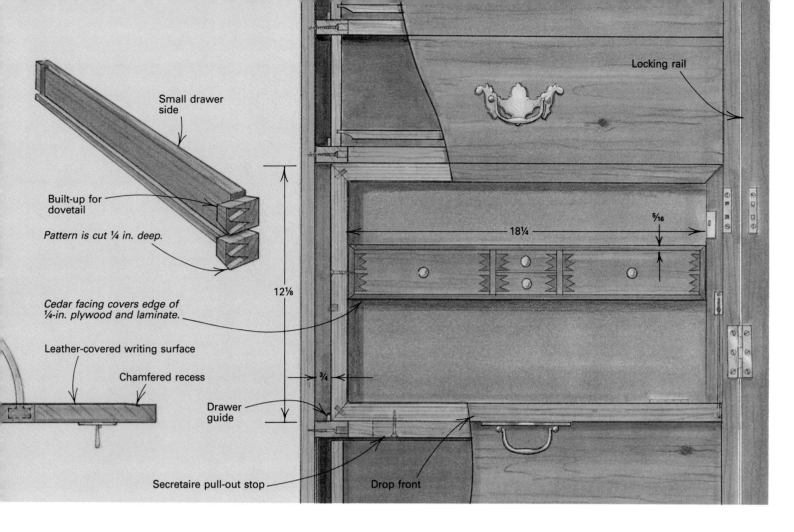

Small drawer side

Built-up for dovetail

Pattern is cut ¼ in. deep.

Cedar facing covers edge of ¼-in. plywood and laminate.

Leather-covered writing surface

Chamfered recess

Drawer guide

Secretaire pull-out stop

Drop front

Locking rail

18¼

12⅛

¾

5/16

The assembled secretaire cabinet is now slid into its space in the chest. To provide a stop for the sliding cabinet, I remove the drawer below, reach in and screw a strip of wood to the bottom of the cabinet that will bump the front rail of the U-frame when the top, front edge of the cabinet is even with the drawer front above it (see figure 3 above).

Locking rail and base – The 1½-in.-wide hinged rail, which closes and locks over the drawers to keep them from falling out when the chest is transported, is mounted with three brass butt hinges mortised into the rail and carcase. A chest lock and escutcheon plate are mortised into the right side of the carcase, and the keeper is let into the back side of the rail. The fixed rail is glued to the edge of the carcase's left side to maintain symmetry. Before the rails are mounted, they are contoured as shown in figure 2 on p. 49.

The base frame consists of four rails and legs mortised and tenoned together. The rails meet the legs ¼ in. down from the top of the legs. I chisel out a ¼-in. recess from the back side of the legs so the carcase can rest in this recess on the legs and on the top edge of the rails. The chest is retained by the portion of the legs that extends up around its corners.

Owing to the irregular grain, especially around the knots, I found the best preparation for finishing to be a hand scraper followed by hand-sanding with a cork block and 120-grit paper. Sanding with coarser grits or with power sanders simply raises the grain. Finishing knotty cedar can be a real challenge: The knots harbor the tree's resin, and for many years the resin tends to bleed through any finish, forming a gummy residue that gradually picks up household dust and other airborne particles. The only remedies I've found are to refinish the piece after, say, five years, or to accept the residue as a natural phenomenon. I doubt if even shellac, which is known for its sealing ability, could hold back this resin. Naturally, the older the piece of furniture, the less bleeding will occur.

I finished my Wellington chest with five coats of interior-grade polyurethane, rubbing the chest down with 0000 steel wool between coats. However, I've also used tung oil with equal, if not better, success. The same preparation is required, and the final finish appears a little softer than the polyurethane finish. The advantage of the oil finish is that when bleeding occurs, you can recondition the surface by scraping the resin from the offending areas and applying another coat of oil. With polyurethanes, you need to completely strip the finish and refinish from scratch.

After finishing, glue the leather into the chamfered recess on the inside of the drop front. I used Weldwood Plastic Resin glue, which is available at most hardware stores. I find that leather stretches some while gluing, so I advise you to run a test first to see if your leather is going to stretch; if necessary, cut the leather a little small to start with so you won't have to trim it after it's covered with glue. I made beveled strips that fit into the chamfered recess to help clamp the leather in place while the glue dries overnight. □

Vernon Harper, a graduate of the School of Furniture, Birmingham, England, was the lecturer in Commercial Carpentry at Bermuda College from 1980 to 1986. He now lives in Ontario, Canada.

Sources of supply

Brass hardware for the Wellington chest is available from Ball and Ball, 463 W. Lincoln Highway, Exton, PA 19341; (215) 363-7330. Hardware is listed by part name and 1987 catalog number:

    Chippendale pulls, C51
    Knobs for small drawers, G17-136
    Quadrant stays, J38
    Drop-front catches, J39
    Chest lock for rail, TJB-056
    Hinges for rail, H35-313
    Table hinges for drop front, H36-343

Building a Roll-Top Desk

Interlocking slats form an all-wood tambour

by Kenneth Baumert

I can recall my first encounter with a roll-top desk. My parents and I were visiting my uncle's home and were impressed with all the compartments and little drawers in his desk. Many years have passed since that visit, and I now realize that the greatest asset of a roll-top desk is not all the storage areas provided by the drawers and pigeon holes, but the tambour curtain that can be drawn over the working area to transform a cluttered utility desk into an elegant piece of furniture.

Before building my roll-top desk, I did a little research to determine what would be a typical design. The roots of the roll-top stretch back more than two centuries to the "bureau à cylindre" or cylinder desk, which was built in France in the 1700s. The curved solid cover, called a cylinder fall, "disappeared" as it was rotated into a large housing chamber within the desk. Another French cousin of the roll-top was the "secrétaire à abattant," which had a hinged, solid wood cover. This desk contained the small drawers and pigeon holes now found in the roll-top. Finally, a third relative of the roll-top, the tambour desk, came into prominence in En-

gland and America during the Hepplewhite and Sheraton periods of the late 1700s. It featured horizontal tambour doors that generally did not cover the writing surface. It wasn't until 1850 that Abner Cutler, owner of the Cutler Desk Co. in Buffalo, N.Y., combined elements from these desks and patented a desk with all the features we associate with roll-tops today: A curving tambour curtain that pulls down from above to completely enclose the pigeon holes and writing surface.

Although there have been many variations on the basic roll-top desk through the years, the most common method for constructing the tambour has always been to glue the slats to a canvas backing. This somewhat awkward process requires a special clamping board large enough to hold all the slats tightly together while the cloth backing is glued onto them. I used this method on my first roll-top, simply butting the slats together edge to edge. This may work on smaller tambours, but on my 4-ft.-wide roll-top, the slats at the convex part of the S-curve gradually separated from each other. Even though I could solve this problem by alternately rab-

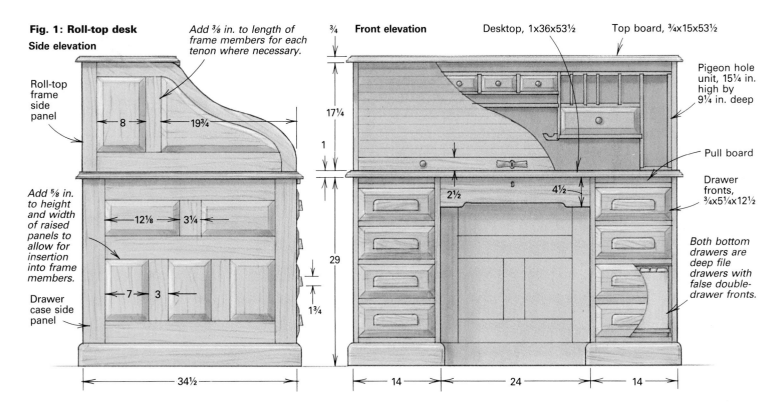

Fig. 1: Roll-top desk
Side elevation

Add ⅜ in. to length of frame members for each tenon where necessary.

Roll-top frame side panel

8   19¾

Add ⅝ in. to height and width of raised panels to allow for insertion into frame members.

12⅛   3¼

Drawer case side panel

7   3

34½

¾   **Front elevation**

Desktop, 1x36x53½   Top board, ¾x15x53½

17¼

1

2½   4½

29

1¾

14   24   14

Pigeon hole unit, 15¼ in. high by 9¼ in. deep

Pull board

Drawer fronts, ¾x5¼x12½

Both bottom drawers are deep file drawers with false double-drawer fronts.

From *Fine Woodworking* magazine (December 1989) 79:48-53

beting the edges of the slats like shiplap boards, so they would overlap and strengthen the cloth-back curtain, I wanted to eliminate the cloth backing completely. So, I sat down at the drawing board and designed an interlocking joint for the edges of the slats—kind of an elongated ball-and-socket joint—that holds the slats together without any backing at all. The mating parts of this joint are cut with a dado blade and standard router and shaper cutters. The interlocking tambour design, along with a mechanism for locking the six lower-case drawers by closing the tambour, help make this roll-top both a challenging project and a unique piece of furniture worthy of its long heritage.

Understanding the basic construction—The desktop in the photo at right is 36 in. deep and 53½ in. wide. The desk requires approximately 170 bd. ft. of hardwood lumber and about 25 bd. ft. of a secondary wood, such as poplar or pine, for drawer sides and slides. Drawer bottoms require two sheets of ¼-in. plywood or the equivalent amount of solid wood. I use ⁵⁄₄ stock for the writing surface so I can end up with a 1-in.-thick top after straightening and planing it. All the other parts are milled to their appropriate thickness from ¼ stock. The top board, drawer fronts, tambour stock and frame members of the frames and panels all are ¾ in. thick after milling. The raised panels and drawer sides are ½ in. thick and the pigeon holes are made from both ½-in.- and ¼-in.-thick stock.

One of the challenges presented by a complex piece of furniture like this is that it must be designed to be easily disassembled into its component parts for transport. Figure 2 on the following page shows how the parts go together. The two identical frame-and-panel drawer cases are glued up as individual units and form the foundation of the desk. Next, I attach the roll-top frame to the desktop with screws running from the underside of the top through elongated holes to allow the wide, solid top to expand or contract. Then, I attach the desktop and roll-top assembly to the drawer cases with figure 8-shape desktop fasteners, available from The Woodworkers' Store, 21801 Industrial Blvd., Rogers, Minn. 55374-9514, and various other mail-order companies. The circular shape of the figure 8s lets them rotate slightly to allow expansion and contraction, making them ideal for attaching solid tops. Four

A roll-top desk combines the best features of a utilitarian workspace with the elegance of a piece of fine furniture. The tambour on the author's oak desk, above, is made with interlocking slats, instead of being the more common cloth-back tambour.

figure 8s are screwed to the top edge of each case, as shown in figure 2. The desktop is then placed on top of the cases and the locations of the figure 8s are marked on it. Then, the top is removed and shallow mortises are drilled with a brad-point bit at the marks on its underside. The figure 8s fit into the mortises so the top will pull down tight to the frames when the screws are driven home. Be sure to angle the screws that go through the figure 8s and into the top so you can drive them in without hitting your knuckles on the side of the drawer case. To complete the base assembly, the center drawer is slid into place on guides screwed to the sides of the drawer cases.

The interlocking slats of the tambour are now fed into the access grooves at the top of each of the curved side panels. The top board is attached with figure 8s screwed to the roll-top frame in the same way the desktop is fixed to the drawer cases. Finally, with the tambour open, the pigeon hole unit is slid into place. It's made to just fit between the side panels and below the fully opened curtain. Felt glued to its bottom lets it slide easily without marring the surface of the desk. A narrow strip tacked along the back of the desktop acts as a stop to make sure the pigeon holes aren't slid so far back that they interfere with the opening of the curtain.

An optional knee-hole panel can be installed with knock-down hardware between the drawer cases. I prefer the heavy, solid look that this knee-hole panel gives the desk, especially when the desk is used in the center of a room instead of up against a wall. I originally used four regular 90° metal angle brackets to join the knee-hole panel to the drawer cases, but I've since found a somewhat more elegant solution, identified simply as "joining devices" in The Woodworkers' Store catalog. These three-part knock-down brackets, shown in the detail of figure 2 on the next page, provide a tight connection and disassemble and reassemble without having to remove and replace screws. The two brown plastic mating portions of the device screw to the parts to be joined and a metal joining plate slides over them to make the connection.

Making the frames and panels—As you can see in figure 1 at left, the basic building blocks of the desk are all frame-and-panel assemblies, except for the desktop and top board, which can be glued up and cut to size at this time. You'll need a left, right and back panel

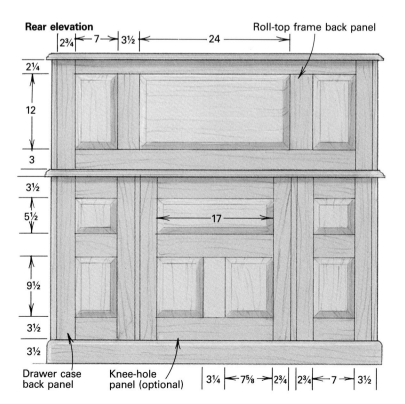

Rear elevation

Roll-top frame back panel

Drawer case back panel

Knee-hole panel (optional)

assembly for each of the drawer cases and, if you choose, a knee-hole panel assembly to go between them. The roll-top frame requires a back panel assembly and the two curved side panel assemblies. To begin, determine the overall dimensions of the desk you're building based on the size of the desktop, and prepare a parts list. Then, cut out, groove, tenon and bevel all the frame-and-panel parts for the base of the desk and the roll-top frame at one time.

I cut the grooves in the frame members with a dado blade on the tablesaw. These grooves accept the tenons from adjoining frame members and also provide the space to house the floating, raised panels. To simplify machining I've standardized the groove for all the pieces at ¼ in. wide by ⅜ in. deep. Where the back panels of the drawer cases and the roll-top frame join their respective side panels, a ¼-in. by ⅜-in. tongue, machined the full length of the frame member, is glued into a groove in the inside surface of the vertical frame members of the appropriate side panels. While you're cutting grooves and tenons, don't forget the parts for the drawer guide frames (see figure 2 below), as they also use the same size groove and tenon.

I originally cut the rectangular raised panels with a dado head on the tablesaw, but this was very time-consuming because of all the sanding needed to clean up the bevels. When I tried to make the cut in one pass with a panel-raising cutter on the shaper, I had to reject a significant number of panels because of chipping. Even when I made multiple passes, there was some chipping across the grain. To eliminate this chip out, I switched to a two-tool operation on the tablesaw and shaper. First, I make a ¹⁄₆₄-in.-deep scoring cut on the tablesaw at the inner edge of the bevel. Next, with the sawblade set to the same angle as the shaper's panel cutter, I saw off most of the waste. Finally, the shaper is set up to make the finish cut.

By slightly changing the settings on the tablesaw and shaper, you can bevel the ¾-in.-thick drawer fronts right after the panels are made. Experience has taught me to belt sand the outer surfaces of the drawer fronts and panels before cutting the bevels to avoid rounding the crisp edges of the raised panels. To sand the cross-grain bevels, I clamp the panels to the workbench and begin sanding with 80-grit paper on an electric block sander. Oak panels usually don't need to be sanded finer than 120-grit;

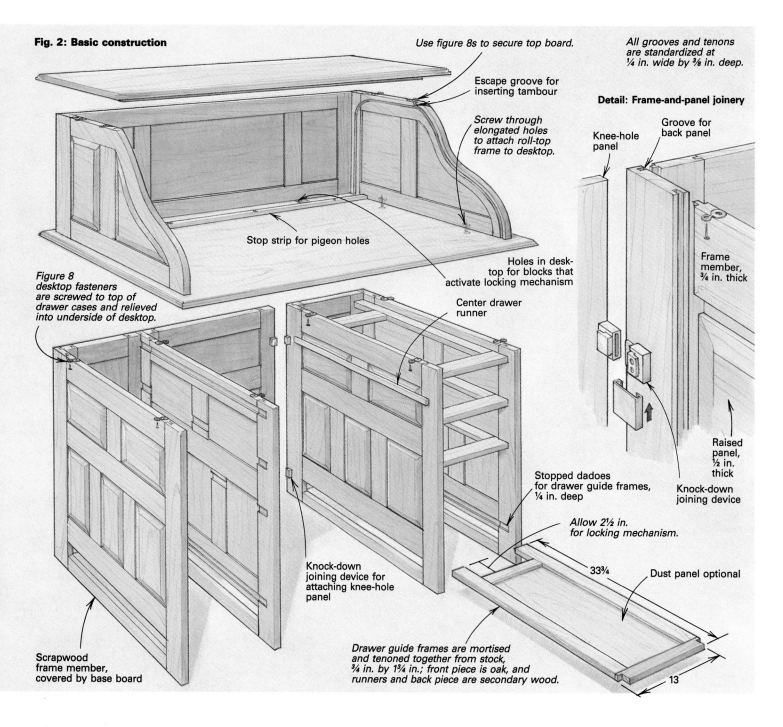

Fig. 2: Basic construction

Use figure 8s to secure top board.

All grooves and tenons are standardized at ¼ in. wide by ⅜ in. deep.

Escape groove for inserting tambour

Screw through elongated holes to attach roll-top frame to desktop.

Detail: Frame-and-panel joinery

Knee-hole panel

Groove for back panel

Stop strip for pigeon holes

Holes in desk-top for blocks that activate locking mechanism

Frame member, ¾ in. thick

Figure 8 desktop fasteners are screwed to top of drawer cases and relieved into underside of desktop.

Center drawer runner

Raised panel, ½ in. thick

Knock-down joining device

Stopped dadoes for drawer guide frames, ¼ in. deep

Allow 2½ in. for locking mechanism.

Knock-down joining device for attaching knee-hole panel

33¾

Dust panel optional

Scrapwood frame member, covered by base board

Drawer guide frames are mortised and tenoned together from stock, ¾ in. by 1¾ in.; front piece is oak, and runners and back piece are secondary wood.

13

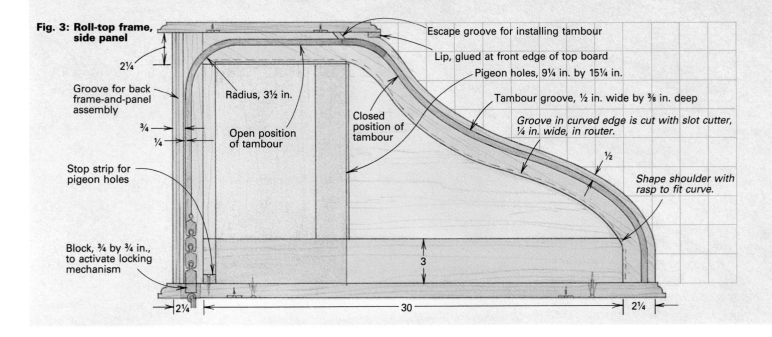

Fig. 3: Roll-top frame, side panel

2¼

Groove for back frame-and-panel assembly

Radius, 3½ in.

¾

¼

Open position of tambour

Closed position of tambour

Stop strip for pigeon holes

Block, ¾ by ¾ in., to activate locking mechanism

Escape groove for installing tambour

Lip, glued at front edge of top board

Pigeon holes, 9¼ in. by 15¼ in.

Tambour groove, ½ in. wide by ⅜ in. deep

Groove in curved edge is cut with slot cutter, ¼ in. wide, in router.

½

Shape shoulder with rasp to fit curve.

3

2¼

30

2¼

walnut and birch are usually sanded to 220-grit.

Work out the design for the curved frame-and-panel sides for the roll-top frame full scale on paper. When the tambour is open, only the handle slats should show and when the tambour is closed, there should be only one or two slats hidden behind the lip on the front edge of the top board (see figure 3 above). To test this relationship, lay a string along the path of the tambour groove on your drawing, and mark the length of the string when it's lying in the closed tambour position. Now, move the string to the open tambour position and compare the distances. Because the depth of the desktop is already established, you must vary the height of the side panel assembly and the slope of the curve until the two distances are equal.

Once you've established the profile of the roll-top frame, you can bandsaw the curved frame members and sand them smooth with a drum sander chucked in the drill press. Then, rout the groove in the inside edge with a bearing-guided ¼-in.-wide slotting bit. With rasps and files, I fit the shoulders of the tenons to the curve where the bottom frame piece of the side panels join the curved frame. After the frame pieces are complete, use them to lay out a pattern for the curved panels. Bandsaw the panels to shape and bevel them with a horizontal panel-raising shaper cutter in conjunction with a guide bearing. If you don't have one, you can use a bearing-guided router bit with a profile that will remove most of the waste, and then finish up with chisels and sandpaper to match the bevel on the other panels.

After all the frame-and-panel parts are grooved and tenoned, assemble them into the modules that will make up the desk. Take care when gluing the joints to avoid locking the panels to the frames; the panels must float freely so they can expand or contract with changes in humidity. In addition, be sure you have a flat area to lay out your clamps or you might end up with twisted case sides. After the cases are glued up, I run a baseboard around them, mitering it at the corners and screwing it to the case from inside the bottom rail. Since the first 3½ in. of the bottom rail gets covered by the baseboard, I save oak by leaving a gap and using scrapwood or secondary wood at the very bottom (see figure 2 on the facing page).

After removing the clamps from the frame-and-panel assemblies, sand the frame pieces with a small electric pad sander to about 100-grit. Keep the sander on the frame members and be careful not to round over the crisp corners of the raised panels. I go over the cases again with 100-grit after they are glued up and then usually finish-sand them to 120-grit.

Before gluing up the drawer cases, you need to lay out and cut the dadoes on the inside of the case sides to receive the drawer guide frames. I cut these stopped dadoes on the tablesaw, and then use a router to clean them out to within about 1 in. of the front, and right up to the groove for the back panel assembly at the rear of the case sides. Then, notch the front corners of the guide frames to fit the stopped dadoes (see figure 2). I use the tablesaw to ensure square and accurate notches. When the guide frames are all notched to fit, glue up the drawer cases. Make sure the cases go together square or you'll spend hours fitting the drawers to out-of-square openings.

With the base of the desk in clamps, you can turn your attention to the roll-top frame. Before gluing the curved side panels to the upper back panel, you'll need to rout the tambour groove, as shown in figure 3 above. The easiest way to do this is with a ½-in.-dia. pattern cutting bit and a Masonite template. Pattern cutting bits come with interchangeable bearings that fit on the ¼-in. shaft *above* the cutting portion of the bit, and they are available from Trendlines, 375 Beacham St., Chelsea, Mass. 02150. The top bearing makes it possible to use a Masonite template bandsawn to fit right up to the inside edge of the desired groove. Clamp the template and side panel to the top of your bench and rout the ⅜-in.-deep groove. The next step is to mark the location of the escape grooves for inserting the tambour slats and rout them freehand. Now you can glue the side panels to the upper back panel and attach the roll-top frame to the desktop. The top board can't be screwed in place until the tambour is installed, but this is a good time to mount the figure 8s to the side panels and mark and drill to recess them in the underside of the top. As shown in the photo on p. 53, a thin strip is glued below the front edge of the top. The purpose of this small lip is to fill the gap created by the curve of the tambour as it goes under the top. However, this piece should be made and glued in place only after the tambour is installed to be sure it doesn't interfere with the tambour's motion.

Drawers and locks—Each of the drawer cases that compose the base of the desk contains three drawers and a pull board, as shown in figure 1 on p. 52. Both bottom drawers are deep file cases that can hold either manila folders or Pendaflex hanging files. The fronts of the file drawers incorporate a visual ploy common to this style of roll-top: a false double-drawer front. The narrow, center drawer runs on wooden guides screwed to the side cases (see figure 2 on the facing page). Additional drawers, as many or few as you prefer, can be made to fit the pigeon holes.

My desk drawers have dovetails on all four corners and are flush

Fig. 4: Locking mechanism

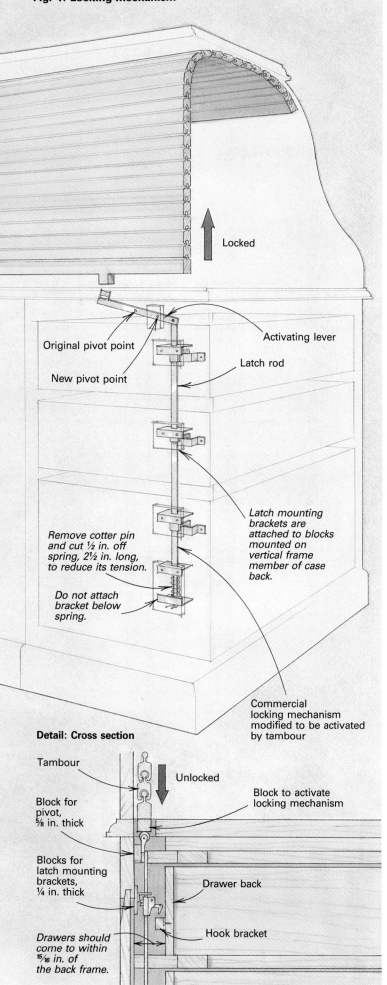

Locked

Original pivot point

New pivot point

Activating lever

Latch rod

Remove cotter pin and cut ½ in. off spring, 2½ in. long, to reduce its tension.

Do not attach bracket below spring.

Latch mounting brackets are attached to blocks mounted on vertical frame member of case back.

Commercial locking mechanism modified to be activated by tambour

Detail: Cross section

Tambour

Unlocked

Block for pivot, ⅝ in. thick

Block to activate locking mechanism

Blocks for latch mounting brackets, ¼ in. thick

Drawer back

Drawers should come to within ¹⁵⁄₁₆ in. of the back frame.

Hook bracket

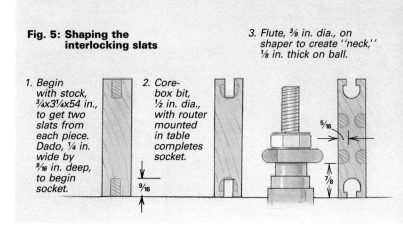

Fig. 5: Shaping the interlocking slats

3. Flute, ⅜ in. dia., on shaper to create "neck," ⅛ in. thick on ball.

1. Begin with stock, ¾x3¼x54 in., to get two slats from each piece. Dado, ¼ in. wide by ⁹⁄₁₆ in. deep, to begin socket.

2. Core-box bit, ½ in. dia., with router mounted in table completes socket.

⁹⁄₁₆

⁵⁄₁₆

⅞

mounted, meaning they fit within the case frame so their front edges are flush with the case. Flush drawers make it imperative that both the cases and the drawers be built perfectly square; the fit around the drawer front is right there for all to see. The wooden drawer pulls are easily made if you begin with a long piece of stock. Clamp this long board in a vise and lay out for several pulls, marking both the length of the pull and the location of the finger notch for each. Then, with the long piece still in the vise, rout all the notches with either a 45° bevel or a core-box bit. Bevel the front face of the pull stock on the tablesaw, and sand this beveled face. Now, crosscut each handle from the long stock and round the corners.

There are only two key holes in the desk, as shown in the photo on p. 53: one on the bottom slat of the tambour to secure it to the desktop and one for locking the center drawer. The side drawers lock automatically and simultaneously when the curtain is closed, and conversely unlock when the curtain is open.

I couldn't find a locking system designed to be activated by the tambour of a roll-top desk. But Selby Furniture Hardware Co. (321 Rider Ave., Bronx, N.Y. 10451) has a mechanism (part #L-7CTRDSK U) that locks all the side drawers when the center drawer is closed. With a few modifications, I made the mechanism work off the weight of the tambour. Metal rods with spring-loaded latches are screwed to the inside back of each of the drawer cases, and activating levers are connected to the top of each of these latch rods. To work off the center drawer, as the mechanism is designed to function, the latch rods are placed so the activating levers extend over to each side of the center drawer. Each lever is screwed to the back frame of the drawer cases so it will pivot when its free end is forced up by triangular metal brackets screwed at the back of each side of the center drawer. So, when the center drawer is closed, the brackets push up on the lever and the lever's pivoting action forces the latch rod down, engaging the latches with hook brackets on the back of each drawer and locking all the side drawers simultaneously. When the center drawer is open, a spring at the base of each latch rod pushes the rod back up, disengaging the latches and unlocking the drawers. However, this system is cumbersome because the center drawer has to be left partially open for the side drawers to be unlocked. By modifying the mechanism, as shown in figure 4 at left, I made it work off the weight of the tambour.

I reversed the position of the activating levers so that instead of the brackets on the center drawer pushing up on the levers to lock the drawers, the tambour will be pushing down on them. This means that the springs at the bottom of the latch rods, instead of pushing down on the bottom mounting bracket, will be pushing up against the first mounting bracket from the bottom. Since the bottom mounting bracket moves with the latch rod, it must not be screwed to the frame of the desk. Although the springs were easily squeezed by the force of the brackets on the center drawer, the

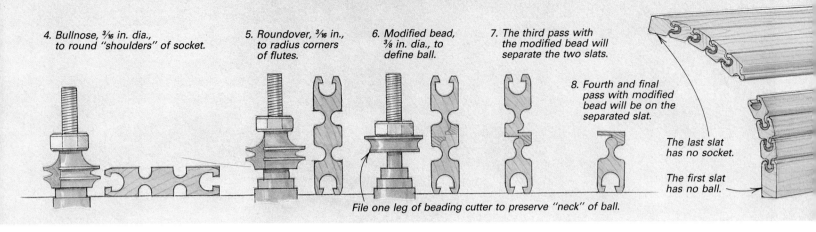

4. Bullnose, ³⁄₁₆ in. dia., to round "shoulders" of socket.

5. Roundover, ³⁄₁₆ in., to radius corners of flutes.

6. Modified bead, ³⁄₈ in. dia., to define ball.

7. The third pass with the modified bead will separate the two slats.

8. Fourth and final pass with modified bead will be on the separated slat.

The last slat has no socket.

The first slat has no ball.

File one leg of beading cutter to preserve "neck" of ball.

weight of the tambour was not sufficient to compress them. To remedy this I cut ½ in. off the 2½-in.-long springs and moved the fulcrum point of the activating levers closer to the lifting point to increase the levers' mechanical advantage.

Now that I've installed a few of these mechanisms, I find it's easier to mount the lock on the desk back before gluing the drawer case together. The lock is mounted with the curtain contact point 1 in. above the drawer case. A 1½-in. square is cut in the desktop and blocks glued to the last slat of the tambour activate the lock through these openings. The final step is to mount the hook brackets on the back of each drawer for the spring-loaded hooks to grab.

Shaping the tambour slats—One of the keys to shaping the interlocking joint on the edges of the slats is beginning with 3¼-in.-wide boards. This width allows you to get two slats out of each piece, which speeds up the process, and gives you a substantial piece of wood to work with, which keeps your hands away from the cutter. The 3¼-in.-wide boards should be milled ¾ in. thick and crosscut a little longer than the finished length of the slats. I prefer to sand the surfaces of the stock before machining the slats so the only clean up I have later is on the rounded-over corners.

Figure 5 above shows the progression of cuts I use to make the joint. The socket for the elongated ball-and-socket joint is begun with a ¼-in.-wide dado cut on the tablesaw and completed on the router table using a ½-in.-dia. core-box bit. You need to set the router table fence so the core-box bit will center on the dado groove to begin cutting. Once you're in the groove, the ¼-in.-dia. shaft of the core-box bit will guide itself along the dado.

The ball portion of the joint is formed on the shaper. First, I make four cuts with a ³⁄₈-in. flute cutter to define the ⅛-in.-thick "neck" of the ball. Then, I change to a multiple profile cutter, as shown in step #4 of figure 5 above, which has the next two shapes I need: a ³⁄₁₆-in. bullnose to contour the "shoulders" of the socket and a ³⁄₁₆-in. roundover for what will be the outer edges of the slats (step #5 of figure 5). The bullnose cut is made with the stock flat on the table; all the other passes are made by running the stock on edge. I readjust the fence and the height of the cutter in between the bullnose and roundover operations. The final ball shape is formed with a ³⁄₈-in. beading cutter that I modified by grinding back one of the protruding cutting wings so it would leave the neck of the ball. To avoid weakening the piece prematurely, make the first two cuts on opposite sides from opposite edges. The third pass will separate the two slats (see step #7 of figure 5) and the fourth and final cut will be done on an individual slat.

The whole operation results in a significant amount of chips and sawdust because the process removes approximately 40% of the blank. It may be desirable to hog out as much of the waste as

possible with a dado head on the tablesaw; some woods are less forgiving than others and won't tolerate heavy shaper cuts without splintering. Depending upon the quality of the wood, you should machine 5 or 10 extra slats to ensure that you end up with the 25 to 30 good slats needed for a desk. Don't forget to make a wide slat with only a socket for the handle slat, and make another with only a ball for the last slat. Also, the small blocks that fit through the holes in the desktop and disengage the locking mechanism when the tambour is open are glued to the last slat.

I don't crosscut the slats to final length until after I've screwed the roll-top frame to the desktop so I'm sure to get an accurate measurement. The slats should be about ⅛ in. shorter than the distance between the curtain grooves. Then, I cut a rabbet on the back side of both ends of each slat to leave a ⁷⁄₁₆-in.-thick tenon. Calculate the length of the tenon to leave the back of the slats ¹⁄₁₆ in. shorter than the distance between the roll-top side panels. The tenons for the handle slat have to be somewhat thinner and rounded so this wider piece will negotiate the curves.

Building the pigeon holes—I build the pigeon hole unit after the rest of the desk is complete so it can be dimensioned to fit between the side panels with very little to spare. When laying out the pigeon holes, consider how the desk will be used and design the compartments to suit that particular purpose.

All pigeon hole pieces are cut to size and sanded. Make the top and end pieces a little wider than the shelves and dividers so they can be rabbeted for a back piece. The grooves for joining the parts are all dadoed on the tablesaw. To ensure that the compartments all come out square, it's important to lay out and cut all the grooves from the same end of the horizontal shelves. This can be tricky, so take your time and check your spacing before you glue up the unit. Don't be surprised if you have to trim some of the pieces to length to account for the depths of the dadoes. Gluing up the pigeon holes is a delicate process because some grooves are only ¼ in. wide by ⅛ in. deep.

After all the component parts have been built and fitted together, the desk should be disassembled and the parts finished separately. I apply up to seven coats of polyurethane to the writing surface to completely close the pores. The other portions of the desk get three or four coats of polyurethane, and I sand between coats. The tambour slats are finished individually with a liberal amount brushed into the interlocking sockets. Once the finish is completely set, all wearing surfaces, such as the tambour's ball joints and the tambour grooves in the curved panels, as well as the drawer guides, are coated with a hard carnauba wax to ensure free and easy movement. □

Kenneth Baumert is a mechanical engineer and woodworker in Emmaus, Pa.

Post-Office Desk
Simple construction in the Southern tradition

by Carlyle Lynch

This simple desk was about all there was to some of the early post offices in rural settlements of 19th-century Virginia. Local woodworkers built the desks with a wide variety of native hard and soft woods, and the design often reflected their whimsey. The maker of the piece shown here is unknown, but the desk was almost certainly made in Grottoes, Va., or in a nearby village in the Shenandoah Valley.

Not fancy but well made, this walnut desk can afford a few subtle refinements without losing its character. For instance, its Spartan array of pigeonholes and shelves could be made symmetrical. Additional pigeonholes, proportioned and arranged differently, might enhance the idea of the post-office look. The simple, thin flat door panels might alternatively be replaced by raised panels, as suggested by the cross section in detail 4 of the drawing on the facing page. For historical purposes, I've drawn and measured the desk as it is, leaving to conjecture only hidden construction. Occasionally I'll depart from some visible detail, but I'll own up to it in the text. You are not so bound: Use the plan only as a guide or as a spur to your imagination.

The desk consists of two pieces: The dovetailed cabinet simply sits on the table, which has a leg-and-apron frame. The aprons are mortised and tenoned to turned legs. Molding nailed to the tabletop butts against the front and sides of the cabinet to hold the cabinet in position. The simple molding design helps unify the cabinet and table sections, and although most easily shaped with a router, I prefer the more subtle appearance created by hand-shaping.

Building the table and legs – Construction is straightforward. Begin by turning a set of legs for the frame. The leg design is quite simple and reflects the taste of the craftsman. The outside corners of the front legs are shown rounded, but it was not uncommon for them to be left square. The legs were, of course, turned individually; one leg was turned by eye, then it was used as a model to scale and mark out the cove-and-bead locations for the other legs. Making duplicates this way led to small differences from leg to leg, which lent an appealing sort of charm to the piece.

The table-frame joinery is next. The top rail on the original is ⅞ in. thick; the drawer rail is ¹³⁄₁₆ in. thick. Since boards were planed by hand in those days, the difference is probably due more to convenience than design. The human eye can easily pick up that ¹⁄₁₆ in. difference however, and you may find the variation more pleasing than not. The front rails are flush with the legs, but the back and side aprons are set in ³⁄₁₆ in. This seemed a little too much, so I've changed it to ⅛ in.; you may want to make it even less. I've used ⁵⁄₁₆-in.-thick tenons, and they can be as long as 1¼ in., which is allowed for in the materials list. Lay out and cut the mortises and tenons. Cutting them with traditional hand tools is not difficult, and the satisfaction gained is worth the effort.

There are two options for attaching the tabletop to its frame. Detail 1 on the facing page shows pocket holes bored for screws in the side and back aprons—the first option. The top drawer rail is also bored for pocket holes, but be careful to angle the holes enough so a screwdriver will clear the lower rail when you attach the tabletop to the frame. Detail 3 shows the second option, which requires cutting short grooves in the aprons to accommodate button clamps fashioned from pieces of scrapwood. Both methods were used in furniture of the period, but I prefer to use button clamps; the clamps hold the tabletop snugly to its frame but allow the top to move freely as it expands and contracts.

Assemble and dry-clamp the frame to check for fit and squareness. Make any adjustments, then glue it up. If you have a limited number of clamps, you can peg the tenons, as the original maker did, to hold pieces together until the glue dries. After the joints have dried, glue and nail the drawer guides and runners to the side aprons.

The drawer is made traditionally using hand-cut, half-blind

In the mid-19th century, desks like the one shown here were sufficient to serve the postal needs of a small Southern rural community. Few letters were written in those days, perhaps because postal rates were comparable to those of today.

From *Fine Woodworking* magazine (November 1988) 73:72-74

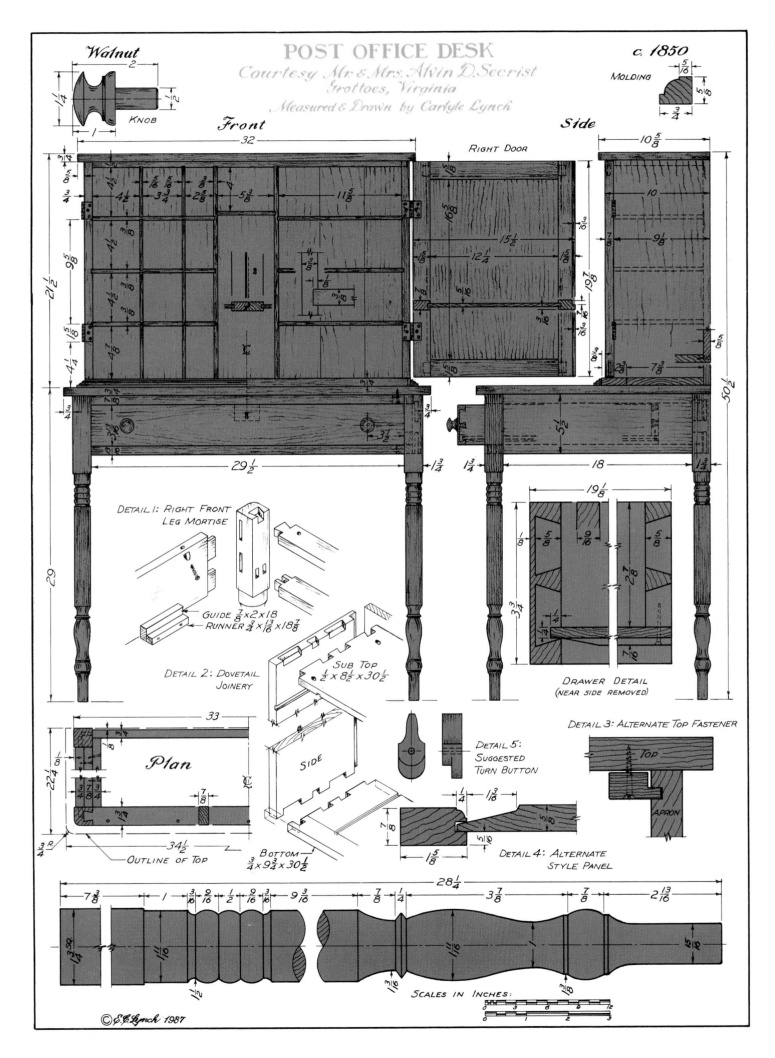

POST OFFICE DESK
Courtesy Mr. & Mrs. Alvin D. Secrist
Grottoes, Virginia
Measured & Drawn by Carlyle Lynch

c. 1850

Walnut

KNOB

MOLDING

Front

Side

RIGHT DOOR

DETAIL 1: RIGHT FRONT LEG MORTISE

GUIDE ⅞ x 2 x 18
RUNNER ¾ x 13⁄16 x 18⅞

DETAIL 2: DOVETAIL JOINERY

SUB TOP
½ x 8½ x 30½

SIDE

DRAWER DETAIL
(NEAR SIDE REMOVED)

DETAIL 3: ALTERNATE TOP FASTENER

TOP

APRON

DETAIL 5:
SUGGESTED
TURN BUTTON

Plan

OUTLINE OF TOP

BOTTOM
¾ x 9¾ x 30½

DETAIL 4: ALTERNATE
STYLE PANEL

SCALES IN INCHES:

© E. C. Lynch 1987

dovetails at the front and through dovetails at the back. The bottom is $^7/_{16}$-in.-thick pine, with three edges beveled to fit a $^1/_4$-in. slot cut in the front and sides of the drawer. The bottom is held in place by square nails driven into its rear edge up into the back of the drawer. Because nails tend to work loose over time, you may want to substitute screws. The $2^7/_8$-in. depth of the drawer seems a little shallow to be practical; to increase it a bit, use thinner pine or $^1/_4$-in. plywood for the bottom, increase the number of dovetails and make them smaller to allow the drawer bottom to sit lower.

The walnut drawer knobs were turned on the lathe. As with the legs, their design seems to have been a matter of the turner's taste. They were probably spindle-turned, cut off and finished by hand. It's easier, after turning the tenon, to use a spigot or three-jaw chuck to hold the tenon end while turning the knob. Cut kerfs across the grain of the tenoned ends. Then, when you install the knobs, position the kerfs vertically and drive small wedges (dipped in glue) into them to hold the knobs tight. The holes for the knobs can be filed slightly elliptical (along the grain direction) from the inside, forming a taper, which will increase the effectiveness of the wedge.

Adjust the drawer to slide smoothly in the frame, set it aside and make the frame top. Unless you are extremely fortunate to have a single piece of walnut wide enough, you'll have to glue up two or more pieces to meet the 22½-in. width. Two strips of pine screwed to the underside of the top through slotted holes will serve as drawer kickers. Once you fit the top to the frame, you'll be ready to start working on the cabinet.

Constructing the cabinet—The cabinet consists of walnut sides fastened to a walnut-edged pine bottom and a ½-in. pine subtop. The top piece is ¾-in.-thick walnut, which overhangs the front and sides and is attached by screws running up through the subtop. Attaching the sides to the subtop, then screwing on the top, avoids the more complicated joinery that would be necessary, because of the overhang, to join the sides directly to the top. The subtop also simplifies cutting the dadoes for the partitions. Since the subtop isn't visible when the doors are closed, there's no need to stop the dadoes.

The subtop and bottom can be rabbeted to the sides and held with glue and nails; I prefer the look of half-blind dovetails. Both methods are authentic. Before assembling the parts, cut shallow dadoes in the sides, subtop and bottom to hold shelves and partitions. Traditionally, these were cut through and so are visible from the front except at the bottom, where a 2⅜-in.-wide plain strip of walnut is edge-glued to the pine bottom after cutting the dadoes. This strip projects ⅜ in. beyond the front of the doors and is long enough to be flush with the sides. On the original piece, the pine bottom is ⅛ in. thinner than the walnut strip, creating an unnecessary dust catcher, so I made them the same thickness. Also before assembling, rabbet the back inside edges of the sides to accept ⅝-in. tongue-and-groove or ship-lap slats, which form the back of the cabinet. The subtop and bottom don't need to be rabbeted, because they are cut narrower than the sides and allow the back to butt against their full thickness. The inside partitions and shelves are a mixture of pine and poplar, fashioned from whichever was conveniently available. The arrangement of the nooks, wood variety and subtle dimensional differences between the vertical partitions and shelves works to avoid a monotonous look.

The design of the doors is quite simple: They're made using unadorned rails and stiles with thin flat panels. Brass butt hinges are gained into the door stiles and sides at the positions shown. The butting stiles of the doors are rabbeted so the right door

overlaps the left when closed. A wardrobe lock holds the right door to the left where a simple metal catch engages a keeper on the cabinet bottom. A nice alternative to the metal catch and keeper is a neatly designed turn button of walnut, as shown in detail 5 on the previous page. Neither the drawer nor the doors use escutcheons for the keyholes, but brass-thread escutcheons would be appropriate for use with the wood drawer knobs.

The desk is most appropriately finished by applying a traditional, hand-rubbed oil. □

Carlyle Lynch is a designer, cabinetmaker and retired teacher. He lives in Broadway, Va. More of his drawings are available from Garrett Wade, Lee Valley Tools Ltd., and Woodcraft Supply. Other articles by Lynch are on pp. 34-36, 40-43, and 77-79.

BILL OF MATERIALS

Amt.	Description	Wood	Dimensions
Base:			
4	Legs	walnut	1¾ x 1¾ x 28¼
2	Side aprons	walnut	¾ x 5½ x 20½, 18-in. s/s
1	Back apron	pine	¾ x 5½ x 31½, 29½ in. s/s
1	Top rail	walnut	⅞ x 1¾ x 31, 29½ in. d/d
1	Drawer rail	walnut	¹³/₁₆ x 1¾ x 32, 29½ in. s/s
1	Top, round front corners	walnut	¾ x 22½ x 34½
1	Drawer front	walnut	¾ x 3¾ x 29⁷/₁₆
2	Drawer sides	pine	⁹/₁₆ x 3¾ x 19
1	Drawer back	pine	⅝ x 2⅞ x 29⁷/₁₆
1	Drawer bottom	pine	⁷/₁₆ x 18⅝ x 28¹³/₁₆
2	Knobs, turn to pattern	walnut	1¼ x 1¼ x 2½
2	Drawer guides	pine	⅞ x 2 x 18
2	Drawer runners	pine	¾ x ¹³/₁₆ x 18⅞
2	Drawer kickers	pine	⅞ x 1 x 18
1	Top molding, miter ends	walnut	⅝ x ¾ x 32½
1	Top molding, makes two, miter one end	walnut	⅝ x ¾ x 23
Cabinet			
2	Sides	walnut	¾ x 9⅛ x 20¾
1	Top	walnut	¾ x 10⅝ x 32
1	Inside or subtop	pine	½ x 8½ x 30½, 29¼ in. d/d
1	Bottom front strip	walnut	¾ x 2⅜ x 30¾, 29¼ in. d/d
1	Bottom	pine	¾ x 7⅜ x 30½, 29¼ in. d/d
1	Back, tongue-groove or ship-lap	pine	⅝ x 30¼ x 20¾
6	Shelves, ⅛-in. gain into sides and partitions	pine	⅜ x 8½ x 11⅞
2	Center partitions	walnut	⅜ x 8½ x 19¾
1	Shelf	pine	⅜ x 8½ x 5⅝
6	Partitions	pine	⁵/₁₆ x 8½ x 4¾
2	Bottom partitions	pine	⁵/₁₆ x 8½ x 5⅛
4	Door stiles	walnut	⅞ x 1⅝ x 19⅞
4	Door rails	walnut	⅞ x 1⅝ x 13¾, 12¼ in. s/s
2	Door panels, fill edges before installing	walnut	⁵/₁₆ x 12¾ x 17⅛

Hardware: 2 pairs brass butt hinges, 1⅝-in. pin by 1¾ in.; 1 drawer lock with barrel key, ¹¹/₁₆ selvage to key pin; 1 wardrobe lock with barrel key; 1 door catch for left door or wood button.

s/s = shoulder to shoulder   d/d = dovetail to dovetail

Kentucky Quilt Cabinet
A cabinetmaker tackles two-board construction

by Warren A. May

A custom cabinetmaker has to be ready to make pieces of furniture that the general marketplace doesn't provide. At the same time, a craftsman is better off doing work that he feels a sympathy for. I had the chance to satisfy both requirements recently when some customers complained that they couldn't find furniture roomy enough to store quilts and other bulky items. Quilting is a popular hobby and home-industry in this part of Kentucky, and even if the quilters themselves didn't need a storage cabinet, I was sure the quilt collectors would.

The design is taken from the two-board hutches made by rural handymen all over this country. It's called two-board construction because of the sides—one long board on each side runs from floor to top to support the upper shelves and doors. A second, shorter board is attached on each side to support the counter and the lower shelves and doors. My adaptation, instead of shelves and doors at the bottom, has a pair of deep drawers. With some minor changes in the plans, this piece would be very easy to adapt to make a gun cabinet, a hi-fi center, a kitchen cabinet, or even a tool cabinet.

I have seen a lot of the old hutches, and I'd say the old joinery standards were, well, quick. Typical construction was a simple nailed butt joint reinforced with a nailed cleat on the inside. Shelves were laid atop nailed cleats as well. The two side boards often were not even glued along their length—the lower shelf cleats held them together. Lumber thickness varied randomly within any one piece, and so did cleat widths. It's as if whoever built these pieces was in a great hurry to get on to more important work, such as pulling stumps or cutting firewood.

These hutches served as storage and display pieces; sometimes the top doors were glazed so the contents would show, perhaps an imitation of the high-style city furniture, where china and porcelain figurines might have been kept visible yet out of harm's way. Ironically, all the glazed hutches I've seen had curtains inside so that the contents *wouldn't* show.

Hutches might be found in any room of the house, but most of them seemed to end up in the kitchen, storing canned goods and other non-perishable items. Inevitably, the doors sagged in time and rubbed a groove in the counter (I raised the doors in mine to prevent this). Some pieces were repaired with as much abandon as they had been made in the first place, and most have accumulated six or eight coats of paint, with apparently never the same color twice in a row. I love these old hutches because of the story they tell about past times. I remember one day seeing an old cabin that had sagged down a couple of feet on one side as the earth beneath it gradually eroded away. On the front porch was a two-board hutch that had managed to keep together and

keep its balance all the while—it was about 20° out of square when I saw it, but it hadn't given up. In fact, I managed to purchase it, straighten it up again, and give it a second chance. It has a place of honor in the gallery my wife, Frankye, and I run. Country crafts look just right in it, something you can't say about display cases made of glass and stainless steel.

So, when it came to making a cabinet for traditional quilts, I was predisposed to a two-board design. I felt that I could avoid the design's construction flaws without losing its character.

I like to run my shop, which is in a corner location down the

The quilt cabinet owes its lines to traditional hutches, but the joinery and detailing have come a long way from the originals.

Carcase construction

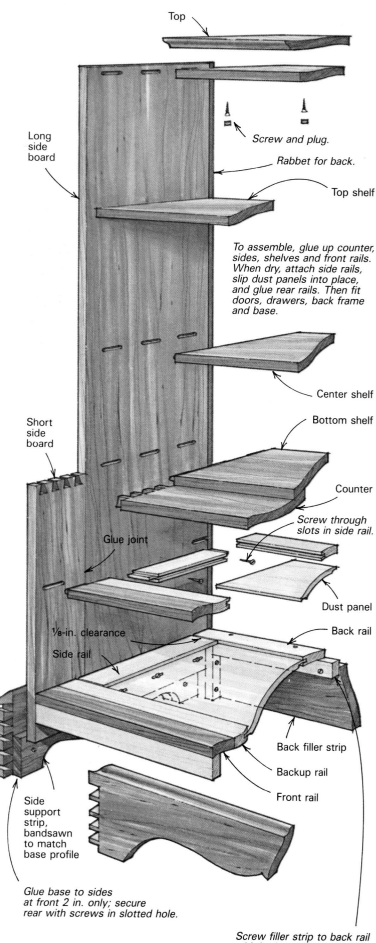

Top

Long side board

Screw and plug.

Rabbet for back.

Top shelf

To assemble, glue up counter, sides, shelves and front rails. When dry, attach side rails, slip dust panels into place, and glue rear rails. Then fit doors, drawers, back frame and base.

Center shelf

Bottom shelf

Short side board

Counter

Screw through slots in side rail.

Glue joint

Dust panel

Back rail

1/8-in. clearance

Side rail

Back filler strip

Backup rail

Front rail

Side support strip, bandsawn to match base profile

Glue base to sides at front 2 in. only; secure rear with screws in slotted hole.

Screw filler strip to back rail with horizontal cleat to form rabbet for back frame.

A mitered through dovetail is made the same as a regular dovetail, except that the top corners are tablesawn at a 45° angle before the rest of the joint is cut. Notice the author's reminder to himself not to cut the top layout line for the first pin.

street from the gallery, so that most operations can be done by one man. My helper and I are likely to get customers stopping by at any hour of the day, and this way one of us can get on with the job while the other goes to talk. Over the years, I've worked out a router-joinery method that's clear enough so that either one of us can take up where the other leaves off, and which even allows one-man glueup when necessary.

If you consider the construction of the quilt cabinet, you'll get the idea. The sides are solid wood, and the crossmembers (whether shelves or front and rear drawer rails) fit into routed mortises, which are easily made with a straight bit and a right-angle fence clamped to the work. For a stock thickness of 3/4 in. or 7/8 in., I have found that a 3/8-in.-thick tenon works best, with a length of 7/16 in. Mortises are 1/2 in. deep, to allow some end clearance, and can be routed in one pass in most woods.

I use several short mortises along the width of shelves rather than a long dado for two reasons. First, it is easier to fit the parts; second, the sides are stronger. At the top and bottom corners of my cases, I offset the tenons toward the inside of the cabinet, as shown in the plans, so as to leave more wood and help prevent end-grain breakout. I make tenons with a dado blade on the tablesaw, then clear the waste between them with bandsaw and chisel. The back of the case fits into a rabbet and is secured with brass screws. This allows the back to be removed for finishing the piece, which makes for a much cleaner job.

The top part of the quilt cabinet shows how such a construction would work for a simple bookcase. Just rout mortises for as many shelves as you would like, assemble by working the shelves in one at a time, then screw on the back. I like a solid top applied afterward, with a molded edge. The bottom can be similar to the top if the bookcase is hung on the wall; if it stands, you can apply a base and filler strip, as at the bottom of the quilt cabinet. I like the idea of a filler strip instead of carrying the sides all the way down, because it keeps the end grain away from the floor, where it might pick up moisture.

When my helper and I make a chest of drawers—the bottom half of the quilt cabinet is an example—the router-joinery method is very straightforward and allows easy assembly. To begin

Hutch plans

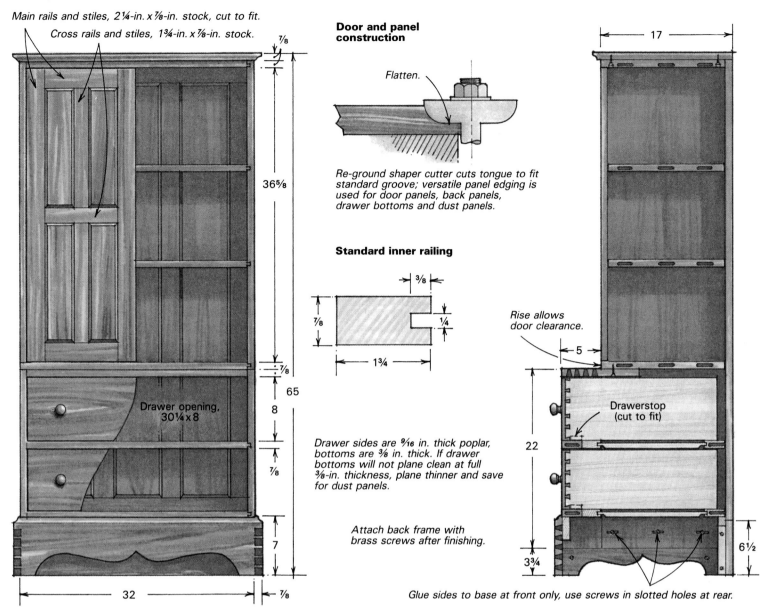

Main rails and stiles, 2¼-in. x ⅞-in. stock, cut to fit.

Cross rails and stiles, 1¾-in. x ⅞-in. stock.

⅞

36⅝

⅞

65

8

⅞

7

32

⅞

Drawer opening,
30¼ x 8

Door and panel construction

Flatten.

Re-ground shaper cutter cuts tongue to fit standard groove; versatile panel edging is used for door panels, back panels, drawer bottoms and dust panels.

Standard inner railing

⅜

⅞

¼

1¾

Drawer sides are 9/16 in. thick poplar, bottoms are ⅜ in. thick. If drawer bottoms will not plane clean at full ⅜-in. thickness, plane thinner and save for dust panels.

Attach back frame with brass screws after finishing.

17

Rise allows door clearance.

5

Drawerstop
(cut to fit)

22

3¾

6½

Glue sides to base at front only, use screws in slotted holes at rear.

with, we make up a standard yellow-poplar drawer rail in large lots, then use it for interior rails in all pieces. This alone saves a lot of confusion. The same profile, in show-wood, can be used for rails and stiles for doors and back panels, so we usually run off some in cherry and walnut as well. To shape the edges of the panels themselves, I re-ground a standard shaper cutter as shown above, to raise the panel and cut the ¼-in. lip at the same time. We leave this cutter on the shaper most of the time, because in addition to door panels and back panels, the shape is handy to thin down the edges of both drawer bottoms and dust panels.

In making a chest with drawers, we cut the sides of the case to size first, then rout mortises for the front and back drawer rails. Front rails are routed to fit flush with the edge, back rails are set in to allow room for the back framing. The front rails are show-wood, of course, and on a wide drawer, we often back them up by gluing on a strip of the standard yellow-poplar rail to give extra strength and to minimize any chance of warping.

For a chest, the first stage of assembly consists of gluing the front rails into the sides and clamping things square. When the glue is dry, we add the front backup rails, if any, and side rails, securing them as shown in the drawings. Then we slip in the dust panels and attach the back rails. The top can then be

screwed on from beneath and various forms of base moldings and feet can be added. Although it's nice to have company, all this can be a leisurely one-man job.

Of course, the quilt cabinet is more complicated than a simple chest of drawers. To build this piece, first dovetail the counter to the short side boards. Measure this to determine the shoulder-to-shoulder length of the shelves and drawer rails. Then disassemble the dovetail joint and glue the long side boards to the short ones. Proceed to rabbet the sides for the back framing, then rout the mortises for the shelves and rails. Next, measure all this to get the true sizes of the drawers and doors. Once the overall proportions are established, you can let the piece build itself to its own measurements as it goes along.

It will be necessary to dry fit the dovetails at the counter, but I'm not sure whether to recommend that you dry fit the whole thing. We have found that another advantage of using the same joinery from piece to piece is that you quickly learn what tolerances to allow so that joints practically weld themselves together. If you dry fit too often, the wood becomes overcompressed and some of this strength is lost. □

Warren May lives in Berea, Kentucky.

Constructing a Walnut Chest

A "keep-all" scaled down to fit any room

by Ronald Layport

All you need to build complex pieces of furniture is persistence and a command of basic joinery techniques. For me, learning woodworking has been a matter of reading, studying antique cabinetry and, most of all, lots of practice. My first and only woodworking class was in the fifth grade, when I learned to use basic hand tools and a bandsaw to make cutting boards and other simple objects. It wasn't until a few years ago that I began to build, in a serious way, on those elementary skills. So even if your woodworking experience is as limited as mine, I encourage you to tackle the projects that appeal to you. Most are more manageable than they might appear at first glance.

The project shown in the photo below and on the top of p. 67 is

Although the keeping chest looks huge, it's barely 5 ft. tall, less than 2 ft. wide and 14 in. deep. The secretaire's light, curly maple drawer fronts and cherry framework contrast with the dark walnut chest.

what I call a "keeping chest." It appears to be massive, yet it's barely 5 ft. high, less than 2 ft. wide, and only 14 in. deep. The chest is small enough to be slipped comfortably into tight spaces, yet it is distinctive enough to provide a startling contrast to the large, high-ceiling rooms of my turn-of-the-century home. When the doors are closed, the paneled, dark walnut exterior of the chest contributes to the piece's unassuming character. The simple brass hardware on the doors and drawers also enhances this understated quality. When the doors are opened, however, the strong, contrasting colors of the figured cherry and curly maple drawers in the removable secretaire are revealed. In addition, the panel in the pull-out writing surface is a piece of highly figured walnut with strongly contrasting heartwood and sapwood. The back of the chest is attractively paneled and finished, so the piece can stand away from the wall, if desired. As you can see from the photo on the bottom of p. 67, I've also designed the top of the chest to include a secret cash compartment, which challenges the truly curious individual to discover how to open it.

I work out of a small shop in the basement of my home. By any standards, it is modestly equipped. For a long time, a 10-in. table-saw and 14-in. drill press were my only power tools. Working almost exclusively with hand tools is slow in terms of output, but I find handwork is an enjoyable aspect of woodworking. Shaping wood and solving joinery problems with only handsaws, planes, chisels and scrapers has taught me more about the craft than I would have ever learned working only with power tools.

I'm not a "hand-tool purist" however; as my skills have developed, I've added machines to expand my capabilities and make my work go more quickly. About the time I came up with the idea for this keeping chest, I added a jointer and thickness planer to my shop. These tools broaden my design possibilities, making it easier for me to include thin stock and tighter tolerances in my designs.

My power tools are legitimate members of my design staff, waiting patiently to rough out parts, flatten stock and perform other routine and, at times, tiresome operations I used to do with hand tools. Most of all, the machines free up my time so I can concentrate on the things I like to do best: developing ideas, working out design problems, and cutting dovetails, mortises and decorative moldings with hand tools. The time spent making a tool for shaping the bead on a door stile or sweetening a tiny molding is its own reward.

Although all of my pieces are original designs, they are influenced by my fascination with the work of the itinerant cabinetmakers of the mid-1800s. These builders understood the limitations of their tools and materials; their design solutions reflected these limitations, resulting in many one-of-a-kind pieces. The honesty of their work,

Fig. 1: Keeping chest construction

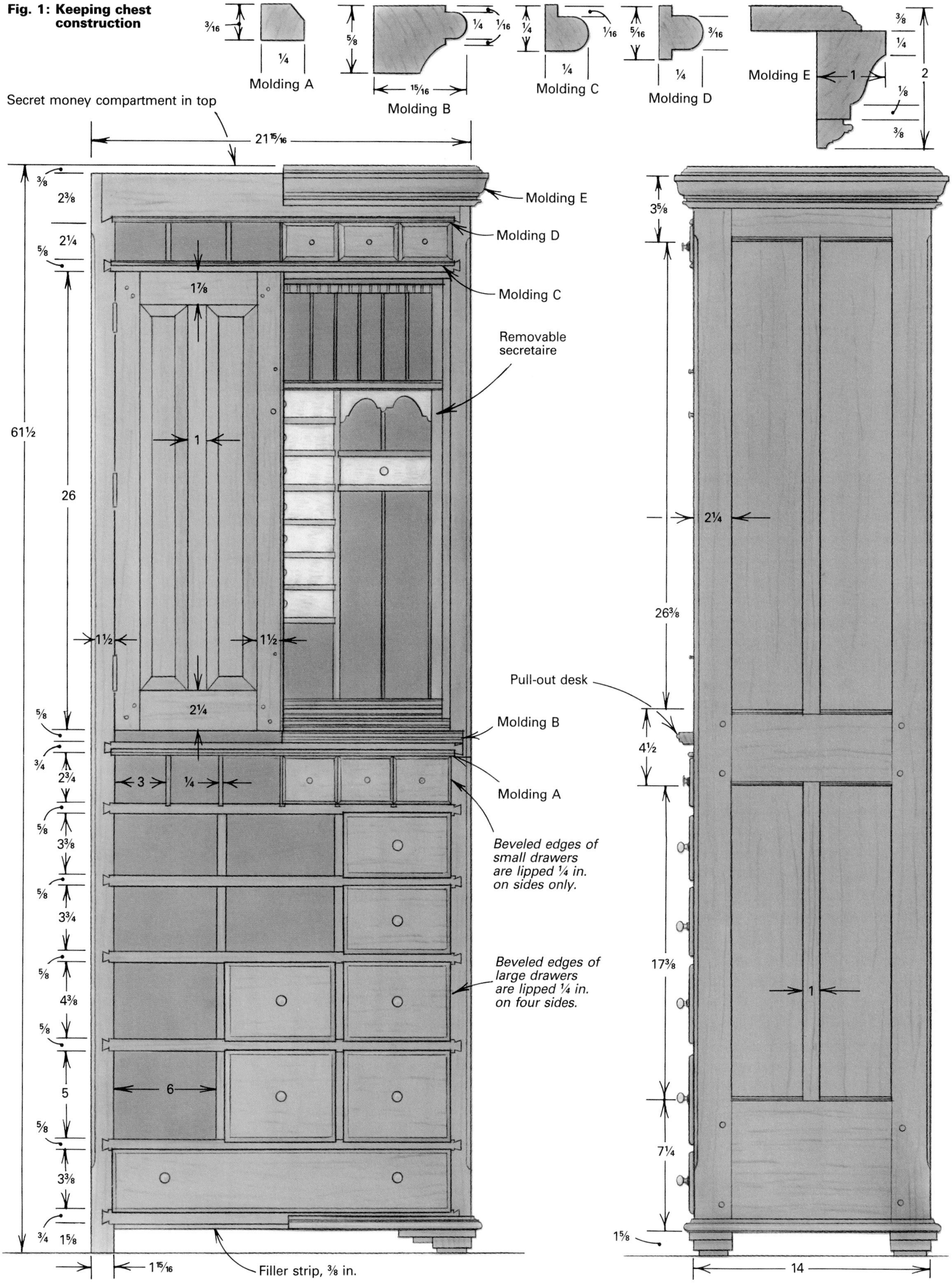
Molding A
3/16
1/4
Molding B
5/8
15/16
1/4
1/16
Molding C
1/4
1/4
1/16
Molding D
5/16
3/16
1/4
Molding E
3/8
1/4
1
2
1/8
3/8
Secret money compartment in top
21 15/16
3/8
2 3/8
2 1/4
5/8
Molding E
Molding D
Molding C
Removable secretaire
1 7/8
1
61 1/2
26
1 1/2
1 1/2
2 1/4
5/8
3/4
Molding B
Molding A
2 3/4
3
1/4
5/8
3 3/8
Beveled edges of small drawers are lipped 1/4 in. on sides only.
5/8
3 3/4
5/8
4 3/8
Beveled edges of large drawers are lipped 1/4 in. on four sides.
5/8
5
6
5/8
3 3/8
3/4
1 5/8
1 15/16
Filler strip, 3/8 in.
3 5/8
2 1/4
26 3/8
Pull-out desk
4 1/2
17 3/8
1
7 1/4
1 5/8
14

Drawings: Roland Wolf; photos: Chuck Fuhrer

including its flaws, reveals their humanness and teaches me to be patient with myself while I strive to reach their level of excellence.

Designing the chest—Each of my pieces is designed to satisfy a particular need for a specific person. This ensures that the piece will be put to practical use and not just idly admired. This chest was designed for my son, who is the family collector, record keeper and banker; thus, it needed lots of drawers to stash keys, newspaper clippings, small tools, telephone numbers and whatever else might strike his fancy. I thought a pull-out writing surface and secret cash compartment would facilitate his loan business with family members. And so the idea of a keeping chest evolved in my mind as a way of satisfying my son's needs, as well as my desire to pass on something of lasting value to him.

I usually work from very rough, conceptual sketches. Once I'm satisfied with the overall design, I concentrate on detail sketches to resolve construction problems and to develop a strategy for building the piece that is within the range of my skills and tools. Because of the complexity of the chest, I also made full-scale drawings so I could better visualize each detail. These full-scale drawings also helped me work out a unique interlocking framework, which allows for wood movement while providing support for the chest's many drawers.

Constructing the chest—Building this chest isn't difficult, despite the complexity of its design. I'd recommend that you begin by carefully studying the drawing on the previous page and those on the following three pages. I work on one section at a time. As I rough-cut the pieces for each section, I label all the parts clearly. This organized approach makes for greater accuracy and speeds construction. After rough-milling all the parts, I plane them to their final width and thickness, but leave the pieces a little long until I'm ready to cut the joints.

I built the side panels and drawer frames first, and then added the back corner stiles to the side panels, before gluing up the carcase. The drawer frames slide into dadoes in the side and back stiles, which simplifies alignment and ensures carcase squareness. After adding the back panels, I installed the face frame, moldings and feet. One of my objectives in building this piece was to hone my drawermaking skills; making the 34 drawers gave me experience akin to an apprenticeship. After completing the drawers, I turned my attention to making the paneled writing shelf, hidden cash compartment, doors and the removable secretaire. To finish the chest, I scraped and sanded all the components, and then applied three coats of warm linseed oil with a pad of 0000 steel wool, followed by a coat of low-luster tung oil, also rubbed out with 0000 steel wool. Finally, I installed the hardware and applied a coat of wax.

Making the panels and assembling the carcase—The pinned mortise-and-tenon frames for the side panels are made from 1⁵⁄₁₆-in.-thick stock. The ¼-in.-thick flat panels, float in ⁵⁄₁₆-in.-deep grooves. Dadoes are also routed across the inside surface of the stiles for each of the 10 drawer frames. To eliminate alignment errors when the drawer frames are installed, I place the side panels together, front edge to front edge, when routing these dadoes. The molding on the rails is milled before the panels are assembled. I make a ¾-in.-wide by ⁹⁄₁₆-in.-deep rabbet on the back inside edge of each side panel where the rear panel stiles will be glued and clamped to the side panels. The rear panel stiles are rabbeted along their length for the back panel and dadoed for the drawer frames.

The maple drawer frames are assembled with pinned mortise-and-tenon joints. I cut ⅛-in.-deep dadoes into each frame's top and bottom crossmembers to house the drawer guides and vertical separators. I rout adjacent drawer frames together for accurate alignment. Because the frames are not all alike, it's a good idea to check the dimensions and other details, shown in figure 1 on the previous page, frequently as the work progresses.

The next step is to install the drawer frames and construct the back panel. Because of the dadoes already cut in the side panels and back stiles, aligning the 10 drawer frames is fairly simple. After a trial dry fit, I glue and clamp the drawer frames to the side panels, usually making only minor adjustments to keep everything square and aligned.

The back panel construction details are shown in figure 2 on the facing page. I place the carcase face down on the floor and fit the back panel's top rail to the stiles. The two middle stiles can then be shaped, as shown in figure 2, and installed. I resaw and plane the three flat panels to ¼ in. thickness and thread them between the backs of the drawer frames and under the rabbeted edges of the stiles and top rail. Next, I fit the bottom rail in position. Finish nails, run through the stiles into the drawer frames, secure the stiles and allow the panels to float free.

Completing the internal framework—Once the dadoed drawer frames that make up the horizontal members of the framework have been installed, all that remains to be added are the vertical members and the face frame. If the dadoes were cut accurately and the carcase assembled squarely, this stage of the work proceeds very smoothly. I always feel I am handsomely rewarded for the care I invested in the early stages of the project.

The framework for the three-by-four array of drawers is assembled in three steps. First, I cut and slide the maple vertical supports into the back end of all dadoes. Then, the ⅝-in. by ½-in. drawer guides are cut and glued into the dadoed slots. Finally, the front vertical supports are inserted. As you can see in the construction details shown in figure 3 on the facing page, the frame components are sized and matched so the whole assembly locks together mechanically. Glue isn't necessary, but I do put some in the bottom dadoes as added insurance. This same method is used for attaching the face frame. The vertical members are notched in the back to mesh with the internal framework and also are notched in the front where they crosslap with the face frame's horizontal members. The dovetailed ends of the horizontal pieces fit into the dadoed side panels, as shown in figure 3. Both vertical and horizontal face frames are glued along their entire length to the internal framework.

Making the framework for the two sets of small drawers is less complex. Here, after installing the face frames, I simply insert ¼-in.-thick scrap cherry pieces, with the grain oriented vertically, into the dadoes. They should fit loosely to allow for wood movement, so no glue is used. These dividers are faced with walnut strips, which are glued flush to the face frame in the bottom dadoes only.

Drawers and doors—I use standard construction methods as described in *FWW on Boxes, Cases and Drawers* (The Taunton Press, 1985), building the main chest drawers first and the nine secretaire drawers later. Through dovetails connect the cherry sides to the back; half-blind dovetails join the sides to lipped walnut drawer fronts. The small drawers are lipped on the sides only. I shaped the edges of the larger drawer fronts with a molding plane and scrapers; they can also be shaped with a router. I beveled the front edges on the small drawers with a handplane. The dovetails, all 358 of them, are cut by hand. Paneled bottoms for the larger drawers are made from ¼-in.-thick stock. The panels' bottom edges are beveled with a handplane and float in ³⁄₁₆-in. dadoes cut into the front and sides; for the small drawers, I use ³⁄₁₆-in.-thick scrap pieces. Brads, nailed up through the bottom into the back of each

Fig. 2: Back panel

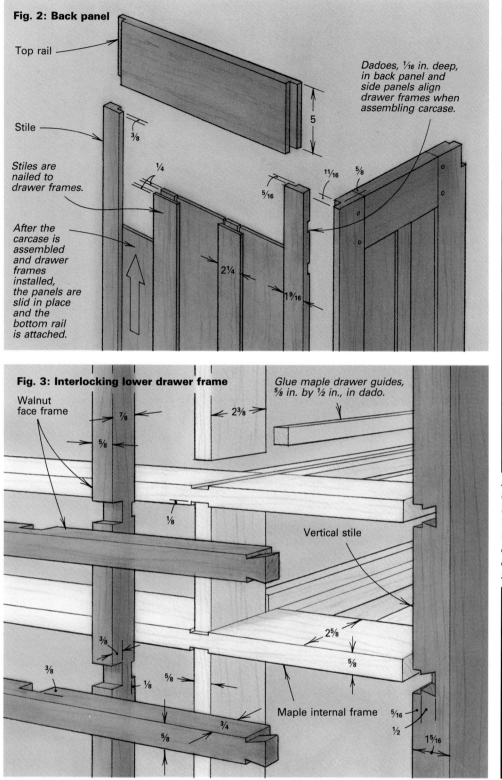

Top rail

Stile

Stiles are nailed to drawer frames.

After the carcase is assembled and drawer frames installed, the panels are slid in place and the bottom rail is attached.

Dadoes, 1/16 in. deep, in back panel and side panels align drawer frames when assembling carcase.

5

3/8

1/4

5/16

11/16

5/8

2 1/4

1 9/16

Fig. 3: Interlocking lower drawer frame

Glue maple drawer guides, 5/8 in. by 1/2 in., in dado.

Walnut face frame

7/8

2 3/8

5/8

1/8

Vertical stile

3/8

2 5/8

5/8

3/8

1/8

5/8

Maple internal frame

5/16

1/2

1 5/16

3/4

5/8

Above: The back of the chest is finished so it can stand away from the wall. Below: The lid of the secret cash compartment, built into the top of the chest, is opened by pushing up on a dowel hidden in one of the underlying drawers. The compartment's cherry dividers are dadoed to fit but are not glued, so they can be easily removed for cleaning.

drawer, holds the bottoms in place. Because I dimension the drawers for an exact fit, trimming isn't necessary after they are assembled.

The chest is fitted with frame-and-panel doors. I added a vertical center stile, tenoned to the rails, to visually enhance the vertical look of the chest. To keep them lightweight, the pinned, mortise-and-tenon frames were made from 9/16-in.-thick stock. The raised panels were roughed out on the tablesaw, finish-shaped with a handplane and allowed to float in the frames. After the doors are assembled, the mating edges are rabbeted so the doors will overlap when they are closed. Finally, I use a shopmade scraper to form a vertical 1/16-in.-dia. bead along the vertical mating edges of the doors.

Adding the frills—A variety of molding styles add interest and visual balance to the chest. I take my time in making moldings and improvise as I proceed. You can shape your moldings with a router, but I enjoy roughing them out on the tablesaw, and then using molding planes, shop-built scrapers and gouges to complete the job. The tiny moldings, above and below the small drawers at the top of the chest, are secured with glue and tiny brads; larger moldings are just spot-glued on.

The molding at the top of the chest is assembled from three separate pieces, and it frames the secret cash compartment, as shown in the bottom photo above. The compartment's frame-and-panel lid rests on the chest's carcase, flush with the top molding,

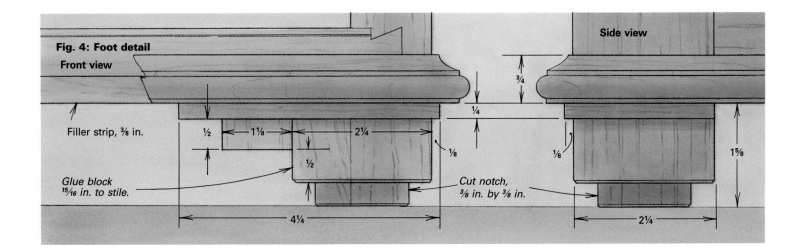

Fig. 4: Foot detail

Front view

Filler strip, ⅜ in.

Glue block ¹⁵⁄₁₆ in. to stile.

½

1⅛

2¼

½

¾

¼

⅛

⅛

Cut notch, ⅜ in. by ⅜ in.

4¼

Side view

1⅝

2¼

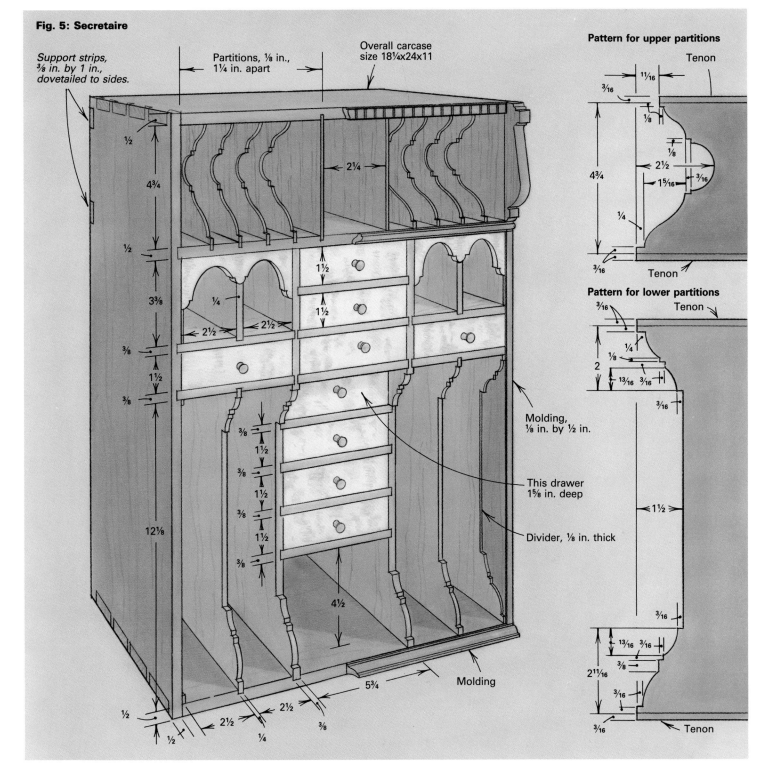

Fig. 5: Secretaire

Support strips, ⅜ in. by 1 in., dovetailed to sides.

Partitions, ⅛ in., 1¼ in. apart

Overall carcase size 18¼x24x11

½

4¾

½

3⅜

⅜

1½

⅜

12⅛

¼

2½

2½

1½

1½

2¼

¾

Molding, ⅛ in. by ½ in.

This drawer 1⅝ in. deep

Divider, ⅛ in. thick

⅜

1½

⅜

1½

⅜

1½

⅜

½

½

2½

¼

2½

⅜

5¾

4½

Molding

Pattern for upper partitions

Tenon

¹¹⁄₁₆

³⁄₁₆

⅛

⅛

4¾

2½

1⁵⁄₁₆

³⁄₁₆

¼

³⁄₁₆

Tenon

Pattern for lower partitions

Tenon

³⁄₁₆

¼

⅛

2

1³⁄₁₆

³⁄₁₆

³⁄₁₆

1½

³⁄₁₆

1³⁄₁₆

³⁄₁₆

⅜

2¹¹⁄₁₆

³⁄₁₆

³⁄₁₆

Tenon

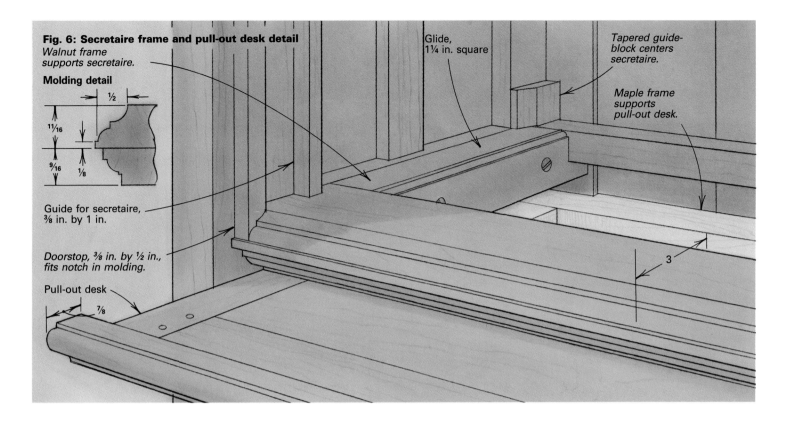

Fig. 6: Secretaire frame and pull-out desk detail
Walnut frame supports secretaire.

Molding detail

½
11/16
9/16
1/8

Guide for secretaire, ⅜ in. by 1 in.

Doorstop, ⅜ in. by ½ in., fits notch in molding.

Pull-out desk

⅞

Glide, 1¼ in. square

Tapered guide-block centers secretaire.

Maple frame supports pull-out desk.

3

and it is hinged at the back and held in a raised position with a 6-in. forged-brass chest stay. I bought mine from Garrett Wade Co. Inc., 161 Ave. of the Americas, New York, N.Y. 10013; (212) 807-1757; catalog #A101.01. I installed a vertical dowel, with a small knob on each end, through a hole in the bottom of the cash compartment, so that it extends into one of the underlying small drawers; to open the lid, reach in the small drawer with your finger and push up on the dowel.

The top of the frame for the six small drawers also serves as the bottom of the cash compartment. The separators, made from ³/₁₆-in.- and ⅛-in.-thick cherry stock, are dadoed together but not glued, so they can be removed easily for cleaning. I added another small walnut molding to hide the top outside edges of the cherry separator structure.

This chest looked best to me with its bottom slightly off the floor. Therefore, I laminated walnut scrap pieces, as shown in figure 4 on the facing page, to form feet and provide this visual "lift." Like the rest of the chest, the feet are intricate but not fussy.

I used walnut sapwood and heartwood for the panel, which is flush-fit in the mortise-and-tenon frame of the pull-out writing shelf. Molding, fastened to the frame's front edge, serves as a stop when the shelf is not being used, and it visually separates the upper and lower sections of the chest. A dowel installed at the back edge of the shelf rides in a stopped dado in the underlying frame and acts as a pull-out stop.

As a final touch in dressing up the chest, I used a molding plane and gouge to relieve the sharp edges along the length of the carcase stiles.

Removable secretaire—There are two reasons for making the secretaire section separately: it's more easily constructed and it's heavy enough that you'll want to remove it when you move the chest. The case is dovetailed, as you can see in figure 5 on the facing page, and it has no back. I used walnut to visually tie it to the chest. The walnut mail slot dividers float freely in stopped dadoes. The framework below the mail slots is cherry, which softens the color transition from the dark walnut chest to the light tiger

maple drawers, which are dovetailed and flush fitted.

Figure 6 above shows how the secretaire is supported in the chest by a walnut frame fastened to the carcase with screws. This frame also holds the writing surface in place. Tapered blocks attached to the carcase ensure that the secretaire is properly centered. Additional trim and moldings around the secretaire and attached to the carcase were installed to give it a built-in appearance.

Finishing up—I don't do much sanding; I prefer scrapers, which leave subtle traces of my handwork, such as scribe lines and molding imperfections, yet flatten and smooth the wood to my satisfaction. Three coats of boiled linseed oil is enough to seal and protect the wood and to develop a low sheen to complement the wood's color and grain. I heat the oil almost to its boiling point before each application. Linseed oil is flammable and should not be heated over an open flame; I also wear heavy rubber gloves when working with it. I rub out the oil with 0000 steel wool and allow it to sit for about 30 minutes before I wipe it dry. I let the chest sit for a day or so and then apply a coat of Sutherland Wells Low Luster Tung Oil, available from Garrett Wade Co., catalog #99RO2.01, which is also rubbed out with 0000 steel wool. For this piece, I applied a thin coat of water-soluble Solar Lux (NGR) Aniline Dye Stain (available from Behlen & Brothers, Route 30 N., Amsterdam, N.Y. 12010; 518-843-1380, and Garrett Wade Co.), which I like because it highlights the red and yellow tints in the walnut. Again, I use steel wool to remove the dye until I have the effect I want. A final coat of linseed oil, rubbed dry, restores a soft patina, and one or two coats of paste wax, applied a couple of days later, completes the job.

The final steps are to install the doors, the lid to the cash compartment, the drawer pulls and the door latch. All of the hardware is solid brass; I ordered it from Horton Brasses, Nooks Hill Road, Box 120F, Cromwell, Conn. 06416; (203) 635-4400. ☐

Ron Layport is an amateur woodworker and lives in Pittsburgh, Pa. He is currently building a curley maple sideboard, his first commissioned piece.

Shaker Casework

Simplifying the glories of Sheraton and Chippendale

by David Lamb

Even though I'm not a Shaker, I've lived most of my life in the Canterbury, N.H., Shaker Village where my stepfather is curator. For several years I was the village's resident cabinetmaker and operated a shop that was open to the public during the summer. Even though the Shaker cabinetmakers were gone by the time I learned my craft, I think the furniture, cabinetry and philosophy they left behind have profoundly influenced me, and that's apparent in both my contemporary and traditional work.

I don't just copy Shaker furniture, although I like the simplicity, balance and delicate refinement of many of the original pieces. As a craftsman and designer, I tend to start with ideas presented in the old pieces, then add my own touches to simplify or elaborate on these themes. Whenever I work from a Shaker original, my goal is always to take the good, throw out the bad, and try to bring each piece to its highest possible level. I make a coffee table, for example, that is a take-off on the large work tables at Canterbury. I incorporated the contours of its turned legs, its dovetailed drawers, and the small dropleaf on the back side in a very compact, functional and visually pleasing design for a piece of furniture the industrious Shakers just didn't have in their homes.

Not all Shaker work is particularly good. You'll see many Shaker pieces with shoddy, nailed joints and lots of visible saw marks. Even some of these cruder pieces, most likely built by Shaker farmers or other tradesmen filling in for trained woodworkers, have pleasing designs. If I were going to adapt one of these cruder pieces, perhaps one of the simple wall cabinets installed in many Shaker workshops, I would replace the dadoed-and-nailed joints with dovetails and probably add raised or flat panels for the cabinet doors, but strive to preserve the proportions and simplicity of the original.

Most of the best Shaker work was done between 1800 and 1860, when Shaker communities throughout the country were prospering and the religious fervor of the sect was at a high level. Because Shaker furniture was built over such a long period by numerous workers in more than 20 different communities, it's difficult to define what makes Shaker work "Shaker." The finest pieces demonstrate an extraordinary level of craftsmanship and attention to detail, along with a passion for efficiency and function. The Shakers created an incredible range of tables and carcases, both freestanding and built-in, often filled with custom-fitted drawers, as well as cupboards, shelving units and benches designed to meet the needs of groups of people trying to live together communally.

Sewing desks, the design source for the piece shown on the facing page, are a good example of the Shakers' skill at blending delicate framing elements, highly figured wood, and well executed joinery into an eminently functional piece. The desk features a good work area and supplemental slide-out writing/work surface. Placing drawers on the side, as well as the front, allowed two Shaker sisters to work together efficiently in a relatively small area. In addition to the functional aspects, some of these pieces featured precisely cut joints and such dazzling visual contrasts as bird's-eye maple panels framed with walnut.

There is nothing unusual about Shaker joinery, except that it was consistently well done in the finer pieces. The Shakers favored dovetails—both through and half-blind—and made good

Shaker sewing desks are eminently functional, as well as a skillful blend of delicate framing elements, highly figured wood and well executed joinery. Having drawers on two sides of the piece allowed two Shaker sisters to work together efficiently, in a relatively small area. This chest is based on one probably built in the Enfield, Conn., community about the middle of the 19th century.

use of mortise-and-tenon joints. On this piece, for example, the quirk bead worked on the rails and stiles is mitered at the joints to make everything fit nicely.

Frame-and-panel constructions, executed in cherry, maple and walnut, were favored for refined home furnishings, such as the sewing cabinet. This type of construction was very popular with cabinetmakers, but it was by no means new—its roots can be traced back to the time of the pharaohs. By using frame-and-panel techniques, cabinetmakers could build large pieces of furniture using short and narrow pieces of wood, without having to resort to extensive glue-up to make solid, and somewhat unstable, sides and backs. These short pieces could be joined together with mortises and tenons or dovetails, joints well-suited to the skills of craftsmen schooled in handtool techniques, to create very strong and stable cases. The cabinetmakers also favored highly figured wood, such as burls, crotches and branch figures, which were often available only as small pieces. These pieces were traditionally resawn so they could be matched together to create consistent grain patterns, and frames were an ideal way to display and accent these matched grains. The thinner, resawn pieces were also well suited for fitting into grooves plowed into the frames.

Although the Shakers benefited from the fact that the thin panels floating in frames tended not to split with the changing seasons, they apparently were most concerned with making efficient use of natural materials and with displaying wood grains, rather than with wood movement, one of the chief reasons we use the method today. Like their contemporaries, the Shakers didn't worry much about wood movement—they often rigidly nailed moldings perpendicular to the grain of the sides—but they worked before central heating introduced serious expansion and contraction problems. When beautiful, wide pieces of old pine were available, carcases often had solid sides. The tops of tables and cases were single solid boards or edge-joined of just two or three wide pieces.

The major design sources for the Shakers undoubtedly were the same as those of their more worldly contemporaries: mainly Sheraton, Hepplewhite, and country Chippendale styles. The Shakers simplified these designs greatly, though. If you examine fashionable early 19th-century pieces (*Fine Points of Furniture*, Crown Publishers, Inc., New York, shows quite a few), you see many that are strikingly similar to Shaker pieces, once you imagine them stripped of all the elaborate turning, carving, veneer, inlay, applied molding, and brass work. Many small tables, especially those built at Canterbury, mirror the Sheraton fondness for thin tapered legs with balls near or at their feet. Gone, however, are the elaborately molded edges of the Sheraton top and apron. Canterbury workers also built solid-side bureaus and blanket chests that had bracket feet with cyma curves or ogee cutouts and moldings, which reflect Chippendale forms. Shaker woodworkers who learned the craft before joining the community would have been very familiar with these contemporary styles.

The drive to simplify contemporary designs, avoid excess ornamentation, and maintain rigid quality standards can be traced directly to the Shakers' religious beliefs. Work was a form of prayer, and timeless perfection was the only acceptable goal. The community itself and its millennial laws provided guidelines for wood use, embellishments, color, what was acceptable and what wasn't, and what the piece would be used for. Even though the communities were scattered from Ohio and Kentucky to Maine, the ministry traveled frequently, promoting consistency and high standards from community to community.

Very few Shaker pieces are signed, so it's sometimes difficult to determine who made what and where. Achievement for its

Fig. 1: Shaker sewing cabinet

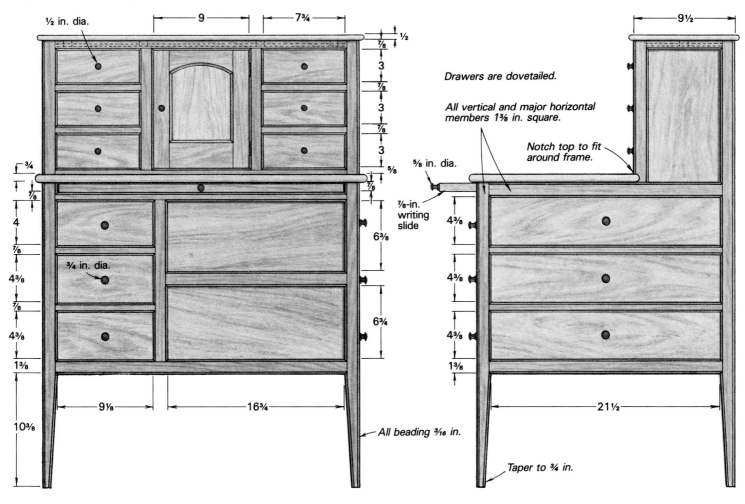

½ in. dia.

9

7¾

½

⅞

3

⅞

3

⅞

3

⅝

9½

¾

⅞

4

⅞

4⅜

⅞

4⅜

1⅜

10⅜

¾ in. dia.

⅝

⅞

6⅜

6¾

9⅛

16¾

Drawers are dovetailed.

All vertical and major horizontal members 1⅜ in. square.

Notch top to fit around frame.

⅝ in. dia.

⅞-in. writing slide

4⅜

4⅜

4⅜

1⅜

21½

All beading ³⁄₁₆ in.

Taper to ¾ in.

Fig. 2: Writing slide and cupboard door

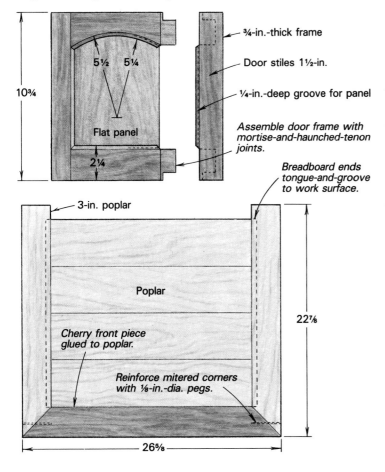

5½   5¼

10¾

Flat panel

2¼

3-in. poplar

Poplar

Cherry front piece glued to poplar.

Reinforce mitered corners with ⅛-in.-dia. pegs.

22⅞

26⅝

¾-in.-thick frame

Door stiles 1½-in.

¼-in.-deep groove for panel

Assemble door frame with mortise-and-haunched-tenon joints.

Breadboard ends tongue-and-groove to work surface.

own sake was not encouraged. Rather than encourage recognition for an individual, the Shakers stressed perfection as a way of reaching a higher plane of existence. Even without the cabinetmaker's signature, many pieces show undeniable similarities in the way proportions, turnings and tapers were handled. Many of the tables made at Canterbury are so similar, for example, they were probably all made by the same man. Pieces from New England and Mt. Lebanon, N.Y., all have what I can only describe as a nice feel about the way their makers gently tapered their table legs and created a pleasing balance with the unusual overhang of the tops and subtly shaped edges. In all the communities, delicate handturned pulls were favored. Despite these similarities, I don't think any of the ministers and craftsmen ever sat down to formulate a Shaker "style." The designs were more the result of religious tenets on simplicity and harmony, and a passion to ensure that form was inseparable from function. Displaying wood grain was itself a new development among the Shakers. The early religious leaders had proclaimed wood grain to be distracting, capable of inflaming the passions, and had ordered everything painted. When the restrictions against more natural finishes were relaxed, many Shaker communities stripped the paint off much of the furniture, doors, and other woodwork in their homes.

Another significant design factor was that the Shakers didn't produce furniture for commercial sale, except for chairs and stools manufactured at the Mt. Lebanon community. They made communal furniture to fit in specified locations and to meet specific needs. This explains why some pieces are asymmetrical—they had to fit a particular spot in a particular building. Since the Shakers had a reverence for taking care of all things, whether it

From *Fine Woodworking* magazine (May 1986) 58:30-36

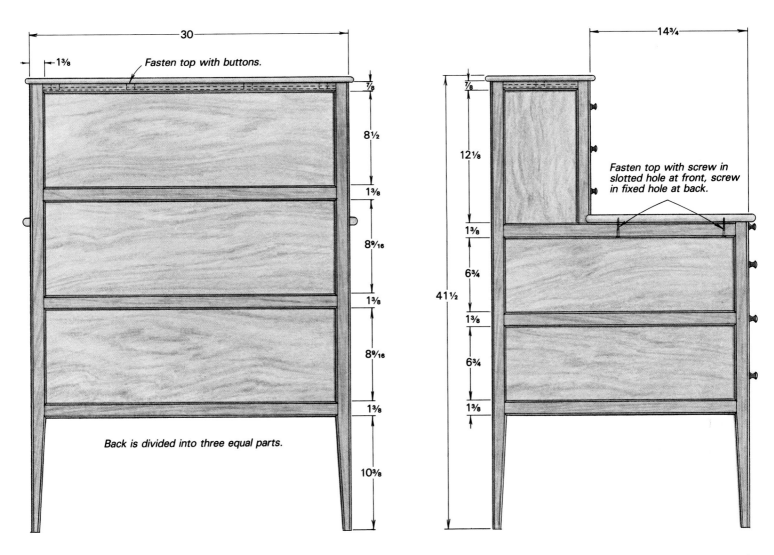

Fasten top with buttons.

30

1⅜

⅞

8½

1⅜

8⁹⁄₁₆

1⅜

8⁹⁄₁₆

1⅜

Back is divided into three equal parts.

10⅜

14¾

⅞

12⅛

Fasten top with screw in slotted hole at front, screw in fixed hole at back.

41½

1⅜

6¾

1⅜

6¾

1⅜

was children in the schools, animals in the fields or furniture, furniture could be more delicately designed than pieces destined for harsher treatment in the secular world.

I began work on my sewing chest by examining a walnut and poplar cabinet now displayed at the old meeting house in Canterbury. The chest is believed to have been built in the Enfield, Conn., community about the middle of the 19th century. I was interested mainly in size and proportions, rather than in deciphering the details of the original joinery and construction methods. I recorded the dimensions on a story stick, which I made from a piece of heavy cardboard. A story stick, which is as long as the longest frame piece (in this case the back post), contains all the information needed to construct the case—location of rails and stiles, top height and thickness, taper of legs, etc. The stick does not detail joinery. The cabinetmaker's knowledge of construction makes that information unnecessary, but during stock preparation you must remember to provide enough wood for cutting the joints. To record overall dimensions and proportions, I also made sketches of the front and side views of the piece, along with details. Later, I modified the original proportions a little, making the legs more graceful and slightly longer for today's taller people.

Like other 19th-century woodworkers, the Shakers relied heavily on handtool techniques. I like to cut joints by hand, hand-plane and scrape pieces whenever practical, but I'm not against machines. Neither were the Shakers, and I know they would approve of my shaper, tablesaw and planer, for they used them themselves. The Shakers excelled at taking advantage of whatever technical innovation appeared on the market. The Canterbury Village, for example, had electricty before anyone else in

the area because they built their own generating plant. Local farmers would wait and see what new products the Shakers bought before they invested any of their own money. The Shakers also made many of their own machines—they built the first machine to make tongue-and-groove boards, for example.

The paneled construction is such a good showcase for wood grains that I decided to build with cherry and poplar for the interior, secondary wood. I rough cut all the pieces needed for the chest at once, leaving things slightly oversize, then planed them to the proper width and thickness. I left each piece slightly long until I cut the joints. I don't make a materials or cutting list before I begin, but am particularly careful about labeling each piece and laying them out in units, for example all the top rails and stiles together, to make sure that I don't overlook any parts. This is a fairly complicated structure, so you should study the plans carefully before beginning.

When you lay out the mortises and tenons for the frame, you must set back the tenon shoulders, as shown in figure 3, to accommodate the mitered beading. I run ³⁄₁₆-in. beads on my shaper before cutting the joints. I could not find a commercial beading cutter with the profile I wanted, so I ground a custom knife from bar stock. I also mortise-and-tenon the front ends of the drawer runners into the drawer rails, and the back ends are screwed to posts, partitions and sub-posts, which are attached to the partition needed to support the side drawers. The Shakers usually nailed or glued theirs, but I like the added strength and neatness of the mortises. I tend to overbuild sometimes, compared to the delicacy of the original works, but I feel that the added strength is necessary because I don't know how

Drawings: Lee Hov

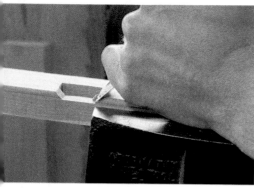

After sawing through the bead with a backsaw, Lamb pares away most of the waste with a sharp chisel, above top. Lamb carefully pares down to the miter line he previously marked, above center. The tenon shoulders, above, are chiseled the same way: one heavy cut, then light paring cuts to fit the joint. At right, the case is assembled dry to make sure everything fits. The panels are added when the frame is glued up.

roughly the piece will be treated once it leaves my shop.

After cutting all the tenons on the tablesaw and the mortises on my drill press set up for slot mortising, I square up the slots with a chisel, and trial fit the mortises and tenons together. Next I put a dado head on the saw to plough ¼-in. grooves for the panels. I carefully cut and pare the bead miters, as shown in the photo series above, on the rails and posts. I do this by eye, although you could cut a 45° angle block to guide your chisel. I first mark the miter locations on the post, then remove the bead in front of the mortise area with a handsaw and chisel. Saw the waste as shown and clean down to the bottom of the bead with chisel paring cuts from the front of the post. Next, cut the miters by chiseling from the top edge to the bottom of the bead. Do this in at least two cuts—one to remove the bulk of the waste, and one to clean up. It's a good idea to leave the miter somewhat heavy for later final fitting. Next, I fit the tenon partially into the mortise and draw in a matching miter angle. I carefully pare away on the rail until the two pieces fit tightly. Here, again, cut the miter in two steps. This is finicky work, but not as hard as it looks, and I think it's typical of the elegant, understated details

that appealed to the skilled craftsmen working under the sect's strict guidelines. Before going any further, I dry-fit the base unit together, as shown in the photo above. Because of the number of frame pieces, everything must fit together perfectly before you add any glue, or the real assembly will be a nightmare.

The top unit is an unusual construction, consisting of a separate face frame and a back frame formed by the extended rear legs. The unit's bottom and center cupboard are solid-wood construction. The cupboard is through dovetailed at the top and dadoed to the bottom. I used 1⅜-in.-thick breadboard ends to cap the bottom piece. These oversized ends rest on the top side rails of the lower case and hold the bottom level with the front rail of the upper cabinet face frame. The cupboard back is fitted into grooves let into the sides, top, and bottom. The cupboard also contains a shelf that is housed in dados about one-third to one-half the way down from the top. Tongues on the front edges of the solid cupboard and bottom fit into grooves milled into the back of the face frame. Next, I dry-fit the unit together and, if everything fits properly, I mortise the door frame for hinges. I glue up the top face frame and the cupboard and bottom assembly separately. When

Fig. 3: Carcase construction

Attach drawer runners, vertical supports, auxiliary strips (shown in blue) after assembling carcase and attaching bottom.

Frame-and-panel detail

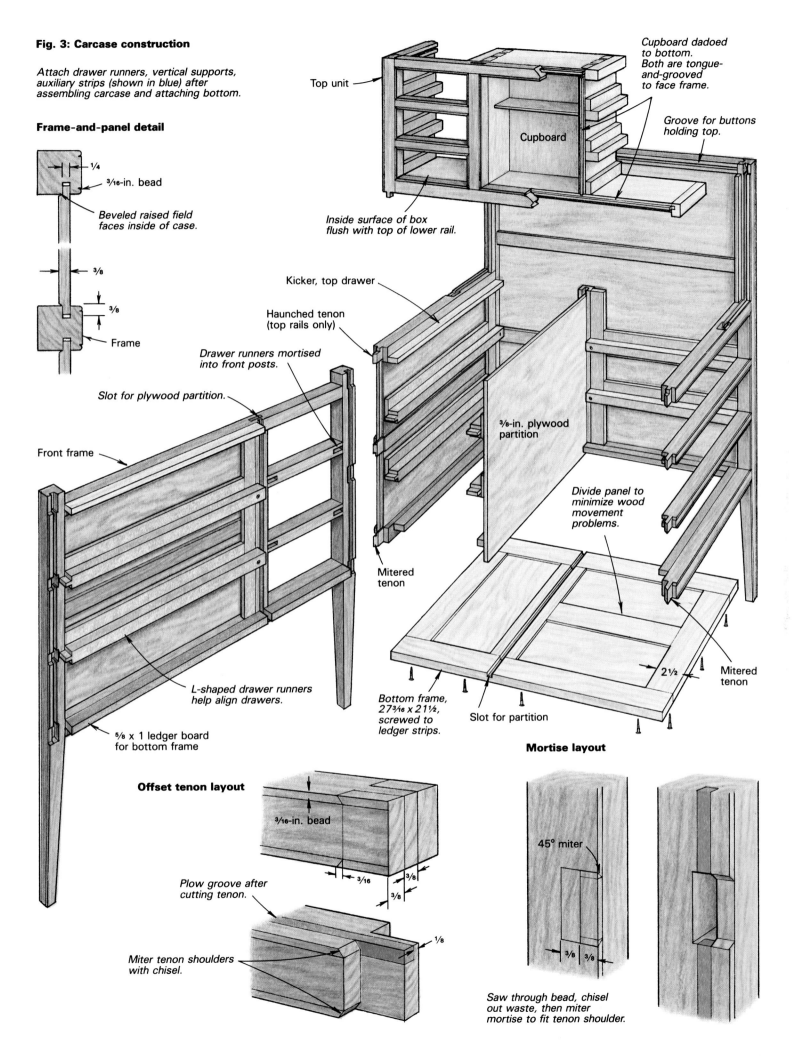

1/4

3/16-in. bead

Beveled raised field faces inside of case.

3/8

3/8

Frame

Top unit

Cupboard

Cupboard dadoed to bottom. Both are tongue-and-grooved to face frame.

Groove for buttons holding top.

Inside surface of box flush with top of lower rail.

Kicker, top drawer

Haunched tenon (top rails only)

Drawer runners mortised into front posts.

Slot for plywood partition.

Front frame

3/8-in. plywood partition

Divide panel to minimize wood movement problems.

Mitered tenon

L-shaped drawer runners help align drawers.

5/8 x 1 ledger board for bottom frame

Bottom frame, 27 3/16 x 21 1/2, screwed to ledger strips.

Slot for partition

2 1/2

Mitered tenon

Offset tenon layout

3/16-in. bead

3/16

3/8

3/8

Plow groove after cutting tenon.

Miter tenon shoulders with chisel.

1/8

Mortise layout

45° miter

3/8 3/8

Saw through bead, chisel out waste, then miter mortise to fit tenon shoulder.

Shaker designs offer an excellent way to display highly figured hardwoods. The delicately turned legs and gracefully shaped overhang on this bird's-eye maple chest are also hallmarks of the best Shaker work. This frame-and-panel chest is 21 in. deep, with a 3-in. overhang on the front, and 45 in. wide, including a 4½-in. overhang on each side. A ¼-in. bead highlights the drawer fronts and the inside edge of the frame of the side panels.

the glue is dry, I glue these two together. Assembly of the rest of the piece must wait until the panels are made and fitted.

I resaw the panels from 1⅛-in. stock, bookmatching and edge gluing the pieces together. I don't worry too much about the actual finished panel thickness, as long as they are all the same. The shaper raises the panels and puts a ¼-in.-thick tongue on all the edges. I aim for a snug fit in the panel grooves at first, then use a pad sander to finish sand the outside faces. Each panel is completely scraped and sanded before assembly. After sanding to 220-grit paper, I also wet the panels to raise the grain and sand again with 220 grit. Doing this now eliminates a lot of the raised grain that will result when I apply shellac to the finished case. I also sand the beading on the frame at this time.

Now I'm ready to glue up the frame. First, I assemble the front and back frames and panels separately, leaving the panels unglued and free to float. After cleaning up these assemblies, I connect them with the side rails, then install the frame-and-panel bottom. Before gluing the already-assembled top face frame and cupboard to the lower case, I install the bottom and the ⅜-in.-thick plywood partitions separating the two lower drawer sections.

To install the bottom, I apply a 1-in. by ⅝-in. strip around the inside of the carcase, flush with the top of the rails. I mill out a rear sub post to match the front divider and groove it to accept the plywood partition. I position the post against the back rails and screw it in place, exactly in line and square to the front post. I build the frame-and-panel unit as shown in figure 1 from 2½-in. by ¾-in. stock, and push it up from the bottom until it is snug against the applied strip, and level with the lower desk rail. The bottom is screwed to the strips, which also act as drawer runners. Once the bottom is in place, I insert the plywood partition from the top, fit it into the groove I cut in the bottom, and glue it in place. At this time, I also install drawer guides and apply strips to the inside top side rails and front to act as kickers for the top drawers and to support the writing slide.

The tops each have a shallow nosing worked around the edges. The upper top is attached to the frame with 10 buttons let into grooves cut into the top rails. The lower countertop, which is the actual working surface, must be held tightly against the lower rail of the face frame. I used a fixed screw through the side

rail to hold the work surface tight to the upper cabinet and a slot-housed screw in the front end of the side rails. Since the ends of the top extend beyond the front face of the upper cabinet, the back edge of the top must be notched to fit around the cabinet.

The slide-out writing surface is made from poplar edged with 3-in.-wide cherry, mitered at the corners. I edge-glued the front piece to the poplar, but attached the poplar side pieces with wide tongue-and-groove joints glued only at the front end and the first few inches of the panel, and spot glued in the center.

The drawers are next. I fit the fronts to the openings first, again allowing for seasonal expansion by fitting them tight if I'm working in the summer and loose in the winter. Conventional half-blind dovetails join the drawer fronts to the sides, through dovetails join the sides to the back. I've never noticed any standard rules on dovetail angles and spacing used by the Shakers, so I just lay them out to suit my eye. Here I used fairly delicate tails, about ⅜ in. at the widest. Once the drawers have been fitted, I install stops on the drawer runners.

I made the door using standard mortise-and-haunched-tenon joints, but chamfered the edges of the door frame instead of cutting a small bead, as with the rest of the frame elements. A bullet catch with a brass strike inset in the threshold of the door frame keeps the door shut. I also turned a small walnut doorstop and inserted it in the door jamb directly behind the door pull.

I turned ¾-in.-diameter drawer pulls for the lower drawers and ½-in. to ⅝-in.-dia. pulls for the slide, door, and upper drawers. I don't know of any mathematical rules or proportions the Shakers used for their pulls, but over the years I have gravitated to making the length of the pull roughly equal to its largest diameter. This makes a delicate looking pull that feels right to your fingers. I turn six or seven pulls at a time on a single blank. After sawing the individual pulls apart, I mount each tenon in a Jacobs chuck mounted in the lathe headstock, to sand the face of the pull.

After handscraping the chest and sanding it with a pad sander, I applied a thin cut of shellac. I use light coats and build up the finish gradually. I rub down all the surfaces between coats with 400-grit wet/dry silicon-carbide paper. The inside of the case is finished in the same way. The insides of the drawers and the two tops are finished with a 50/50 mixture of oil and varnish. I apply the oil mixture with a brush, let it stand until it's tacky, then rub vigorously with a clean lint-free cloth until it doesn't look wet anymore. Do small sections, a couple of square feet at a time, since the mixture dries rapidly. Apply enough coats to build a film roughly as thick as the shellac. When I'm satisfied with the finish, I wax the surfaces and polish. I think these two finishes are very compatible. I'm particularly fond of the look of a good shellac finish, but think the oil/varnish mixture is better for areas subject to abuse or water and alcohol.

I am continually amazed by the quality and beauty of the original Shaker pieces, and by the inspiration they offer modern workers. And, they are challenging enough to interest even the most accomplished craftsman. Shaker designs also provide a way to display the most beautiful, highly figured woods without detracting from the beauty of the piece itself. So good is the design that, no matter what the decor of your home—modern or traditional—a Shaker piece seems to fit right in. □

David Lamb builds Shaker-inspired traditional and contemporary furniture at 370 Shaker Road, just down the road from the Canterbury Shaker Village. For information about visiting the village, write Shaker Village Inc., Canterbury, N.H. 03224. The village is open from mid-May through Columbus Day.

Provincial Corner Cupboard

No-frills country joinery

by Carlyle Lynch

Corner cupboards have long been popular for transforming useless room corners into efficient storage areas that seem to blend right into the walls. Even though these triangular pieces were designed to be purely functional, early craftsmen couldn't resist turning them into beautiful showcases of their own skill. Often they added distinctive touches like the arched panel doors on the cupboard shown above, which is now in the Great Hall of the Tuckahoe Plantation in Richmond, Va.

The simplicity of this one-piece walnut and riftsawn yellow pine cupboard suggests that it was made by a country craftsman at Tuckahoe shortly after the plantation was built in 1712. Tuckahoe, now a national historic landmark, is noted for its architecture and furnishings, so it's not surprising that a cabinetmaker working there would have tried to make the cupboard special. Later, as the cabinetmakers' art flourished in America, corner cupboards were embellished with more intricate moldings, bracket feet and delicately framed glass doors.

My measured drawing and bill of materials (pp. 78 and 79) show the lumber thicknesses of the original, but more conventional stock sizes will work all right. The carcase sides and doors can be 7/8 in. or 13/16 in. thick. You could make the back panels from 1/2-in. boards and work the cornice from 3/4-in. stock.

While it's impossible to know exactly how the original maker went about constructing the piece, I think that this practical worker might have made the shelves, bottom and top first, then simply nailed or pinned the two sides and back center piece to them. This formed a rigid skeleton to which the rails, molding and doors could be added. Even though the cabinetmaker used nails (you can feel them if you insert a thin knife between the shelves and sides), it's difficult to see any nail holes on the sides. I suspect that he filled the holes with tiny plugs, carefully matching the grain of the sides—pretty sophisticated work.

Since the hexagonal shelf units are 19 in. deep, you'll have to edge-glue several narrower boards to get the required width. Saw the pieces a little longer than needed in case individual boards shift slightly in the clamps. You can trim the shelves to size after the glue has cured. For additional strength, or perhaps because the cabinetmaker didn't bother to thickness-

plane parts that wouldn't show, the waist shelf, top and bottom on the original are thicker than the other shelves.

The sides and back center piece are made from single long boards. On each side, bevel the front edge 22½° so it can butt against the beveled door to form a 45° corner, and rabbet the back edge for the back panels. Bevel both edges of the back center piece to 45°. Now nail these pieces to the shelves—one way would be to prop up the hexagonal top on the floor and tack a side to it, then prop up the bottom and tack the side to it. All the shelves are permanent, so while the assembly is still on the floor, nail the remaining shelves to the side, then nail on the second side. The cupboard framing should now be rigid enough for you to flip it over and nail the back center piece to the shelves.

Next pin the top, waist and base rails to the cupboard. The rail ends are beveled 22½° and appear butted to the sides, forming a 45° angle between them. I suspect, however, that blind tenons or splines (figure 2) may have been used for extra strength. Once the rails are in place, nail the shiplapped boards to the back center piece, shelves and sides.

The basic cupboard is now ready for some decorative touches. Make and apply all moldings—the profiles used on the original are shown on the plan. Miter the waist molding to fit the 45° angles on the sides. For the cornice, make a coving cut on the tablesaw, then form the beads with a shaper or router. If you are really ambitious, you could also hand-carve or plane the molding. If you're less zealous, you may be able to find patterns close enough to the originals at a well-stocked mill shop.

Next make the doors. Make sure you work carefully—it's too late to change the carcase, should you make the doors undersize (which is why some cabinetmakers prefer to make the doors first, then build the carcase to fit). Through mortise-and-tenons are used on the original door frames, but figure 3 on p. 79 **shows an easier way to build the frames with blind mortises. Cut** all the door stiles and rails to size, then mold and plow the inside edges to accept the panels before you lay out and cut the mortises and tenons. On the original, the grooves are about 1/4 in. to 5/16 in. deep. To assemble the frames, you'll have to miter the molded edges of the stiles so they can be fitted to the rails. A 45° guide block and a sharp chisel will work well to miter the mold-

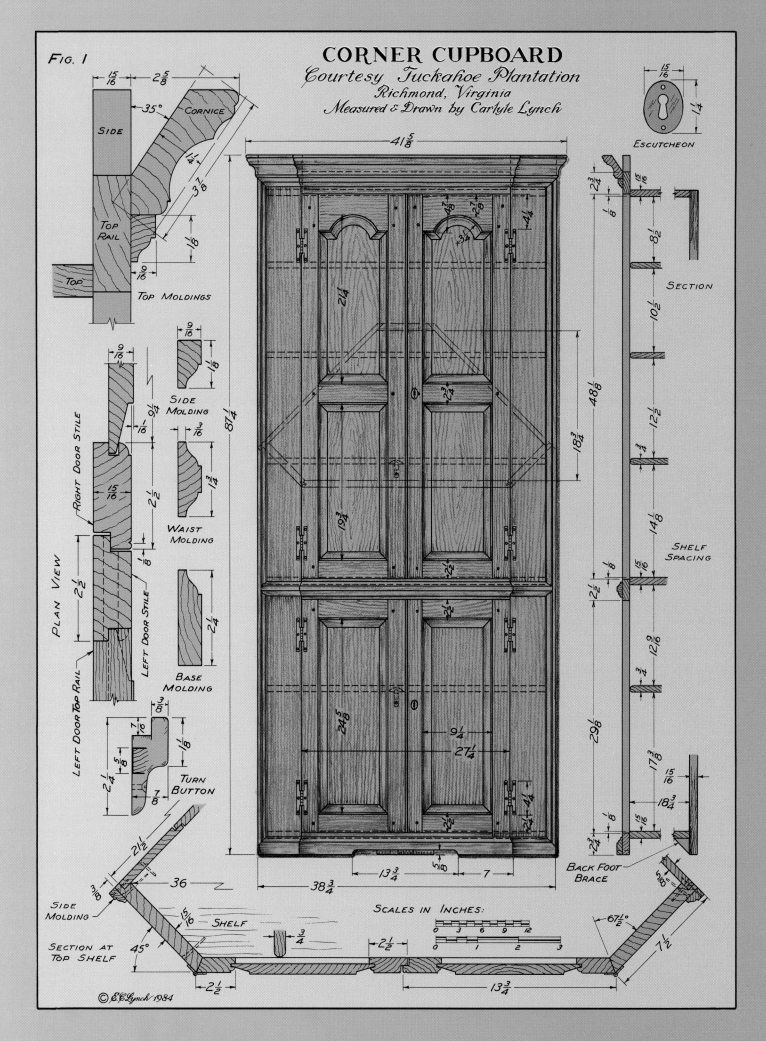

CORNER CUPBOARD
Courtesy Tuckahoe Plantation
Richmond, Virginia
Measured & Drawn by Carlyle Lynch

FIG. 1

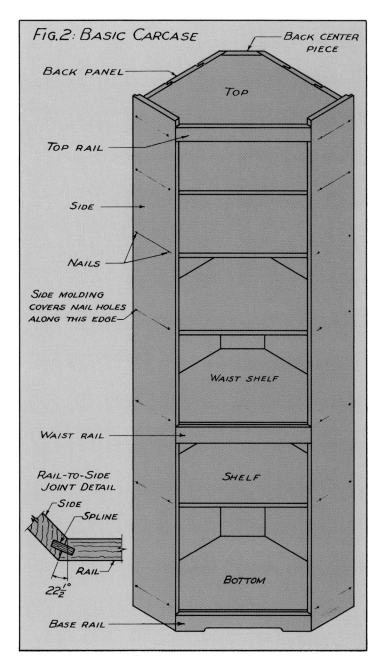

FIG.2: BASIC CARCASE

- BACK CENTER PIECE
- BACK PANEL
- TOP
- TOP RAIL
- SIDE
- NAILS
- SIDE MOLDING COVERS NAIL HOLES ALONG THIS EDGE
- WAIST SHELF
- WAIST RAIL
- RAIL-TO-SIDE JOINT DETAIL
  - SIDE
  - SPLINE
  - RAIL
  - 22½°
- SHELF
- BOTTOM
- BASE RAIL

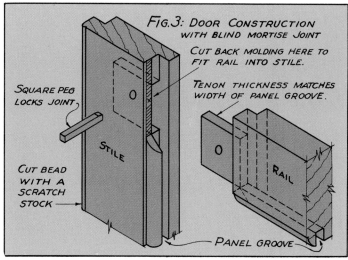

FIG.3: DOOR CONSTRUCTION WITH BLIND MORTISE JOINT

- CUT BACK MOLDING HERE TO FIT RAIL INTO STILE.
- TENON THICKNESS MATCHES WIDTH OF PANEL GROOVE.
- SQUARE PEG LOCKS JOINT
- STILE
- RAIL
- CUT BEAD WITH A SCRATCH STOCK
- PANEL GROOVE

ing so that it will fit together snug and tight.

Once you know the size of the frames, you can make the panels. The straight ones can be cut with a shaper, with a tablesaw and a router, or by hand. The arched ones will need handwork. Careful work with a chisel will raise the arch and give you a nice sense of accomplishment.

Assemble the doors with glue and clamp them to dry, making sure they're flat and square. Fit the panels loosely (don't glue them) so they'll have room to swell when the weather turns damp. To ensure a tight fit, peg the frame joints with square pins.

Before you install the doors, rabbet one edge of each right-hand door to fit over the left-hand one. With a scratch stock, make a ⅛-in. bead on the right-hand doors. Bevel the hinge edges of the doors to 22½° to match the cupboard sides, and install the hinges with steel screws. After the doors are hung, remove the hardware, then sand and finish the cupboard. I recommend that you fill the grain with dark silica-base filler, then apply two coats of Minwax Antique Oil finish. When I rehang the doors, I usually substitute brass screws for the steel ones. □

Carlyle Lynch, a designer, cabinetmaker and retired teacher, lives in Broadway, Va. Drawings by the author.

BILL OF MATERIALS

Amt.	Description	Wood	Dimensions T x W x L
2	Sides	walnut	¹⁵⁄₁₆ x 7½ x 87¼
2	Top and base rails	walnut	¹⁵⁄₁₆ x 2¾ x 27¼*
1	Waist rail	walnut	¹⁵⁄₁₆ x 2½ x 27¼*
1	Cornice	walnut	1¼ x 3⅞ x 50**
1	Waist molding	walnut	⁹⁄₁₆ x 1¾ x 45**
1	Base molding	walnut	⁹⁄₁₆ x 2¼ x 45**
2	Side moldings	walnut	⁹⁄₁₆ x 1⅛ x 84
1	Top molding	walnut	⁹⁄₁₆ x 1⅛ x 45
4	Shelves	pine	¾ x 19 x 36¼
3	Waist shelf, top, and bottom	pine	¹⁵⁄₁₆ x 19 x 36¼
1	Back center piece	pine	¹⁵⁄₁₆ x 7¾ x 83¼
2	Back panels, shiplapped	pine	⅝ x 21½ x 83¼

Hardware: Eight polished-brass H-hinges, 1½ x 4¼; two wardrobe locks with barrel keys, 1¼-in. selvage to key pin; two polished-brass oval escutcheons.

Amt.	Description	Wood	Dimensions T x W x L
	Upper doors:		
4	stiles	walnut	¹⁵⁄₁₆ x 2½ x 48
2	top rails	walnut	¹⁵⁄₁₆ x 4⅞ x 9¼ s/s
2	center rails	walnut	¹⁵⁄₁₆ x 2¾ x 9¼ s/s
2	bottom rails	walnut	¹⁵⁄₁₆ x 2½ x 9¼ s/s
2	top panels	walnut	⁹⁄₁₆ x 9¼ x 21¼
2	bottom panels	walnut	⁹⁄₁₆ x 9¼ x 19¾
	Lower doors:		
4	stiles	walnut	¹⁵⁄₁₆ x 2½ x 29
4	rails	walnut	¹⁵⁄₁₆ x 2½ x 9¼ s/s
2	panels	walnut	⁹⁄₁₆ x 9¼ x 24⅝
24	Tenon pins	walnut	¼ x ¼ x 1¼
1	Back foot brace	pine	2 x 2 x 2
2	Turn buttons	walnut	⅝ x ⅞ x 2¼

* Long point to long point.
** Makes front and side moldings.
s/s = shoulder to shoulder. Allow 2¾ in. to 3 in. for through tenons.

Kentucky Cupboard

Retaining the essence of the country style

by Warren May

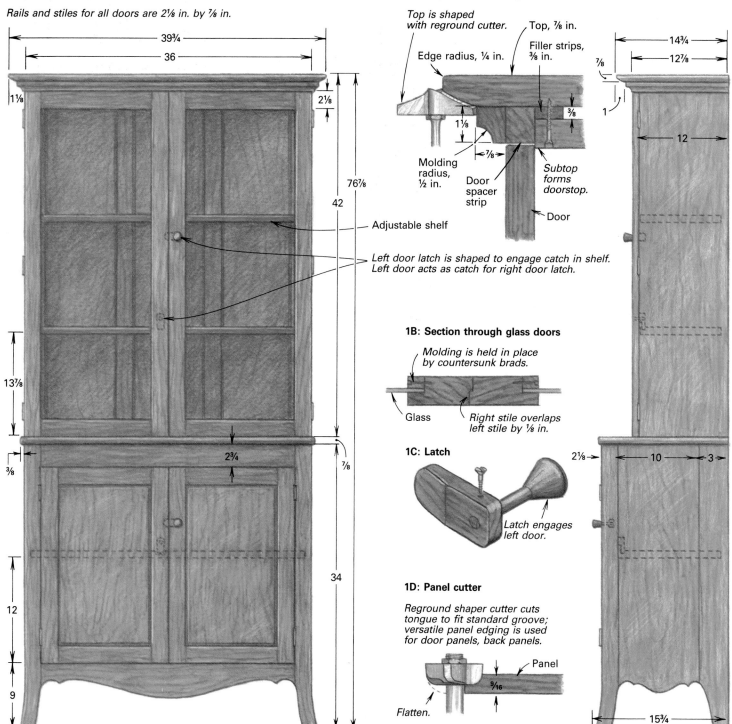

Fig. 1: Cupboard plans

Rails and stiles for all doors are 2⅛ in. by ⅞ in.

39¾
36
1⅛
2⅛
76⅞
42
13⅞
2¾
⅞
⅜
34
12
9

Adjustable shelf

Left door latch is shaped to engage catch in shelf.
Left door acts as catch for right door latch.

1A: Top corner molding detail

Top is shaped
with reground cutter.

Top, ⅞ in.

Edge radius, ¼ in.

Filler strips, ⅜ in.

⅞

⅜

1⅛

⅞

Molding
radius,
½ in.

Door
spacer
strip

Subtop
forms
doorstop.

Door

14¾
12⅞
⅞
1
12
2⅛
10
3
15¾

1B: Section through glass doors

Molding is held in place
by countersunk brads.

Glass

Right stile overlaps
left stile by ⅛ in.

1C: Latch

Latch engages
left door.

1D: Panel cutter

Reground shaper cutter cuts
tongue to fit standard groove;
versatile panel edging is used
for door panels, back panels.

Panel

9⁄16

Flatten.

From *Fine Woodworking* magazine (March 1989) 75:66-69

In the early 1800s, lumber was so abundant that Kentucky became known as the hardwood capital of the world, and there were more than 30 cabinetmakers in the central Kentucky (Lexington) area alone. Even though these cabinetmakers were far from major cities and fashion centers of the day, prosperous rural landowners and prominent townspeople in the area wanted furniture of the trendy Chippendale, Sheraton, Hepplewhite and Federal styles popular in the East. Striving to meet the needs of their patrons, these local cabinetmakers made the fashionable pieces as best they could, but at the same time, developed their own "Kentucky style."

The Kentucky builders took advantage of the ready availability of local hardwoods, such as cherry, walnut and poplar, rather than depend on mahogany or veneers. And even though they often simplified construction procedures and didn't bother wth curved dovetails and other elaborate devices, their pieces were not plain. The furniture was often embellished with inlays that conveyed a strong folk quality and a sense of the individual builder. Various cabinetmaking schools in the area and individual craftsmen, in training their apprentices, solidified these characteristics into an identifiable and lasting style. I've always found the honest melding of function with design and the use of the marvelous local hardwoods in the furniture of this period to be particularly appealing, and I try to incorporate these characteristics into my own pieces, such as the cherry cupboard shown below.

The cupboard is tall, light and functional, with simple, clean lines commonly found on Kentucky-style pieces. The cabinet is made in two sections, which simplifies construction and assembly. I begin by building the legs, then the bottom and upper sections and finally the doors and back. All the rails and stiles are joined with mortises and tenons. The backs of each section are large frames fitted with floating panels.

The top, display section has two shelves: one adjustable, the other fixed. The framed glass doors overlay the sides of the cabinet and are rabbeted along their abutting edges so they "nest" together when the doors are closed. The molding crowning the upper section is formed by shaping the edge of the top and adding a simple underlying cove molding. This molding treatment is the display section's single decorative feature.

The base section has a single, fixed-position shelf. The paneled doors are flush-mounted. Flared, Kentucky-style legs are integral to the sides of the base and are reminiscent of the proud stance of pieces from the Federal period. Both the scalloped sides and bottom apron combine with the legs and top molding to provide a softening contrast to the otherwise straight-line features of the cupboard. To make the most of the wonderful grain of the cherry used throughout, the cabinet is finished with oil and then several coats of lacquer.

Feet first—Even after 20 years of furnituremaking, I still make a full-size "rough-out" to test any new leg design. A pine 2x4 prototype costs only a few dollars but will give you a good feel for how the drawing translates into three dimensions and help you visualize the proportions of the entire piece. The same curve pattern is used for both the front and back legs. I've flared the front legs sideways and forward; the back ones flare only sideways. For this reason, they are laid out and cut differently, as shown in figure 2 below.

I make each leg from a single piece of cherry, because the glue lines and interrupted grain patterns of a lamination would detract from the appearance. Square the stock for the front and back legs, cut the pieces to length and lay out the patterns. The front legs are interchangeable, but the back ones are not and should be marked "right" and "left" to avoid mistakes when the joints are cut. Carefully bandsaw the legs close to the line; later, after the legs are glued to

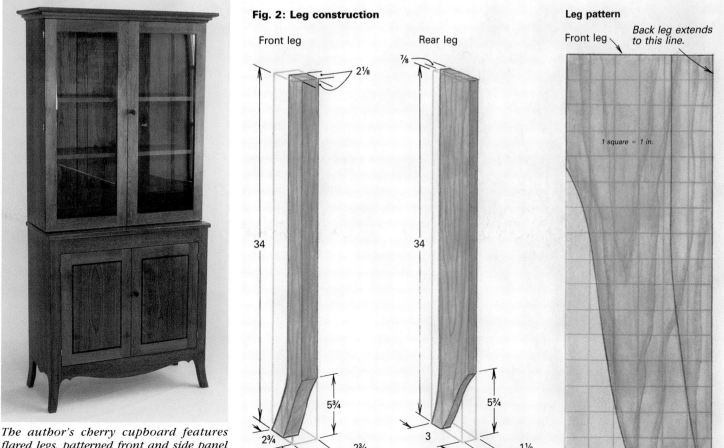

The author's cherry cupboard features flared legs, patterned front and side panel aprons and an unobtrusive top molding, identifying it as 'pure Kentucky.'

Fig. 2: Leg construction

Front leg

$2\frac{1}{8}$

34

$5\frac{3}{4}$

$2\frac{3}{4}$ $2\frac{3}{4}$

Rear leg

$\frac{7}{8}$

34

$5\frac{3}{4}$

3   $1\frac{1}{2}$

Leg pattern

Front leg

Back leg extends to this line.

1 square = 1 in.

Fig. 3: Cupboard construction

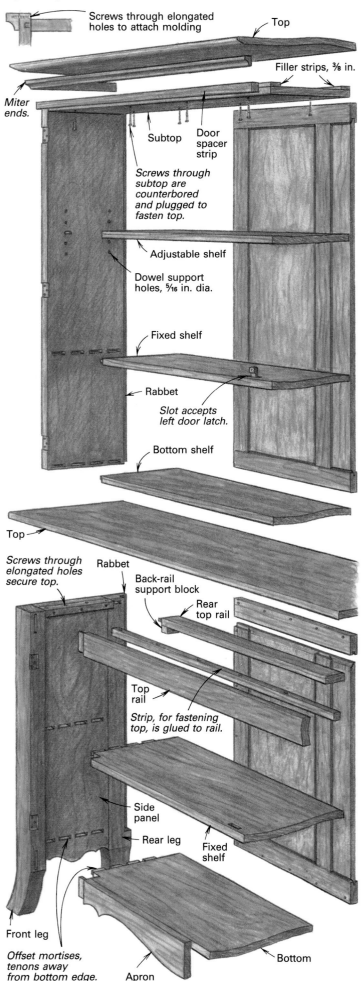

Screws through elongated holes to attach molding

Top

Miter ends.

Filler strips, ⅜ in.

Subtop

Door spacer strip

Screws through subtop are counterbored and plugged to fasten top.

Adjustable shelf

Dowel support holes, 5⁄16 in. dia.

Fixed shelf

Rabbet

Slot accepts left door latch.

Bottom shelf

Top

Screws through elongated holes secure top.

Rabbet

Back-rail support block

Rear top rail

Top rail

Strip, for fastening top, is glued to rail.

Side panel

Rear leg

Fixed shelf

Front leg

Offset mortises, tenons away from bottom edge.

Apron

Bottom

the side panels, these bandsawn curves can be spokeshaved to blend gracefully into the side panel surface and smoothed with a scraper.

Making the base section—You can make each side panel shown in figure 3, left, from a single, wide board, or you can joint and edge-glue two or more narrow pieces to make the needed width. After jointing the mating edges, I apply Titebond yellow glue and simply clamp the pieces together. The long-grain joints are strong and do not require dowels or other reinforcement. I am quite fussy, however, about selecting wood for grain and color match. I also orient the grain for maximum visual effect. For example, placing denser, more intense grain patterns toward the bottom of the tall, narrow sides of the cupboard imparts a welcome sense of balance. I also like to use arching grain patterns on the horizontal rails, which seems to lighten and lift a piece visually.

After cutting the side panels to width, align each one with its front and back legs, then dry-clamp everything together. If you've been careful in your wood selection, the grain pattern along the edge joints between the legs and the side panel should match closely. Now you can mark the decorative bottom curve using the pattern shown in figure 4 on the facing page. I make sure the shape and grain pattern harmonize with the legs; if they don't, I substitute another piece.

The next step is to cut the mortises for the front and rear top rails and the shelves. I rout the mortises with a ⅜-in. spiral cutter, which makes a smoother cut than a straight bit and chatters less. I offset the mortises and tenons for all the rails away from the sidewalls of the legs to leave more wood to support the tenons and to help prevent side-grain breakout. I finish the job by slightly rounding the ends of the tenons with a hand chisel.

Next, I cut the stopped rabbet in the rear legs for the paneled back with a dado blade on my tablesaw. Once the corners, which are not reached by the blade, are squared up with a chisel, the side panels and legs are ready to be glued up. Use caul blocks to ensure uniform clamping pressure, and edge-glue each side panel to its front and back legs.

The front legs serve as stiles to frame the flush-mounted doors, so here you just need to cut the tenons on the rails and apron, and shape the apron. Bandsaw 1⁄16 in. or so proud of the apron curve so you can blend the apron into the curve of the front leg. A sharp knife or round-bottom spokeshave works well for this. For additional support, I screw a small block to the leg under the tenoned back rail.

Fitting the middle shelf and bottom to the base is a bit tricky and requires careful measurement. The bottom must be level with and butt against the bottom apron rail. The middle shelf must set back exactly the door thickness plus 1⁄32 in. for clearance so it can act as the doorstop. Notching around the front legs and marking out the tenons is critical here to ensure that the shelf and bottom fit snugly to all their mating surfaces. Finally, the shelf and bottom must be cut so the back-panel assembly can butt against them at final assembly. Carefully aligning the bottom shelf and gluing it to the apron rail at this point makes it easier to square up the carcase during assembly. Check all joints in a final dry run. Multiple tenons on the shelves should be an "easy fit," but even here, sturdy caul blocks across the sides should be used for clamping in the final glue-up.

The top of the lower cabinet is made with a ⅜-in. overhang on the sides and front. I soften the edges using a router with a stock ¼-in. cove bit. The top is held in place with screws driven up through strips fastened to the inside top edge of each side and front rail. Be sure to use elongated screw holes in the strips to allow for the seasonal expansion and contraction.

Building the top section—Mortise-and-tenon joints are also used for the frames and fixed-shelf top section of the cupboard. The

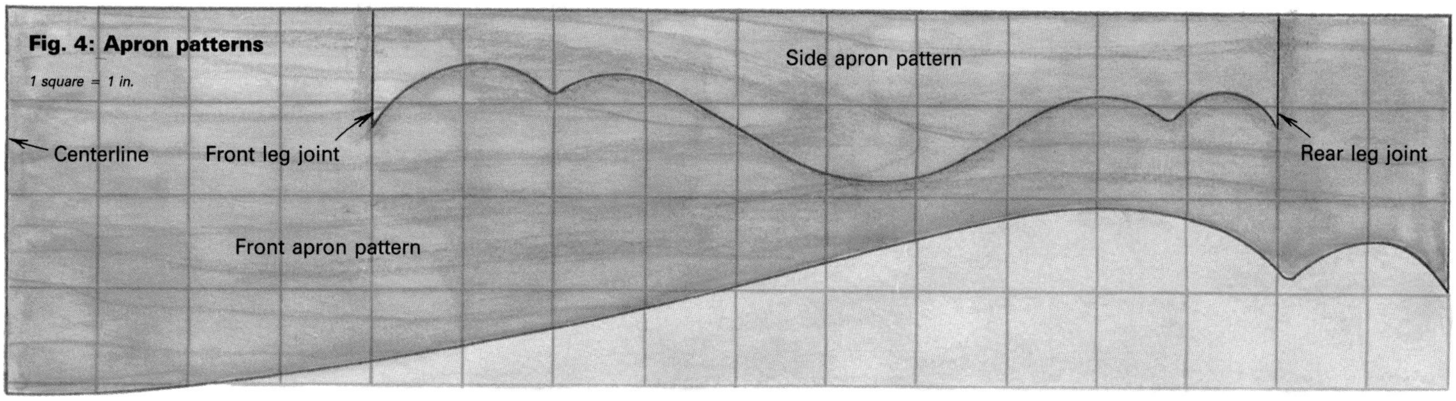

Fig. 4: Apron patterns

1 square = 1 in.

Side apron pattern

Centerline   Front leg joint

Front apron pattern

Rear leg joint

upper display shelf is adjustable, but the fixed lower shelf provides needed rigidity. The cabinet has a subtop that acts as a doorstop. The top, attached by screws driven up through the subtop, overhangs the sides and front, and with its shaped edge, forms the upper part of the top molding. The lower molding is a cove-shape strip installed under the overhang. The top molding works visually with the flared legs to give the cupboard a well-balanced appearance.

Construct the sides, shelves, bottom and subtop as shown in figure 3 on the facing page. Note that the subtop is set down from the top of the sides by ¼ in. This provides a space between the top and subtop, giving me room to screw through the sides to attach the cove molding. This space also means there is plenty of wood to support the joints, so there's no need to offset the mortises and tenons here. I do, however, offset the tenons on the bottom shelf to minimize the risk of tearout. Dado the rabbet for the back, rout mortises, cut tenons and dry-clamp the pieces together for a final check. Again, use sturdy caul blocks for applying even pressure during glue-up.

After assembly, I add ¼-in. filler strips to the subtop and glue on a spacer strip for attaching the molding above the door, as shown in figure 3. The molding is shaped with a stock ½-in.-radius cove bit. The front cove molding can be glued along its entire length. The end moldings are glued only at their mitered ends; they're screwed at the back ends, as described above. I shape the edge of the top in two steps, using first a ¼-in. cove bit to round the top edge and then a ½-in. roundover bit, which I've custom-shaped on my grinder (see figure 1A on p. 80), to extend the curve back from the edge. This bit allows me to emphasize the overhang and at the same time blend its curve smoothly into the underlying cove molding. The top is attached with countersunk screws run up through the subtop. These screws are hidden with wood plugs.

Doors and back panels – Again, I select my wood very carefully for grain pattern and straightness. I also rough-cut the lumber a few days before I need it, to identify pieces prone to warping. Second-choice pieces become the frames for the paneled back; really warped pieces are discarded. On the back, rather than cut mortises in rails for the stile tenons, I groove the entire rail. The groove accepts the tenoned ends of the four stiles as well as the routed edges of the floating panels. I modified this construction procedure slightly for the bottom doors. Here I grooved the stiles to accept the rail tenons and the panel edges. This makes for a strong door, and the tenon is only visible on the top edge. The door panels are resawn and finished to 9⁄16-in. thickness; the backs are ½ in. thick. I shape the edges of the floating panels using a cove bit with one edge ground flat, as shown in figure 1D on p. 80, which permits the panel edge to fit snugly in the frame's groove. The back assembly is then fitted to the routed opening in the back of the carcase and attached with countersunk brass flat-head screws. For the glass doors, I cut stopped grooves in the ends of the stiles to accept the tenoned ends of the rails. I use a ¼-in. dado blade to cut these and then square them up with a chisel. The rabbet for the glass is routed using a ¼-in. straight bit. Here again, I use a chisel to square the corners. The butting edges of the doors are rabbeted to allow the right door to overlap the left one by ⅛ in. when closed. After fitting the glass, I secure it with molding that's attached to the frame with countersunk nails. Note that the glass doors are designed to fit against the front of the upper section, while the lower, floating panel doors are flush-mounted. This visually ties the top and bottom sections of the cupboard together by allowing the full width of the leg line in the bottom section to extend through the full height of the cabinet. To mount the doors, I use extruded brass 1¼-in. by 1⅞-in. desk hinges (available from The Wise Co., Box 118, 6503 St. Claude, Arabi, La. 70032; 504-277-7551), because of their strength and ease of installation. These hinges also add to the appearance of the cupboard, because when installed flush, the gap between the door and the frame is smaller than is possible with conventional door hinges.

Early Kentucky pieces sometimes had wooden spools for pulls and buckles for catches, because these items could be designed to fit any application and were easily repaired or replaced. I prefer the knobs shown in figure 1C on p. 80. I turn the stems and rough out the knob ends on a lathe. The knobs are finish-shaped by hand-sanding. The stem extends through a hole drilled in the door and is secured to a wooden latch, which holds the stem in place and engages a catch when the knob is turned. The catch for the left door is a groove formed in the fixed shelf; for the right door, the back inside edge of the left door acts as the catch.

Finishing up – Most projects will bring rave reviews only if they are well finished. After all fitting, shaping and detailing is completed, I round all edges with sandpaper to about 1⁄32 in. radius. This gives the cupboard a soft look and pleasant feel. I sand first with 80 grit, then dampen the surfaces with water to locate glue residues and to raise the grain before finish-sanding with 120 grit. Planed surfaces, such as panels, need only be hand-scraped and sanded with 120 grit.

After 20 years of experimenting with different finishes, I've settled on an oil-and-lacquer finish I feel best complements the natural beauty of the cherry and walnut hardwoods I use. I apply several coats of my oil recipe (two part boiled linseed oil, two part high-gloss polyurethane, one part turpentine) until the wood is evenly sealed. After two to three days of drying time, I apply two coats of lacquer sanding sealer, sand with 240 grit and finish with two additional coats of high-gloss lacquer. After buffing the surfaces with 0000 steel wool, I apply a protective layer of Lemon Pledge spray wax. ☐

Warren May makes traditional Appalachian Mountain dulcimers and Kentucky-style furniture. He and his wife, Frankye, operate The Upstairs Gallery in Berea, Ky.

Fig. 1: Pencil-post bed

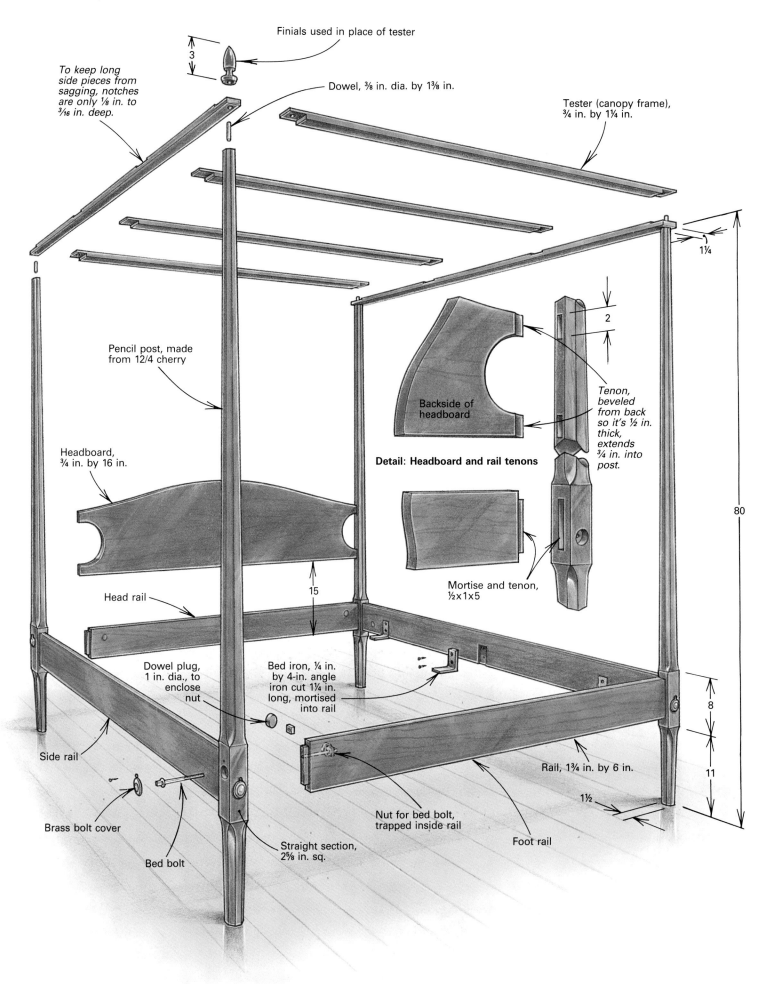

Finials used in place of tester

3

To keep long side pieces from sagging, notches are only ⅛ in. to ³⁄₁₆ in. deep.

Dowel, ⅜ in. dia. by 1⅜ in.

Tester (canopy frame), ¾ in. by 1¼ in.

1¼

Pencil post, made from 12/4 cherry

Backside of headboard

2

Tenon, beveled from back so it's ½ in. thick, extends ¾ in. into post.

Detail: Headboard and rail tenons

Headboard, ¾ in. by 16 in.

Mortise and tenon, ½x1x5

Head rail

15

Dowel plug, 1 in. dia., to enclose nut

Bed iron, ¼ in. by 4-in. angle iron cut 1¼ in. long, mortised into rail

80

Side rail

8

Brass bolt cover

Nut for bed bolt, trapped inside rail

Rail, 1¾ in. by 6 in.

11

Bed bolt

Straight section, 2⅝ in. sq.

Foot rail

1½

The Pencil-Post Bed
Jigs for machining tapered octagons

by Christian H. Becksvoort

The pencil-post bed is a classic form that has been in use for centuries. The high posts were originally designed to hold a canopy frame, or tester (pronounced teester), as shown in the photo at right. Before central heating, a canopy was standard equipment and was often accompanied by thick, quilted curtains on all four sides. Drawing the curtains at night created a room within a room designed to conserve warmth and provide privacy. In warm weather, the heavy curtains were replaced by fine lace netting, which offered protection against insects. Today, the testers are covered with either net or lace canopies or left bare, a decorative reminder of earlier times. I usually turn finials for the tops of the posts so the customer has the option of removing the tester entirely and capping the posts with the decorative turnings.

Traditionally, bedding was supported by a rope mattress woven between the bed rails. Early on, the rope also held the bed parts together, but around 1750, builders switched to bed bolts, which could hold the bedstead securely together even when the rope mattress started to sag. The 6-in.-long bed bolts I use extend through the posts and thread into nuts that are trapped within the side rails *and* the head and foot rails. On conventional, low-post beds, the headboard and footboard are usually glued up and knock-down hardware is used for assembling the side rails. However, it would be difficult, if not impossible, to move an assembled headboard with tall pencil posts upstairs, through doors and around tight corners. Therefore, a pencil-post bed must be made to knock down completely into individual members: four posts, two side rails, a head rail and foot rail, a headboard and a six-piece canopy frame and/or four finials. Besides the eight bed bolts that secure the rails, the bed is held together by the mortises and tenons where the rails and headboard join the posts, and the lap joints on the tester.

Before building this or any bed, check and recheck the actual box-spring dimensions, because they are anything but standard; few people today would want a bed that can accept only a woven rope mattress. I build pencil posts only in full- or queen-size, purely for reasons of proportion. The single-size seems too narrow and tall, while the king-size begins to resemble a cube.

Pencil posts—The evolution of tall bedposts has been from massive square posts to thinner and tapered posts, then to even more delicate, eight-sided tapers, the shape we now associate with pencil-post beds (though most pencils today are six-sided). In addition, I prefer to taper both the upper portion of the post and the shorter, lower portion below the rails. I used to bevel the corners of the tapers with a handplane or spokeshave to create an octagon. This was time-consuming and presented the risk of tearing out the grain as well as the problem of shaping a smooth transition from

A pencil-post bed with traditional tester or canopy frame is shown above. The eight-sided, tapered posts are mortised to receive the four bed rails, which are held in place with bed bolts concealed behind the brass bolt covers. There are no glued joints, so the entire bed can be disassembled for ease of transport.

the bevels to the square portion where the rails join the posts. To simplify this, I devised the two simple jigs shown in figure 3 on the next page. I use the jigs in conjunction with a tablesaw molding head, but they can be used with a shaper or a table-mounted router and a 45° cutter (you'll need 1 ⅛ in. of cutting surface). The posts are first roughed out on the bandsaw, and the tapers are cleaned up on the jointer. Then, the corners of the tapered portions are beveled into octagons by running them over the molding head, using one jig for the upper portion and the other for the lower portion. Cutting the bevels by machine saves time and virtually eliminates tearout and, because of the cutter's arc, automatically leaves a smooth transition from the bevels to the square portion of the post. This results in a completely shaped post right off the ma-

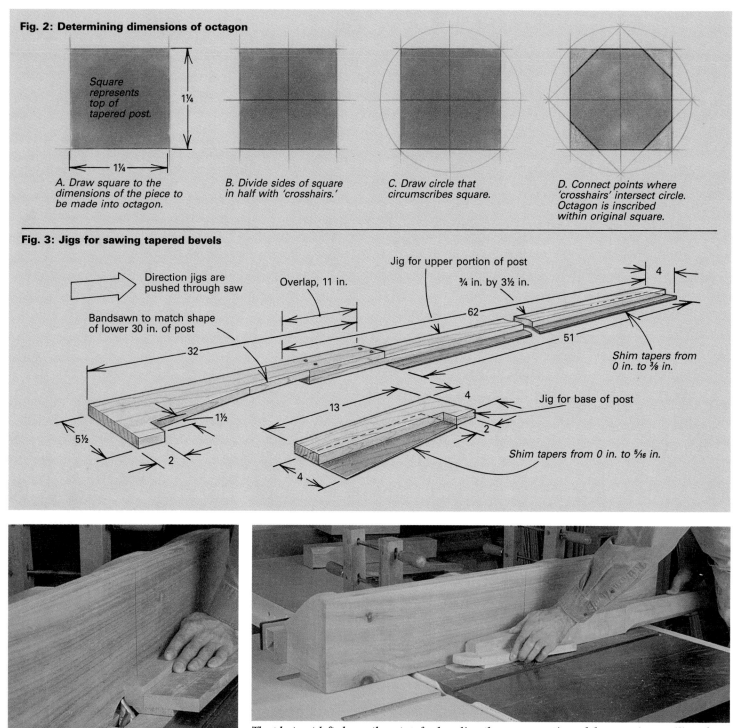

Fig. 2: Determining dimensions of octagon

Square represents top of tapered post.

1¼

1¼

A. Draw square to the dimensions of the piece to be made into octagon.

B. Divide sides of square in half with 'crosshairs.'

C. Draw circle that circumscribes square.

D. Connect points where 'crosshairs' intersect circle. Octagon is inscribed within original square.

Fig. 3: Jigs for sawing tapered bevels

Direction jigs are pushed through saw

Overlap, 11 in.

Jig for upper portion of post

¾ in. by 3½ in.

4

62

Bandsawn to match shape of lower 30 in. of post

32

51

Shim tapers from 0 in. to ⅜ in.

1½

13

4

Jig for base of post

5½

2

2

4

Shim tapers from 0 in. to ⁵⁄₁₆ in.

The photo at left shows the setup for beveling the upper portion of the post. An auxiliary fence and the height of the 45° cutter in the molding head are set to expose 1¹⁄₁₆ in. of cutting edge. Above, the author bevels the base of the post with the smaller jig. The larger jig pushes the post past the cutter; the smaller jig is pushed with the post; both jigs help to safely hold the post against the fence. The lines on the fence and the post indicate where to stop the cut.

chine, with nothing left to do but sand out the machining marks.

To make the posts, I begin with 12/4 stock up to 12 in. wide by 7 ft. or 8 ft. long. Since I don't have a jointer wide enough to true up one face of these planks, I lay out the posts on the rough wood, using a pattern cut from ¼-in.-thick Masonite. My pattern is 80 in. tall, which, adding 3 in. for the finial, gives a total height of just under 7 ft. The untapered portion of my posts, the section that will contain the mortises for the rails, is 8 in. long by 2⅝ in. sq. and begins 11 in. from the bottom of the post. The post tapers from this 2⅝-in.-sq. section to 1¼ in. at the top and 1½ in. at the bottom (see figure 1, p. 84). Because of this taper, you can save a fair amount of wood by reversing the pattern as you lay out the posts side by side.

After all four posts are laid out, bandsaw them apart, leaving them slightly oversize. Then, square up two adjacent sides of the 2⅝-in.-sq. by 8-in.-long section on the jointer, working to the pattern line on the side that's laid out. You only need to true up the area around the square sections, because you'll be bandsawing tapers on the rest of the length of the post. Then, bandsaw the top and bottom tapers on the posts, leaving the pattern lines to work to when cleaning up the shape on the jointer later. Crosscut the posts to length on the pattern lines, then lay out the pattern on the adjacent side of the posts that was previously trued on the jointer. Bandsaw away the waste, then take the posts to the tablesaw and clean up the bandsawn sides of the 2⅝-in.-sq. sections by ripping them 2¹¹⁄₁₆ in.

thick. Take the posts to the jointer and clean up the tapers to the pattern lines. One final pass on the jointer will plane off the sawmarks from the square sections and bring them to 2⅝ in.

To complete the shaping of the posts, you must bevel the corners of the tapers to make them eight-sided. The beveling jigs are designed to cut bevels that increase in width as the post increases in width, so that at any given point, all eight sides are equal in width, forming an equilateral octagon in cross section. Figure 2 on the facing page shows my method for determining the dimensions of the octagonal cross section at the top of the posts. On a piece of paper, draw squares to represent the dimensions of the post's top, bottom and square section, and use this method to determine the octagon's size at each of these points. You will have an octagon with ¹⁷⁄₃₂-in. sides inscribed within the 1¼-in. square representing the tops of your posts and an octagon with ⅝-in. sides for the 1½-in.-wide bottoms of the posts. Draw these octagons on the top and bottom of one of the posts, to use as a reference when setting the fence of the tablesaw and the height of the cutter. The 2⅝-in.-sq. portion of the post will give you an octagon with 1¹⁄₁₆-in. sides. This will be the maximum length of the cutting edge that should be exposed when the molding head's height is set.

The jig for beveling the long, upper portion of the posts, shown in figure 3 on the facing page, consists of a cradle glued to a tapered shim that gradually lifts the post's length off the machine table, thereby yielding a tapered bevel cut. The shim is about 4 in. wide and 51 in. long, and tapers up to ⅜ in. thick. It's glued under the 62-in.-long 1x4 portion of the cradle so about 2 in. of the shim's width overhangs the full length. This overhang will lift and support the post, although part of it will be ripped off with the first pass on the tablesaw. The lower portion of the cradle is bandsawn from a 32-in.-long 1x6, to conform to the shape of the lower 30 in. of the post and to wrap around the bottom end of the post, acting as a push stick. The two parts of the cradle are screwed together, with the shorter portion on top, which raises the push-stick part of the cradle enough to contact the bottom of the post completely. The smaller jig for beveling the bottom of the post is built on the same principle, except in this case, the post pushes the jig instead of the jig pushing the post. This variation makes it easier and safer to control the post for the short, lower portion of the post and vice versa for the longer, upper portion. The shim for the smaller jig is 4 in. by 11 in., tapering from ⁵⁄₁₆ in. to zero. It's glued to a 13-in.-long 1x4, bandsawn to fit the post's taper and to wrap around the post's bottom.

The setup I use, with a tablesaw molding head fitted with shopmade 45° bevel cutters, is shown in the lower, left photo on the facing page. The same basic procedures would apply to a router table or shaper. Our earlier calculations told us that the sides of the octagon at the largest portion of the post are 1¹⁄₁₆ in. wide. So, we now set the cutter and an auxiliary fence to expose 1¹⁄₁₆ in. of the cutting edge so we can cut the tapered bevel in one pass. To double-check this, place the post, with the octagons drawn on its ends, on the larger jig so that the tapered, top portion of the post will run along the saw's fence, as shown in the photo. Raise the cutter so that at the peak of its arc it will bevel the corner right up to the side of the octagon. Slide the fence over to the side of the post and lock it in place, with the cutter centered on the octagon's side. With this setup, you can bevel all four upper corners on each post as well as all four lower corners. The jigs themselves compensate for the different tapers of the upper and lower portions of the post. After setting the fence and the cutter height, use a square and a felt pen to mark on the fence the location where the cutter goes into the table. This is the point where the cutter begins its cut. In addition, mark each post at 11 in. and 19 in. up from the bottom. This designates where to stop the cuts, preserving the square section.

With the shaped post supported by a simple V-block, Becksvoort beltsands the machining marks from the tapered bevels of the octagon. A smooth, continuous motion and a light touch with the nose of the belt sander are requirements for sanding the curving transition from bevel to square.

Push the jig and post, with its tapered side running along the fence as shown in the lower, left photo on the facing page, over the spinning molding head. When the line on the post indicating the top of the square section meets the line on the fence, pull the post and jig away from the fence. Repeat this procedure for the other three corners to form a tapered octagon on the top section of the post. Bevel the bottom of the post in the same way with the smaller jig, as shown in the lower, right photo on the facing page. Stop the cut when the line at the bottom of the square portion lines up with the line on the fence. Repeat the cuts until the four corners are beveled. Once all four posts are beveled top and bottom, you've completed the most difficult part of the bed.

I sand the machine marks from the bevels with a belt sander. With experience, a light touch and a confident hand, I've gotten so I can use the front wheel or "nose" of the belt sander to sand the curving transition without making it wavy (see the photo above). If you don't feel comfortable using a belt sander for this, a cabinet scraper and a hand-sanding block will do the trick.

Rails, mortises and bed bolts — Traditionally, the rails on pencil-post beds were nearly square (2⅝ in. by 3 in. was common), to resist the inward pull of the rope mattress and the downward weight of the bed's occupants. However, today's beds rely on a box spring that only bears *down* on the rails, so the more familiar, 1-in. or 2-in. by 6-in. board-on-edge serves nicely. I mill my rails from straight 8/4 stock to a finished size of 1¾ in. by 6 in. The 6-in. width hides all but 1 in. or so of a standard box spring.

The mortises for the rails are ½x1x5 in. and centered top to bottom and side to side on two adjacent faces of the square section of the posts. This ½-in. depth may seem shallow for bed-rail mortises, but cutting the mortises deeper would only weaken the posts. Besides, the bed bolts hold the tenons tightly in the mortises and help support the downward force on the rails, while the mortises and tenons provide alignment and prevent inward rotation of the rails. In the past, I've done my share of routing, drilling and chiseling mortises, but I now have the luxury of a horizontal mortising machine. However you cut your mortises, be sure they are all the same length and the same distance from the bottom of the posts. Use a square to lay out for the length of the mortises, transferring the lines around the corner of the adjacent faces of the post. Accuracy here will ensure a level mattress support.

After the mortises in the posts are complete, the two side rails

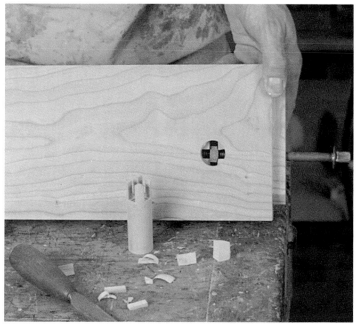

The nuts for the bed bolts are dropped into a 1-in.-dia. hole that intersects the bolt hole. Pie-shape pieces are bandsawn from a 1-in. dowel, chiseled to fit around the nut and glued in place to keep the nut aligned with the bolt hole. The nut is then trapped in place with a glued-in dowel plug.

Fig. 4: Headboard profiles

The style and design of a pencil-post bed can be altered simply by varying the headboard shape.

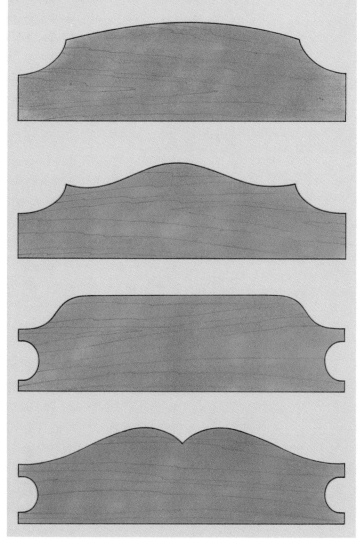

and the head and foot rails are crosscut to length to suit the size bed you're building. Double-check the box-spring dimensions, and don't forget to add 1 in. for the ½-in. tenon on each end of the rails. Add an extra ¼ in. to ½ in. so the box spring is easier to install or remove, and take into account the 7⁄16 in. the rails are set back from the inside corner of the posts. The ½ x 1 x 5-in. tenons are cut on the ends of all four rails, using whatever method is comfortable for you: backsaw, tablesaw, router, or even bandsaw or radial-arm saw. Because these joints will be assembled and disassembled, the tenons should slide into the mortises easily but without excess play. To ease assembly, sand or file a ¹⁄16-in. bevel on the tenon corners and around the perimeter of the mortises.

After fitting the tenons to the mortises, you're ready to drill for the bed bolts. To locate the holes in the posts, I made a rectangular plug that fits into the mortise. On this plug, I marked the vertical center of the mortise and then drilled two 7⁄64-in.-dia. holes through the plug: one ½ in. above center for the head and foot rails; the other ½ in. below center for the side rails. These holes accept a 6d finish nail, which is inserted through the appropriate hole and tapped into the mortise to locate the bolt holes. With the drill press, I drill a ⅛-in.-dia. hole from the mortise through the post to locate the hole on the outside of the post. Then, I turn the post over, and using a 1-in.-dia. Forstner bit, drill a ¾-in.-deep hole to countersink the bolt head. Finally, I change to a ⅜-in.-dia. twist bit and drill back through the ⅛-in.-dia. hole to the inside of the mortise. I repeat the procedure for the other seven bolt holes.

The bolts will extend through the holes in the post and into holes in the tenon ends of the rails. To align these holes, mount a rail horizontally in a bench vise, find the mating post and mortise for that particular rail end and slide the mortise onto the tenon. Hold the post in place with one hand while you drill a ⅜-in.-dia. hole through the post-bolt holes into the tenon ends. Unless you have an extra-long bit, you'll need to remove the post and extend the hole 4 in. deep into the rail to accommodate the 6-in.-long bed bolts. Repeat this procedure for the remaining tenons. The rails are now ready for nut holes.

To locate where the nut will be trapped in the rail, lay the rail on the bench, with its inside face up, and slide a bolt partially into the tenon hole. Align a straightedge with the centerline of the bolt shaft; with a pencil, mark this centerline on the rail. Measure in about 3 in. from the tenon shoulder, along the bolt's centerline, and use an awl to locate the hole you'll drill for the nut. This should fall about ⅜ in. from the end of the bolt. Traditionally, the nut was dropped into a ⅜ x 1 x 1¼-in. slot chiseled into the rail. A plug was then cut and glued into the hole to prevent the nut from falling out. These slots can be chopped by hand or cut with a ⅜-in.-wide hollow chisel or a plunge router and jig. I find it easier to drill a 1¼-in.-deep hole with a 1-in.-dia. Forstner bit. Then, I drop the nut into the hole and screw the bolt through. To hold the nut in place, I bandsaw a ⅜-in. by ⅜-in. cross out of the end of a 1-in. dowel, saw off the four remaining pie-shape pieces and pare them with a chisel until they fit snugly around the bolt and nut, as shown in the photo this page. I glue them into place around the nut, leaving the bolt threaded through the nut until the glue sets, to ensure proper alignment. Then, I plug the hole with a 1-in.-dia. dowel.

Next, I mortise the inside faces of the two side rails to receive the bed irons that support the box spring (see figure 1). You can have a local blacksmith or machinist cut 1¼-in.-long pieces from ¼-in.-thick 4-in. by 4-in. angle iron or bend ¼ x 1¼ x 8-in. stock to 90°. You can also purchase them from one of the sources listed at the end of this article. The irons should be drilled and countersunk for #12 flat-head screws. The mounting screws should be 1 in. to 1½ in. long. Each rail should have one iron 10 in. to 12 in. from

Toying with tradition

Just because the pencil post is a traditional form doesn't mean it has to look traditional. Here are two variations that toy with the pencil-post theme.

A few years ago, I made a "real" pencil-post bed for an architect. The photo (far right) is the model I made from actual pencils. To make a full-size bed, the pencil posts had to be 11 times the actual pencil size. I made four pencils 3⅛ in. by 82½ in. tall. I used cherry, because Port Orford cedar, the usual pencil wood, is a bit too weak and difficult to obtain in 16/4 stock. The posts were cut to six sides and sharpened with a block plane; the grooves and flutes for the eraser holder were carved in, as was the lettering. I painted the posts to match a pencil's colors. The headboard is a section of ruler, to scale.

A friend of mine, David Stenstrom of Portland, Me., built the pencil-post bed in the photo (right) from maple, then had it sprayed to a high-gloss, candy-apple red. The expected clash of style and color results instead in a stunning piece you can't take your eyes off. —C.B.

Photo: Kip Brundage

Don't write-off the diminutive pencil-post bed (right) as just a small pun: Becksvoort made it as a model for a full-scale version. Woodworker David Stenstrom grew tired of his traditional cherry pencil-post bed, so he built another (left) and lacquered it bright red. The form is so simple and the lines so clean that this contemporary treatment doesn't seem at odds with the design of the piece.

each end and one in the middle. I mortise them into the inside face of the rails so the angle is flush with the bottom of the rail.

Headboard and tester—The bedstead is not complete until you've made the headboard. You can choose from a variety of shapes, such as the profiles shown in figure 4 on the facing page, or you can design your own. I prefer a simple curved top with a semicircle cut out of each end. My headboards are 14 in. to 18 in. wide, depending on the bed's size. To determine the length and placement of the headboard, assemble the head rail and two posts. Measure up about 15 in. (the combined thickness of box spring and mattress) from the bottom of the rail, and mark this point on both posts. This is the bottom of the headboard. To determine the headboard's length, measure between the posts where the upper tenons will be and add 1½ in. for the two ¾-in.-long tenons that extend into the posts. I glue up ¾-in. stock to the desired width and bandsaw the headboard to shape. Make the four tenons that anchor the board to the posts about 2 in. wide and bevel them in back so the part of the tenon that extends into the posts is about ½ in. thick. Then, place the bottom of the headboard against the marks on the posts and locate the exact positions of the tenons (mortises-to-be) on the inside facets of the posts. Disassemble the head rail and drill, chisel or rout the mortises. The angle created by the posts' tapers is so minor over the 12-in. distance between tenons that it's easy to compensate for by slightly angling the top and bottom of the mortises with a chisel. The fit should be loose but not sloppy, as this is not a glued joint. Reassemble the entire head unit to check for fit.

Now the posts, rails and headboard can be finish-sanded. If they were shaped and planed with no major tearouts, I begin with 120 grit and sand through 400 or 600.

The tester is made from ¾-in.-thick stock, ripped to 1¼ in. wide to match the width of the post tops and joined with unglued lap joints. If it was glued together, you'd have a large, flimsy, unwieldy frame to contend with when it was removed for transport or storage. The

tester's corners are anchored with dowels in the four post tops.

Determine the size of the tester frame pieces by assembling the bed and measuring from the top of the posts, outside to outside. Make the lap joints in the side frames shallow, ⅛ in. to 3/16 in. deep, to help prevent sagging. Cut four crosspieces, one for each end and two middle pieces; lap their ends to fit the laps in the side pieces.

I use a doweling jig to drill the ⅜-in.-dia. by ¾-in.-deep holes into the tops of the posts for the dowels that secure the tester frame. To aid in clamping the doweling jig to the tapered posts, I cut off a chunk from the thick ends of two of the strips bandsawn from the post tops and use them as spacers. I chamfer both ends of ⅜-in.-dia. by 1⅜-in.-long dowels and insert them in the post tops. Drill ⅜-in.-dia. holes through the corner laps of the tester frame to fit over the dowels in the tops of the posts.

As an alternative to the tester, I also turn finials for the posts. Traditional forms include the ball, acorn, urn, tall urn and flame. I've settled on a modified acorn pattern borrowed from a Shaker chair design. Drill a ⅜-in.-dia., ¾-in.-deep hole in the bottom of the finials to fit over the dowels in the post tops.

The bed featured here is made from cherry with an oil finish, but it looks just as nice in American mahogany, walnut or figured maple. After finishing, the bed irons are attached and decorative bolt covers (usually six) are screwed over the bolt holes. □

Christian H. Becksvoort builds custom furniture in New Gloucester, Me., and is a contributing editor to Fine Woodworking.

Sources of supply

Bed bolts and nuts, wrenches, angle irons and bolt covers (both pressed and cast):

Ball & Ball, 463 W. Lincoln Hwy., Exton, PA 19341; (215) 363-7330.

Horton Brasses, Box 120F, Cromwell, CT 06416; (203) 635-4400.

Period Furniture Hardware, Box 314, Charles Street Station, Boston, MA 02114; (617) 227-0758.

Building a Bent-Back Rocker
Soft rock from hardwoods

by Brian Boggs

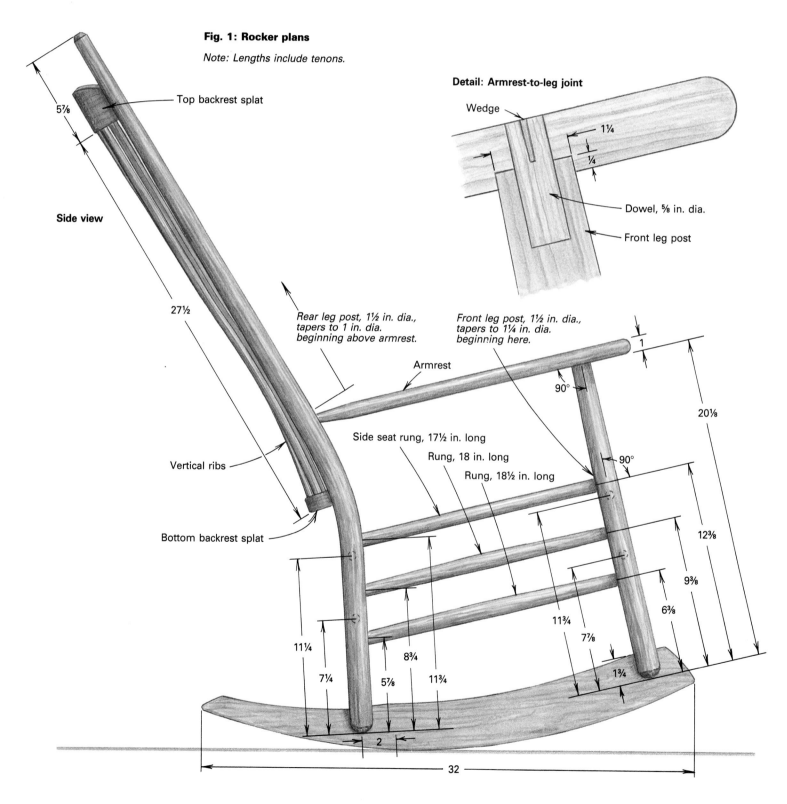

Fig. 1: Rocker plans

Note: Lengths include tenons.

Top backrest splat

5⅞

Side view

27½

Vertical ribs

Bottom backrest splat

Detail: Armrest-to-leg joint

Wedge

1¼

¼

Dowel, ⅝ in. dia.

Front leg post

Rear leg post, 1½ in. dia., tapers to 1 in. dia. beginning above armrest.

Front leg post, 1½ in. dia., tapers to 1¼ in. dia. beginning here.

Armrest

1

90°

20⅛

Side seat rung, 17½ in. long

Rung, 18 in. long

Rung, 18½ in. long

90°

12⅜

9⅜

6⅜

11¾

7⅞

11¼

7¼

5⅞

8¾

11¾

1¾

2

32

Drawings: Lee Hov

After building more than 100 rocking chairs, I've developed a rather non-scientific approach for designing and constructing attractive, strong and comfortable rockers from green hardwoods. My first rocking chair was a straight ladderback chair fit on runners copied from an old chair I liked. Although I was able to construct the chair fairly quickly, I didn't like the piece's visual balance. After more carefully studying how chairs worked, I subsequently altered seat shapes, leg angles, rocker radii and other details to improve the chair's appearance, comfort and my construction methods. The result is the bent-back rocker, shown on p. 95 in the photo at right, which I'll tell you how to build in this article.

Evolution of my rocker design—All rockers, regardless of style—Windsor, ladderback or sculpted—are basically alike. As with any chair, the frame and seat must comfortably support a sitting person's weight. All chairs must withstand everyday use and abuse, such as the sitter moving in the chair, sliding the chair around and leaning back. These destructive forces, working to pull the joints apart, are intensified with a rocker because of the repetitive, dynamic stresses produced by its rocking motion. The character and speed of the rocking motion is controlled by the shape of the runners. By subtly modifying the runners' curve and by adjusting the length of the legs to change how the frame sits on the runners, you can construct a balanced chair that's both easy to get in and out of and is comfortable. These subtle changes will also smooth the rocking motion so the chair won't awkwardly pitch forward or backward, and won't creep or walk across the floor as you rock. And because an optimumly designed frame is consistent with a visually well-balanced chair, your rocker will be attractive. Finally, if you follow the simple rules for working with green wood, you can expect your chairs to survive hard use; you'll be building heirlooms.

The problem with my first straight ladderback rockers was that they were too upright and boxy. They were not exceptionally comfortable, and they provided insufficient lower-back support, which consequently induced sitting in a slouched position. Increasing the angle between the seat and the backrest eliminated the boxy appearance and provided the needed back support. I found that most people were comfortable in chairs with a 105° to 110° angle between the seat and backrest; increasing the angle more than this reduces the amount of head and neck support provided by the back and makes the chair uncomfortable. Curving the backrest to fit a person's shape also increases comfort, but it shifts body weight farther back in the chair. Because of this, I design chairs with curved backrests, like my bent-back rocker, with the minimum recommended angle of 105°.

Since I angled the backrest, I also had to angle the lower, rear leg posts or else the chair appeared to lean back precariously. Even though these unangled rear legs were safe enough, they no longer directly supported most of the weight. Instead, the stresses were concentrated at the points where the lower side rungs joined the rear leg posts and this arrangement would eventually

Front view

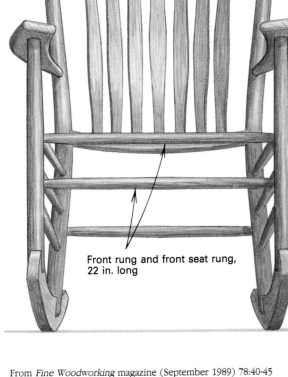

Front rung and front seat rung, 22 in. long

Back view

Rear seat rung, 17½ in. long

Rear rung, 18¼ in. long

From *Fine Woodworking* magazine (September 1989) 78:40-45

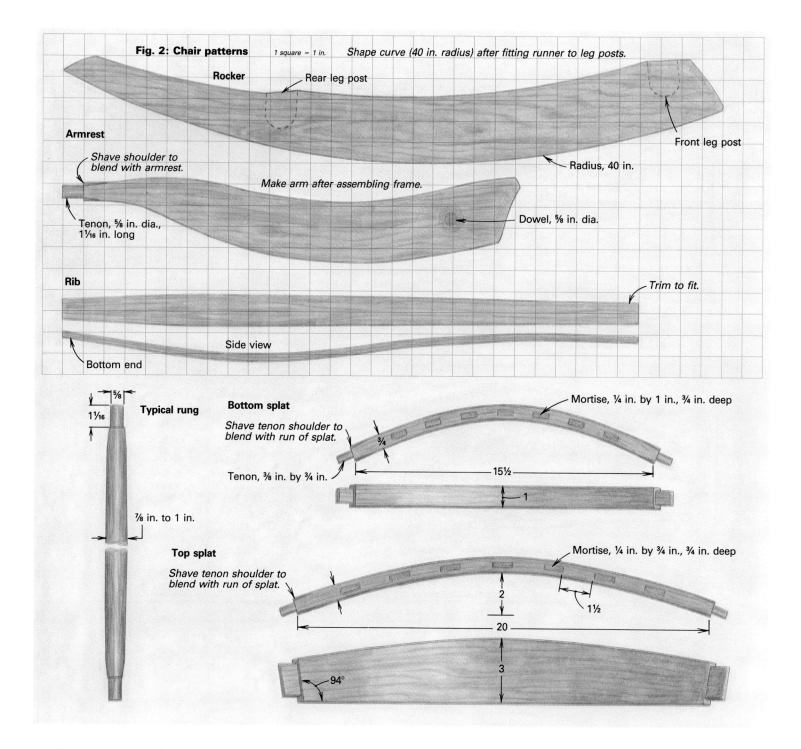

Fig. 2: Chair patterns   1 square = 1 in.   *Shape curve (40 in. radius) after fitting runner to leg posts.*

Rocker

Rear leg post

Front leg post

Radius, 40 in.

Armrest

Shave shoulder to blend with armrest.

Make arm after assembling frame.

Tenon, ⅝ in. dia., 1¹⁄₁₆ in. long

Dowel, ⅝ in. dia.

Rib

Trim to fit.

Side view

Bottom end

⅝

1¹⁄₁₆

Typical rung

⅞ in. to 1 in.

Bottom splat

Shave tenon shoulder to blend with run of splat.

Mortise, ¼ in. by 1 in., ¾ in. deep

¾

Tenon, ⅜ in. by ¾ in.

15½

1

Top splat

Shave tenon shoulder to blend with run of splat.

Mortise, ¼ in. by ¾ in., ¾ in. deep

2

1½

20

3

94°

---

weaken the joints and cause them to fail prematurely. While it didn't eliminate the problem, angling the lower leg backward to match the backrest made the rocker appear more stable and re-positioned the weight more directly over the leg, thus reducing the forces on the joints.

Changes in the backrest had the greatest influence on my rock-er's design because they altered the chair's appearance, structure and comfort. Other less-significant changes generally involved cus-tomizing the chair's size or shape for a particular individual or simplifying construction methods. For example, the armrest looks best to me when it is parallel to the seat; fortunately, the strongest joints result when both the armrest and seat connect to the front leg post at 90°, and it's easy to come up with efficient methods to cut these right-angle joints. To my eye the most attractive and com-fortable chairs have seats that taper gently toward the back and have slightly splayed runners. For a smooth ride that's neither too fast nor too slow with this configuration, I eventually settled on runners that have a 40-in. radius.

The dimensions for my standard bent-back rocker, shown in fig-ure 1 on p. 90, work well for most average-size adults. When I custom-fit a rocker, I scale the standard dimensions up or down as needed, but I maintain the proportions of the original. The simplest approach to customizing is to have the person sit in a standard chair and see how it "fits." Some things are obvious; short, stocky folks need lower, wider chairs than tall, thin peo-ple. But I also look closely for the more subtle, telltale clues: Is the person long legged and in need of a deeper seat? Are the person's knees scrunched up awkwardly, necessitating a change in the seat height? Are the person's shoulders relaxed? Do the forearms rest comfortably on the armrests? With experience, customizing a chair becomes second nature.

Wood selection and joinery—Good joinery methods and wood with proper moisture-content levels are essential for constructing a strong rocker. I split and shave all my chair parts (except for the runners) from green logs. While I prefer oak and hickory, I occa-

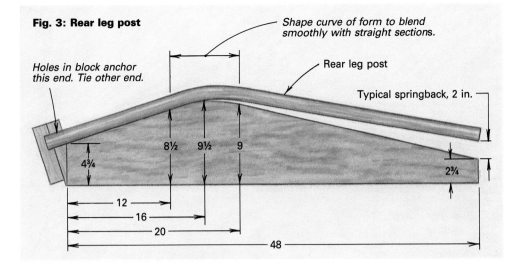

Fig. 3: Rear leg post

Holes in block anchor this end. Tie other end.

Shape curve of form to blend smoothly with straight sections.

Rear leg post

Typical springback, 2 in.

4¾

8½   9½   9

2¾

12

16

20

48

The author is shown working at a shaving horse, rough-shaping a green-wood arm-rest. The job goes quickly because green wood is easy to carve. Boggs removes wood efficiently with a drawknife.

sionally use maple or ash. Select straight-grain logs so the rived parts won't split when they are steam-bent. Although riving wood is hard work, all of the chair parts can be split in about one-half hour. Parts to be tenoned, like the rungs and the armrests, are air dried to about 15% moisture content (MC) and then dried to less than 5% MC in a closed, insulated box, which is heated to about 150° with a 100-w. light bulb. The mortises and tenons are cut to fit together snugly when assembled, but the joints become really tight when the wood reaches its equilibrium moisture content (about 7% in the northeast). This tightening action occurs when the dry tenons absorb moisture and expand, while the wet mortised pieces dry and shrink. For more information on working with green wood, see *Make a Chair from a Tree: An Introduction to Working with Green Wood* by John Alexander (The Taunton Press, 63 South Main Street, PO Box 5506, Newtown, Conn. 06470-5506). I prefer green wood because it can be shaped more easily and more quickly than dried stock. You can build the chair with air-dried stock, however, if you super-dry the tenons. The difference in moisture content between the mortise and tenon is what ensures the tight joinery.

All of the riven parts are shaped with a spokeshave and drawknife. Since it's much better to replace a fouled part than to repair one, I make extra slats, posts and rungs in case something goes wrong. The rungs are kiln dried for a few days before I cut them to length, tenon the ends and shape them. While the rungs are drying, I fire up the steamer and bend the rear leg posts, back splats and vertical ribs. Steamers don't have to be fancy: I simply boil water on a Coleman stove and funnel the steam through a plastic pipe into the closed box that holds the parts. The splats and ribs are steamed for only 10 or 15 minutes, but the thicker leg posts take one hour to two hours. The form used in bending the posts is described in figure 3 above. The rule of thumb for kiln-dried wood is to steam one hour per inch thickness; for green wood, 30 minutes per inch thickness. By preflexing the thin ribs in both directions over an 8-in. radius drum before clamping them in their bent forms, you'll stretch the wood fibers, which will result in a more uniform bend and minimize springback when the pieces are unclamped. Work quickly so you can clamp the pieces before they cool. I leave the parts in the forms to dry overnight or until they're needed.

Building the rocker—The sequence for assembling the chair is pretty straightforward. I begin with the backrest and rear frame, which involves shaping the rear leg posts, splats, rear rungs and vertical ribs as well as cutting the necessary mortises and tenons. I

shape the parts on a shaving horse with a drawknife and spokeshave, as shown in the photo above. Mortises are bored with a ⅝-in. Forstner bit in the drill, but all other joinery is done with hand tools. Next, I build the front frame. Aligning the front frame to the backrest/rear frame assembly and marking out the mortises for the rungs is a bit tricky, but the rest is easy. The armrests are shaped and joined to the front and rear leg posts, the assembled frame is squared up and the runners are installed. All of the tenoned joints are pinned and glued for extra strength. After finishing the frame with boiled linseed oil, I weave a hickory or oak splint seat.

Since the back is the visual focal point of the chair and all other parts must align with it, the backrest/rear frame must be assembled symmetrically and twist-free. To ensure this, chop the mortises for the two back panel splats while the back posts are still square, then round the posts with a drawknife. I cut the splats oversize to allow a ⅞-in. tenon on each end. The tenons are cut with a backsaw and chisel, then the shoulders are shaved off to blend with the run of the splat. This prevents an unattractive gap from developing between the leg post and the shoulder when the leg post dries and shrinks. After shaping the splats freehand, I dry-fit them to the leg posts. Since the top splat is wider than the bottom splat, fitting both splats in the posts gives the backrest its tapered appearance. Installing the curved splats also rotates the leg posts about 8° to 10°, which produces the outward splay of the legs at the bottom.

Next, I mark out and chop the mortises in the splats for the vertical ribs. The ends of the vertical ribs, like the splats, are straight, so chop the mortises perpendicular to the long edges of the splats. I fit the center rib first, and then, alternating sides, fit each rib individually. The tenons on the ribs are not shouldered; if the rib is a bit tight, it's thinned on the back side with a chisel or scraper until it's just snug. Fitting the ribs and contouring their shape is all done by eye. I make a final check by dry-fitting the ribs and slats together. If everything looks right, I glue up the back panel and dry-fit it to the leg posts to hold it in position, making sure the centerline of the middle rib is perpendicular to the splats.

Fitting the two back rungs to the leg posts, which are still dry clamped to the back panel, is straightforward. First, line up the mortises by eye between the leg posts, mark them and bore them with a power drill. I shape the rung tenons and, as before, shave off the shoulders to blend with the contour shape of the rung before gluing the rungs and back panel to the leg posts. Next, drill the ⅝-in.-dia. mortises for the front rungs in the front leg posts. I do this on the drill press after drawknifing them round. Then, I fit and glue the rungs to the leg posts to form the front frame.

Because the seat width tapers toward the back, the front frame is

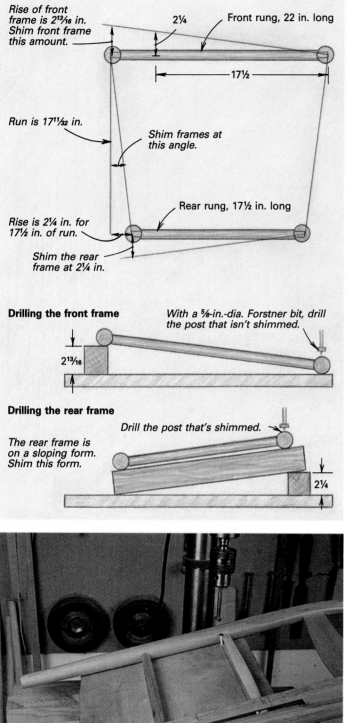

Fig. 4: Setup for drilling side-rung mortises

The side rungs attach to the front and rear frames at an angle that's not 90°. The diagram below shows how to determine the amount to shim the front and rear frames when drilling the mortises.

Rise of front frame is 2¹³/₁₆ in. Shim front frame this amount.

2¼

Front rung, 22 in. long

17½

Run is 17¹¹/₃₂ in.

Shim frames at this angle.

Rear rung, 17½ in. long

Rise is 2¼ in. for 17½ in. of run.

Shim the rear frame at 2¼ in.

Drilling the front frame

With a ⅝-in.-dia. Forstner bit, drill the post that isn't shimmed.

2¹³/₁₆

Drilling the rear frame

Drill the post that's shimmed.

The rear frame is on a sloping form. Shim this form.

2¼

The rear frame is being set up on the drill-press table for boring the mortises for the side rungs. The frame sits on a form shaped like the bent rear leg post. This form and the shim under its far side, which raises the post being drilled, ensure that the mortises are drilled at the correct angle. Later, the front leg posts will be mortised in a similar way.

wider than the back frame. For this reason, the three parallel rungs on each side of the chair join the leg posts at an odd angle. Aligning the front and rear frames without twisting them is tricky, but not all that difficult if you lay out and cut the mortises correctly. You must first mark the vertical position of the mortises: Measure up from the bottom of the leg post to locate the three mortises, as shown in figure 1 on p. 90. All the measurements for the rungs on the front leg are also made from the bottom of the post.

Locating the angular position of the mortises is a bit like laying out rafters for a pitched roof. The difference between the rear and front seat width, divided by two, represents the "rise"; the seat depth, the "run." I use this "rise-over-run" ratio to set up the front and rear frames on my drill-press table to drill the mortises. The procedure for doing this is more fully explained in figure 4 at left. A special support for the rear frame is needed to bore the mortises, as shown in the photo below. This support is angled to accommodate the bend in the rear leg post and allow the mortises to be bored at the correct angle on the drill press. Since the length of the rear seat rung is the same as the run, I shim the post being drilled up by an amount equal to the corresponding rise and bore the mortises for all three rungs. The same procedure is used to bore the other rear leg post.

Boring the front posts is less complicated. The frame is flat and sits directly on the drill-press table. The front seat rung is longer than the run, so the rise, equal to the shim thickness, must be proportionately greater. Unlike the rear frame, the shim is placed under the front leg post not being bored.

The rest of the chair is assembled the same way as the front and rear frames. After tenoning and shaping the side rungs, I glue up everything, making sure the frame is symmetrical and sits without rocking on a flat surface. It's usually necessary to wrestle with the frame a bit to remove any twist that would prevent it from sitting flat. I also make sure the side rungs are parallel and join the front leg posts at 90°.

Armrests—The armrests are roughed out on the bandsaw and refined with a drawknife and spokeshave. The armrests are curved along their length, and I sculpt away much of the wood along their top inside surfaces to provide a comfortable hollow for a person's forearm. With a power drill, bore mortises into the rear leg posts while sighting horizontally along the top of the front leg posts for alignment, as shown on the facing page in the photo at left.

It's difficult to install the armrests because two things must happen simultaneously: The tenoned ends must fit into the rear leg posts and the mortises on the underside of the front section must fit over the tops of the leg posts. Loose-fitting tenons provide enough play to do this, but they also produce a weak joint. My solution is to bore the 1¼-in.-dia. mortises for the front leg posts only ¼ in. deep. Then, I seal the armrests in a plastic bag, so only the ends to be tenoned are exposed, and place them in the kiln. When the ends are dry, I form the joint with a tenon cutter chucked in a power drill or hand brace; you could also cut the tenon by hand. The shallow mortise slips easily over the top of the post, which provides sufficient play for the dry, tenoned end to be fit snugly into the rear post. Finally, I bore a ⅝-in.-dia., 1½-in.-deep hole through each armrest into the posts and install dry dowels. The snug-fitting dowels don't split the wood and they can be safely wedged for a tight fit that will become tighter as the armrests and leg posts dry out and shrink.

Runners—I use 38-in.-long runners glued and pinned into 1¾-in.-deep slots in the bottom of the legs. By making small changes in the depth of the slots, I'm able to alter the chair's tilt to improve its

Above: Boggs' bent-back rocker design evolved as he experimented with changes in early chair models. Left: With a Forstner bit in a power drill, the author bores the armrest mortise in the rear leg post. The front leg post serves as a guide as he eyeballs the mortise position.

appearance and comfort. Each chair I make is tested and adjusted this way before the runners are permanently secured.

If the chair is not entirely twist-free or doesn't sit squarely on all four legs, now's the time to level the chair and adjust the runners to work in unison. I first set the chair on a level bench and check if all four legs are touching or if the chair leans to one side. Shims placed under one or more legs level the chair. Then, measuring up from the top of the bench, each leg is marked and trimmed with a backsaw. After a final check, lay out the slots for the runners.

With the chair upside down, take a long scrap piece, which is the same thickness as the runners, and place it on edge to span the centers of the front and back legs. Mark the runner positions on the bottom of each leg and with the chair upright again, use a square to extend the lines 1¾ in. vertically up the legs. The slots are cut with a backsaw and coping saw and then pared clean with a sharp chisel.

At this point, I'm ready to make the runners. Stock is planed flat, thicknessed to ¾ in. and scraped smooth. Then, I trace the runner pattern on one of the boards, screw the two pieces together and bandsaw both runners. With the runners clamped together, their edges can be block-planed smooth. I plane in both directions to avoid tearout where the grain changes direction. Sanding blocks, made from curved scraps salvaged from bandsawing the runners, are also good for smoothing the curves. I don't fuss with the straight runs along the top edges until the runners have been fit to the slots.

The sides of the runners are scraped until they can be slid into the slots easily. Don't force them or you'll risk splitting the legs. The flat on the top edge of the runners should extend ½ in. from the front leg posts. After temporarily clamping the runners in position, I place the chair upright on a wood floor and go for a test ride. A ¼-in.-thick piece of plywood has some give to it and works well as a temporary seat. Once the chair is going, I put my feet on the front rung and close my eyes to concentrate on the chair's motion. It should feel smooth, like a swing, and both runners should reach the end of their forward and backward swing at the same time. If one runner stops before the other, the chair will veer

toward the stopped side. You can compensate by moving the stopped-side runner forward a bit (or the other runner back) until the two work together.

Next, I completely relax with my feet flat on the floor. You shouldn't have to push back in the chair to get comfortable. If you do, the frame is pitched too far forward on the runners. I shave up to ½ in. from the straight portion of the runners in the rear leg slots to correct this. If the frame tilts back too much, I trim the runners under the front leg slots. If the correction needed is greater than ½ in., I trim the leg posts too.

When the adjustments are complete, mark the leg post positions on the runners. After fairing the curve along each runner's top edge and shaping the ends of the leg posts with a chisel, I glue and clamp the runners in the slots. The runners are secured with ¼-in. square pins once the glue has dried. The tenoned armrest and splat joints are also pinned now. Then, I scrape the parts smooth before applying four to five coats of boiled linseed oil. I don't sand the chair because sanding would eliminate the facets created when the pieces were drawknifed and shaved.

Seats – I use hickory bark for my seats because it wears well and develops a beautiful patina as it ages. This natural fiber is also easy to weave. You can harvest hickory bark yourself in many parts of the country, and it is also commercially available, although supplies are limited. To order hickory bark, contact Unfinished Universe, 525 W. Short St., Lexington, Ky. 40508; (606) 252-3289, or The Caning Shop, 926 Gilman St., Berkeley, Cal. 94710; (415) 527-5010. Oak splints and Shaker tapes also make good seats.

To prevent the seat from sagging, I make a pillow to fit between the woven layers of the bark. The pillow is filled with fine wood shavings and when it is compressed, it is about 1 in. thick. To hold the pillow in place while you're working, tie it to the rungs before you begin weaving the seat. □

Brian Boggs is a professional chairmaker in Berea, Ky.

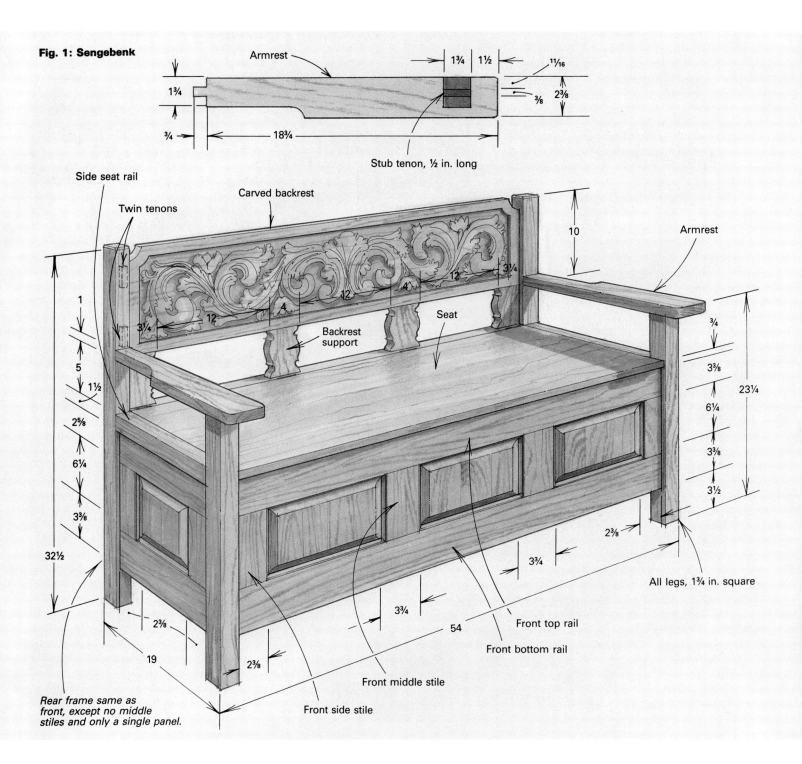

Fig. 1: Sengebenk

Armrest

1¾ 1½

1¾

¹¹/₁₆

¾ 18¾

³⁄₈ 2³⁄₈

Stub tenon, ½ in. long

Side seat rail

Twin tenons

Carved backrest

Armrest

10

Backrest support

Seat

1

5

1½

2⁵⁄₈

6¼

3³⁄₈

32½

2³⁄₈

19

2³⁄₈

3¾

3¾

54

¾

3³⁄₈

6¼

3³⁄₈

3½

23¼

2³⁄₈

All legs, 1¾ in. square

Front top rail

Front bottom rail

Front middle stile

Front side stile

Rear frame same as front, except no middle stiles and only a single panel.

Building a Sengebenk
A Norwegian bench with built-in storage

by Else Bigton and Phillip Odden

Fig. 2: Cross section through rear of Sengebenk

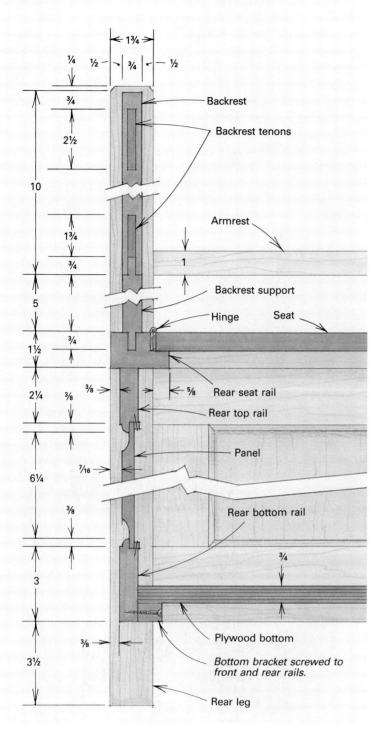

Backrest
Backrest tenons
Armrest
Backrest support
Hinge   Seat
Rear seat rail
Rear top rail
Panel
Rear bottom rail
Plywood bottom
Bottom bracket screwed to front and rear rails.
Rear leg

Traditionally, the sengebenk was an important part of the Norwegian kitchen. During the day it was a seat and at night it became a child's bed. The bench is also a space-saving piece of furniture: Its lid opens to reveal a storage chest. The sengebenk shown was built by Else Bigton from her favorite wood, butternut. The acanthus leaf relief on the back was carved by her husband, Phillip Odden.

it a very comfortable place to sit. Plus, the lift-up seat storage compartment is handy for holding blankets, clothing or anything you might keep in a regular chest. The sengebenk isn't a difficult piece to build and requires only basic mortise-and-tenon joinery and frame-and-panel construction. All the part dimensions are given in the bill of materials on p. 99. The backrest, shown in the photo above, features a traditional Norwegian-style carving (described in the sidebar on pp. 100-101), which can be a nice relief carving project for anyone with basic carving skills, but the bench is also attractive with a plain back.

Developing plans and dimensions—Like much of the other furniture my husband Phillip and I build together in our shop in northwestern Wisconsin, I will build a sengebenk when commissioned by a specific client. The first thing I do is determine the proportions of the piece to suit my client. A comfortable height for the seat can be approximated by measuring the client's favorite chair; and the length of the sengebenk will be determined by the spot in the house that the piece will occupy.

Once I know the important dimensions, I make a scale drawing to work out proportions, including the height of the backrest and height of the arms above the seat. Then, I make a full-size drawing to establish the proportions of the panels and the frames, as well as to confirm all dimensions and construction details. For the bench shown in the photo above, I decided on three panels in the front, for visual interest, and single panels in the rear and on the sides. The size of the side panels is affected by the depth of the bench and the height of the seat. Phillip and I design the decorative pattern to be carved on the front of the backrest, and draw it full size. Finally, I make a cutting list specifying the length, width and thickness of all the necessary parts by taking measurements directly from the full-scale drawing.

As with most of my furniture, I build the sengebenk out of butternut, one of my favorite woods. It carves like a dream, is attractive and is readily available locally. After I make my cutting list, I select lumber for the frames, panels, legs, arms and seat, and thickness plane all the stock.

Constructing the frames and panels—I prepare all the frame parts for the front, rear and sides of the bench seat, and then make the panels and fit them into the frames. First, I rip all the frame stock to width, leaving enough for shaping the edges later. Then,

The sengebenk is a traditional piece of Norwegian furniture used for sitting, sleeping and storage. Because old Norwegian farm houses were small, much of the furniture was designed to be multi-purpose. The sengebenk was usually placed in the kitchen, against the wall next to a trestle table. In the daytime, the bench served as a seat for people working or eating at the table, and at night it became a bed for one or more children. Traditionally, the backrest would flip over to the front via a hinge in the middle of the armrest, to prevent children from falling out of bed. In addition, the bench's seat lifts up to store the bedding inside.

Beyond its customary application, the sengebenk can make a very practical addition to any home; it can be made as long as needed to suit your space, and the addition of a cushion can make

Fig. 3: Frame-and-panel construction

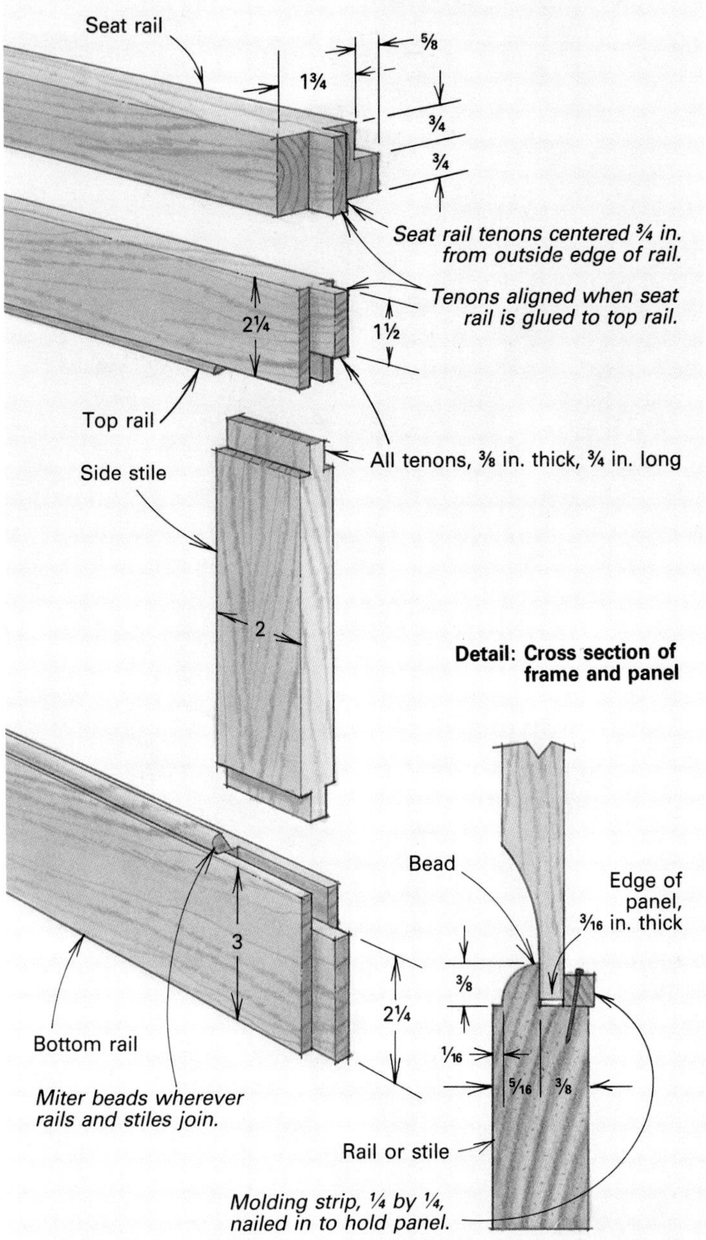
Seat rail
1¾
⅝
¾
¾
Seat rail tenons centered ¾ in. from outside edge of rail.
Tenons aligned when seat rail is glued to top rail.
2¼
1½
Top rail
Side stile
All tenons, ⅜ in. thick, ¾ in. long
2
Detail: Cross section of frame and panel
Bead
Edge of panel, 3/16 in. thick
3
⅜
2¼
1/16
5/16
⅜
Bottom rail
Miter beads wherever rails and stiles join.
Rail or stile
Molding strip, ¼ by ¼, nailed in to hold panel.

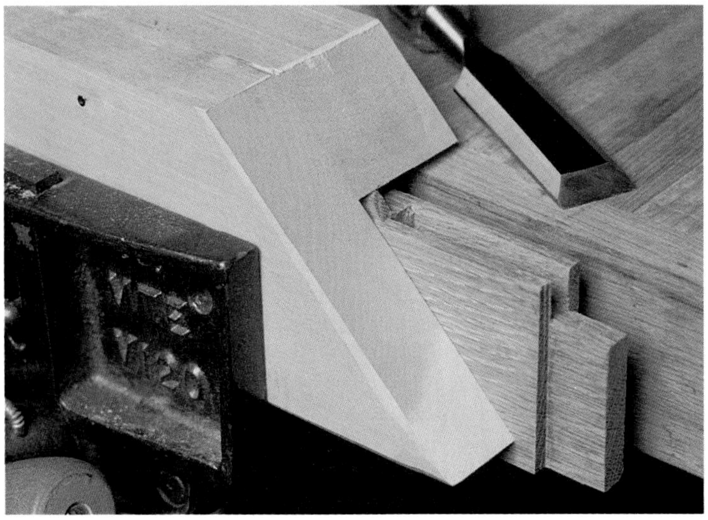

A simple shopmade shooting board allows a chisel to be used for very precise, angled trimming. Here, the shooting board is used for mitering the beads on a rail where one of the side stiles will join via a mortise-and-tenon joint. After mitering, the chisel is used, freehand, to trim the bead at the point to the depth of the rabbet.

each piece is crosscut to length, which includes leaving extra length for a ¾-in.-long tenon on each end of all rails *and* stiles. To give the frames some detail, I cut a quarter-round bead on the inside edges of all the frame members. Instead of using the cope-and-stick method, which requires a special set of matched shaper cutters to simultaneously mold the edges and joints, I use standard straight and roundover cutters to shape a bead and rabbet on each edge, and I cut the required mortises and tenons later. The bead on the front edge of each frame piece is cut with a ⅜-in.-radius cutter (see the detail in figure 3 at left). Then, a straight cutter forms a ⅜-in. by ⅜-in. rabbet on the back edge. The rabbets hold the panels, which will be inserted from the back of the assembled frame and fastened with molding strips. For short frame members, such as the side rails and stiles, it's safer to cut the beads and rabbets on double-width or double-length pieces, and then cut them to final width or length after shaping. This keeps your fingers farther from the cutter during shaping, out of harm's way.

Once the frames are shaped, I spread all the pieces on the workbench and pair up the parts with matching grain and color and pick the best looking parts for the front of the bench. I mark all the parts with a cabinetmaker's triangular proofmark, so I'll know which parts are paired and how they'll be oriented; the top of the triangle always points toward the top on vertical parts. I also number the frame sets, so I'll know instantly where each piece goes.

The next step is cutting the mortises and tenons on the ends of all frame members. The tenons on the stiles fit into mortises on the rails; the rail tenons fit mortises in the legs (see figure 1 on p. 96 and figure 3 at left). I usually cut the tenons with a tenoning jig on the tablesaw; however, you can also cut them freehand with a handsaw. For the mortises, I use my old cast-iron foot-pedal-operated mortising machine, carefully centering the mortises in the width of the stock. Once again, in lieu of a machine, you can chop the mortises by hand or with a router jig—whatever works for you. When you chop the mortises at the ends of the rails, the width of the rail tenons is reduced by the depth of the mortise, but this is fine; the length of the corresponding leg mortises takes this into account.

After the mortises and tenons have been cut and fit, I trim the beads in the corners of the joints using the shopmade shooting board and a chisel, shown in the photo at left. The shooting board is made from two pieces of scrapwood, glued together into an L-shape (when viewed from the end), with the end cut to exactly 45°. The frame piece is clamped into the shooting board, which acts as a fence to guide the chisel for a perfect 45° trim cut. Each bead is trimmed so that the point of the miter comes down to the edge of the mortise, or shoulder of the tenon. I then use a chisel to pare the bead down to the rabbet, so the area where the frame members join together is flat and square. After all the trimming is completed, I trial assemble the frames dry to make sure that everything fits together properly and that all the joints will draw up tightly.

Making the panels is next. I glue up each of the three front and two side panels from short lengths of ½-in.-thick stock, so that the grain in the finished panels will run vertically. The exception is the single rear panel, for which it's easier to run the grain lengthwise. After the panels are glued and dried, I rip and crosscut each panel to its basic dimensions listed in the bill of materials on the facing page, and then trial fit each one in the dry-assembled frame. Each panel is trimmed to fit loosely in its frame opening, to allow for future expansion and contraction. The edges of the panels are then raised, using a three-wing raised panel cutter on the shaper. The gradual curve of the cutter adds visual definition to the panel, and reduces the thickness on the edge to ³⁄₁₆ in.

Backrest and seat assembly—Because the backrest will be carved, I carefully select straight stock with tight grain. Because the bench backrest is joined cross-grain to the rear legs, I try to find boards that show edge-grain on their faces. Boards cut this way (radially) expand and contract only about half the amount of flat-grain cut (tangentially) boards. I do a little test carving on each board to ensure that the wood carves well and doesn't splinter much. I also mark the grain direction on the boards before gluing them, aligning the grain to run in the same direction. This makes it easier to carve across one board into the other. I then clamp the boards together and let the glue dry overnight. After cutting the ends of the backrest square and to length, I notch the top corners with a coping saw, and then cut two 2½-in.-wide tenons on each end, as shown in figures 1 and 2 on pp. 96-97. Making a pair of narrower tenons instead of a single wide one prevents the backrest from splitting, a possibility from even minimal expansion and contraction. At this time, the backrest is carved, as described in the sidebar on the following page.

There are four supports below the backrest that attach to the sengebenk's frame. Each support is 6½ in. long; the middle supports are 4 in. wide and the side supports are 3¼ in. wide. Full-width, ³⁄₈-in.-thick, ¾-in.-long tenons are centered on both ends of each support. After tenoning, cut each support to the profile shown in figure 1 on p. 96. Next, chop the four mortises in the lower edge of the backrest to accept the support tenons, as shown in figure 1. Center these mortises ⁵⁄₁₆ in. from the back side of the backrest so the supports are flush in back. The two end mortises cut into the backrest tenons, which get trimmed to 1¾ in. wide. The bottom tenons on the supports fit into mortises that will be made later in the rear seat rail.

I glue up the seat now, again from edge-grain boards if possible. To make sure the seat will stay flat, I fit two dovetail stretchers on the underside of the seat. First, I glue together all the boards for the seat, save a single 1-in. board at the front edge. Then, I clamp a fence to the underside and, using a dovetail bit in the router, I cut a slightly deeper than ³⁄₈-in. slot in from the front, to within 2½ in. of the seat's back edge. I move the fence over and make several widening passes, until the slot measures 1³⁄₈ in. wide at the top. This is repeated for the other stretcher slot. After cutting the two stretchers from 1-in.-thick stock, rout the male dovetail on the bottom of both strips with the same dovetail bit, this time held in a router table. Make the female dovetails just a hair deeper than the male dovetails so the stretchers will slide in easily, but still fit fairly tight. Next, I chisel away about ³⁄₈ in. of the dovetail on the underside of each stretcher end, so that the dovetail will be hidden and the solid-wood seat has room to shrink and swell. After sanding the stretchers, I drive them in place, and then glue on the 1-in. piece at the front of the seat.

The seat is surrounded on three edges by the seat rails—two on the sides and one in the rear. The rails are made from 2³⁄₈-in. by 1½-in. stock, with a rabbet cut on one edge, as shown in figure 3 on the facing page, to provide a lip that supports the hinged seat. The ends of all the seat rails receive ³⁄₈-in.-wide tenons, centered ⁷⁄₈ in. from the outside face of each rail. The top edge of the rear seat rail also receives four ¾-in.-wide mortises, centered ⁷⁄₈ in. from the rear face of the rail, to accept the bottom tenons on the four backrest supports. After mortising, glue the seat rails on top of their corresponding frame rails, positioning them by lining up the tenons on the ends. Finally, dry-assemble the sengebenk

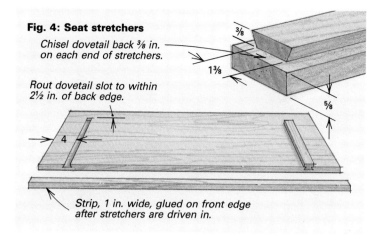

Fig. 4: Seat stretchers

Chisel dovetail back ³⁄₈ in. on each end of stretchers.

Rout dovetail slot to within 2½ in. of back edge.

³⁄₈

1³⁄₈

⁵⁄₈

4

Strip, 1 in. wide, glued on front edge after stretchers are driven in.

and try the seat in place, trimming its ends with a handplane so that it doesn't fit too tightly between the side seat rails.

Legs and armrests—The front and rear legs of the bench are made from 1¾-in.-square stock. The top of each 22¾-in.-long front leg has a ½-in.-long stub tenon that fits into a mortise on the underside of the armrest. All four legs have mortises on two sides to accept the tenons on the ends of the frame rails. Chop all the mortises ³⁄₈ in. wide and make them ¹³⁄₁₆ in. deep, to allow extra clearance for ¾-in.-long tenons. The mortises for the top and bottom frame rails are centered ¾ in. from the outside face of the leg. Mortises for all the lower rails are 2¼ in. long and start 3½ in. from the bottom of each leg; the front top rail mortise is the same length, but starts 14 in. from the bottom. All the remaining top rail mortises house not only the frame rail tenons, but the tenons on the seat rails as well. These mortises also start 14 in. from the bottom of each leg, but are 3¾ in. long.

A 1-in.-long mortise for each armrest is now chopped in the

Bill of Materials

No.	Description	Dimensions (T × W × L)
2	Front legs	1¾ × 1¾ × 22¾ *
2	Rear legs	1¾ × 1¾ × 32½
3	Front top and bottom rails and rear bottom rail	¾ × 3³⁄₈ × 52 **
1	Rear top rail	¾ × 2⁵⁄₈ × 52 **
2	Rear seat rail	1½ × 2³⁄₈ × 52 ††
2	Side bottom rails	¾ × 3³⁄₈ × 17 **
2	Side top rails	¾ × 2⁵⁄₈ × 17 **
2	Side seat rails	1½ × 2³⁄₈ × 17 ††
4	Front and rear side stiles	¾ × 2³⁄₈ × 8¼ **
2	Front middle stiles	¾ × 3¾ × 8¼ **
4	Side stiles	¾ × 2³⁄₈ × 8¼ **
3	Front panels	½ × 13½ × 7 †
1	Rear panel	½ × 7 × 46½ †
2	Side panels	½ × 7 × 11½ †
1	Backrest	¾ × 10 × 52 ††
2	Backrest side supports	⁵⁄₈ × 3¼ × 6½ ††
2	Backrest middle supports	⁵⁄₈ × 4 × 6½ ††
2	Armrests	1 × 2³⁄₈ × 19½ #
1	Seat	¾ × 17¼ × 50¼
2	Dovetailed seat stretchers	1 × 2 × 14¼
1	Bottom (plywood)	¾ × 16¾ × 51¾
2	Bottom brackets	1 × 1 × 50½

* Length includes ½-in.-long tenon on one end.
** Width includes ³⁄₈-in.-deep shaping on edge(s). Length includes ¾-in.-long tenons on both ends.
† Rough width and length, prior to trimming to fit.
†† Length includes ¾-in.-long tenons on both ends.
\# Length includes ¾-in.-long tenon on one end.

1 square = 1 in.

Carving the bench's backrest

The relief carving on the seat back of the sengebenk is a traditional acanthus leaf motif commonly found on decorative furniture and architectural work in Europe and America. My design for the sengebenk, shown above, consists of three symmetrical curls and flowers on each half of the design, and a center crest. To ease the carving process, as shown in the above drawing and on the facing page, you can break the work into three major stages: A. laying out the design; B. roughing out the shapes of the acanthus leaves and flowers; C. refining the forms and adding veins and other details.

Although you can use any carving tools, the best way to create shapes in the relief is to use tools with edges that correspond in size and shape to those in the design. The tools I use to carve the backrest include: an 18mm, #1 skew chisel; a 2mm, #1 spoon skew chisel; 10mm and 16mm,

#5 gouges; a 14mm, #7 gouge; 6mm and 10mm, #8 gouges; 4mm and 8mm, #12 60° V-parting tools; a 5mm, #21 dog-leg chisel. Most of these tools are available from Woodcraft Supply, Box 1686, Parkersburg, W.V. 26102; (800) 225-1153. All of these tool numbers are in the Swiss numbering system; you can find comparable tools from other suppliers, but tools manufactured in other countries will have different numbers.

After the surface of the backrest has been planed smooth and flat, transfer the acanthus pattern, which is shown above and on the facing page, to the wood by carefully redrawing it on a full-size grid of 1-in. squares. Then, transfer the lines to the wood by tracing with carbon paper. Draw one side first, and then flip the patten over and trace the other, symmetrical side.

Begin carving following the steps described on the facing page. As you carve, let

your cuts flow in a continuous, curving line, and let the tool's bevel rub along the wood to keep the depth of cut consistent. After the piece is rough carved, resharpen your tools and begin the fine carving. The goal is to make the carved elements look as though they were created with one continuous cut.

For best results, keep the edges of your carving tools razor sharp. I hone my tools often, first with a soft Arkansas oil stone, and then with a hard Arkansas stone. I also hone a slight bevel on the inside of some of my tools. I prefer to use WD-40 as a lubricant, which makes sharpening easier. Using a lubricant also floats away the metal fragments and keeps the stone clean and cutting well. After honing, I buff the tool edges on a leather wheel charged with buffing compound and chucked in the drill press. Buff lightly, though, or you will round the tool's edge.   —P.O.

front of each rear leg. This mortise starts 22¼ in. from the bottom. Finally, two mortises on the sides of each rear leg are chopped to fit the backrest's twin tenons. To finish the legs, slightly round all the edges, except where the seat rails join, with a handplane, sandpaper or with a small-radius roundover bit in the router.

Next, I rip the 1-in.-thick arms of the sengebenk 2⅜ in. wide. Before shaping the arms, chop the ⅜-in.-wide mortise on the underside to accept the front leg tenon. Also, cut the ⅜-in.-wide tenon on the back end of each arm, to join it to the rear leg. Then, the arms are shaped to the profile in figure 1 on p. 96 and the top edges are rounded over, as you did with the legs.

Gluing and finishing—When all the previous operations are complete, I disassemble the frame and sand all the parts of the sengebenk, except for the carving. I round over any sharp edges and finish-sand all surfaces down to 220-grit.

Everything should now be ready for final assembly. I usually glue up the sengebenk in several steps to make sure I can get everything together before the glue sets up. First, glue the front legs and frame together, applying glue to both the mortises and tenons. Then, clamp the frame, checking it to make sure everything is square and flat after the clamps are tightened. The process is repeated with the rear legs and frame and the carved backrest as well. Finally, I glue the side frames and the armrests to the front and rear assemblies.

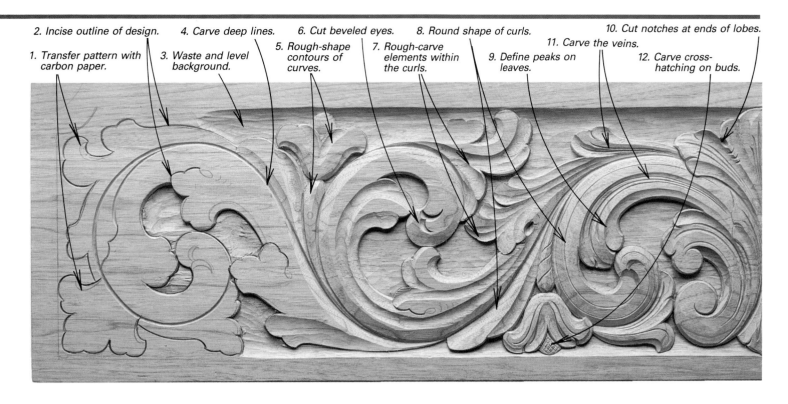

1. Transfer pattern with carbon paper.
2. Incise outline of design.
3. Waste and level background.
4. Carve deep lines.
5. Rough-shape contours of curves.
6. Cut beveled eyes.
7. Rough-carve elements within the curls.
8. Round shape of curls.
9. Define peaks on leaves.
10. Cut notches at ends of lobes.
11. Carve the veins.
12. Carve cross-hatching on buds.

A. The first step in carving the acanthus design is to transfer the carving pattern to the wood with carbon paper (step 1). Incise the outline of each design element (step 2). Use both straight-edge and curved-edge tools, selecting the edge that best fits the shape of the section of line you're working on. Hold the tool plumb, to avoid undercutting, and use a mallet to pound the edge about ⅛ in. into the wood. Next, waste the background using #8 gouges and the #1 plain skew and spoon skew (step 3). Repeat the last two steps until the background is about ³⁄₁₆ in. deep, and use gouges to smooth and level background areas. The background around the edges of the design gradually tapers up to the surface of the board, creating a sort of frame around the edges of the seat back. Define the deep lines on the design (step 4) with the large V-parting tool.

B. Now, with the parting tool and the #1 skew, rough-shape the contours of the individual curls (step 5). Define the two eyelid shapes at the end of each curl (step 6) using a #7 gouge. Make the first cut vertically, as you did when incising the design, and then remove the crescent-shape piece with a second, angled cut. Rough-carve the individual elements within the curls next, using the #8, #7 and #5 gouges (step 7). Use the skew to rough-shape the "bud" on each of the five flowers in the design.

C. Next, the #1 skew is used to round the curls by cutting a series of faceted surfaces (step 8). The skew also defines the transitional peaks (step 9) between details that were rough carved with the gouges (as described in step 7). When the major carving is done, use the #7, 14mm and #8, 10mm gouges to make the notches that define the lobes of each element (step 10). Then, carve in the veins of the plant with the 4mm, #21 V-parting tool (step 11). These veins are cut deeper and wider at the tip of each element, and taper off toward the base of the element. In areas where there are many veins, they converge but never meet. Also use the #21 V-parting tool to carve the cross-hatching on the flower buds. The last thing to do is slightly bevel all the sharp edges with the skew.

Most of our furniture is finished with "natural" Deft oil, which is available from most hardware stores. The oil is easy to apply to both the smooth surfaces of the bench and into the details of the carving, and I like the rich color it brings out in the butternut. The panels are finished separately and put in after they're dry. Each panel is held in its frame by four ¼-in. by ¼-in. molding strips, mitered on their ends and tacked in place with brads. Two bottom brackets, screwed on the inside of both front and rear bottom rails, support the chest bottom, which is cut out of ¾-in. plywood and notched in the corners for the legs.

The only remaining step is to attach the seat to the rear seat rail, which is done with four ¾-in.-wide, 1½-in.-long butt hinges, all centered on the backrest supports. Chisel out shallow mortises for the hinges on the seat first and then screw them on. Next, put the seat in place and mark the rear seat rail. I then chisel out the mortises in the seat rail and screw on the hinges. I've found that using hinges with removable pins makes attaching the seat a lot easier because you don't have to hold the seat up while you drive the screws. □

Else Bigton and Phillip Odden are cabinetmakers and woodcarvers who own Norsk Woodworks in Barronett, Wis. They teach carving classes annually both at their shop and at the Norwegian American Museum in Decorah, Ia.

Chairs of this Philadelphia-Chippendale pattern were produced by the thousands between 1770 and 1800. This utilitarian framework accepts all the fancier variations as well—pierced ladders, open splats, curved front rails, even ball-and-claw feet—without much change in angles or joinery. Landon's reproduction, finish hardly dry, is the one at left.

Making the Chippendale Chair

The way to a chair is to mind your flats and squares

by Eugene E. Landon

Chippendale chairs come in a profusion of designs: ladder-backs, Gothic backs, pretzel backs, some with ball-and-claw feet, some with intricate carving and detailing. The list could go on and on. Yet there's really only one Chippendale chair, because all the variations hang on a common framework. If you can master the chair in this article—it's not really difficult—you should be able to see your way clear to building any of the others. This particular design can be found in *The Philadelphia and Chair-Maker's Book of Prices*, second edition, 1795 (no copy of the first edition has yet been found).

The apparent problem in building a chair is that the seat is trapezoidal and the back posts not only curve, they splay out from the floor upward. This means that most of the chair's mortise-and-tenon joints are not at 90°. To compound the situation, it would seem that all those curves must make it very difficult to cut and fit shoulder joints. Well, the problems look a lot worse than they are. In making this chair we will start with the back posts, then cut each subsequent part to fit in a logical order.

I should say at the outset that you will need some common handtools to build this chair. If you are mostly a machine woodworker, you may never have been taught the virtues of handtools. I remember visiting a woodworking shop at a nearby school. I could hardly believe it, but there wasn't a marking gauge in sight, let alone a mortising gauge. I wouldn't know how to work without gauges, yet they are forgotten tools. You see them for sale in junk shops, garage sales, anywhere there's useless clutter. If you think about it for a moment, there must be *millions* of them out there. It makes you suspect that they might have been used for something, doesn't it?

I could make this chair very easily without electricity, but I could not make it at all without a bevel gauge, my marking gauges, a few sharp chisels, a plane or two, some scrapers, and some rasps and files. If you shy away from such tools, you are not alone, yet trying to duplicate their functions with a machine can be frustrating. For this project at least, I think I can show you that handtools are the right way to go.

The key angle—In building this chair, you would start by scaling up the templates shown on the next page. But if you were reproducing an existing chair in your own shop, you'd begin by determining what I call the chair's key angle—the angle at which the back seat rail meets the back posts, as shown in the photo below. This angle is the same as that at which the chair's back

posts meet the crest rail. If you get this angle wrong, the posts will be out of line and no amount of measuring and gauging from the original will make the chair right—you may still end up with a chair, but you will be playing catch-up all the way.

As long as you have this key angle in your mind's eye, let's examine the main misconception most people have about a Chippendale chair, namely that it is composed of a series of continuous curves. It is not. At every place where a mortise-and-tenon joint comes together there is a planed flat, so that the tenon shoulder lines can be straight. There are short flats where each ladder joins the balloon-shape of the back, and longer flats for the side seat rails. There is even a flat low on the back leg for the side stretcher. The secret to making a chair is to be conscious of these flats, to shape them square to the members, then to fair the adjoining curves to meet them.

Begin with the back posts—The templates in figure 2 were scribed directly off the old chair in the photographs. The side-view template should be laid on the stock, traced, then bandsawn. Two back posts can be bandsawn from a piece of wood 37 in. long, 6 in. wide and 1¾ in. thick. Rough out the side view of the top tenon at this time, but don't saw too tightly to the lines—we'll saw and chisel this tenon to final size later.

Mark the location of the flats for the side seat rails and stretchers, then plane them square. The trick for planing a true flat is shown in the sketch below. Next, use a series of three or four files, from a rough half-round rasp to about an 8-in. smooth file, to remove the remaining bandsaw marks, both front and back. Drawfiling gives the most precision—with the handle of the file in your right hand and the toe of the file in your left, push the file away from you along the work as if you were holding a rolling pin. If your strokes are long, the scratch pattern will give a clear indication of where the high spots are. Chamfers can be stopped using a ½-in.-dia. rat-tail file to achieve the curve.

Files and rasps are precision tools. A coarse rasp may look as if it is butchering the wood, but it is safe to use to remove wood quickly because the scratches are all of uniform depth. The next file in the series replaces the coarse scratch with finer ones, and so on, until the surface is smooth. The whole job should take but a couple of minutes, just remember not to file into the flat spots. At this point, the curve should look continuous; it will look even more so when the chair is together.

The best way to remove the file marks is with a scraper. It

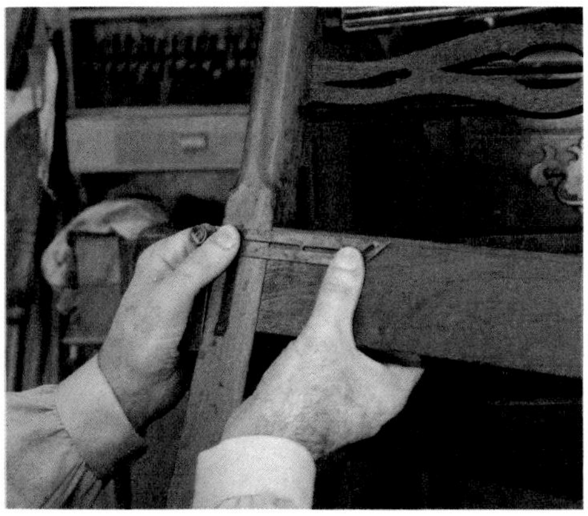

The slope of the shoulders on the back seat rail is a key angle—it determines the splay of the back posts, and thus affects the sizes of all the other parts in the back.

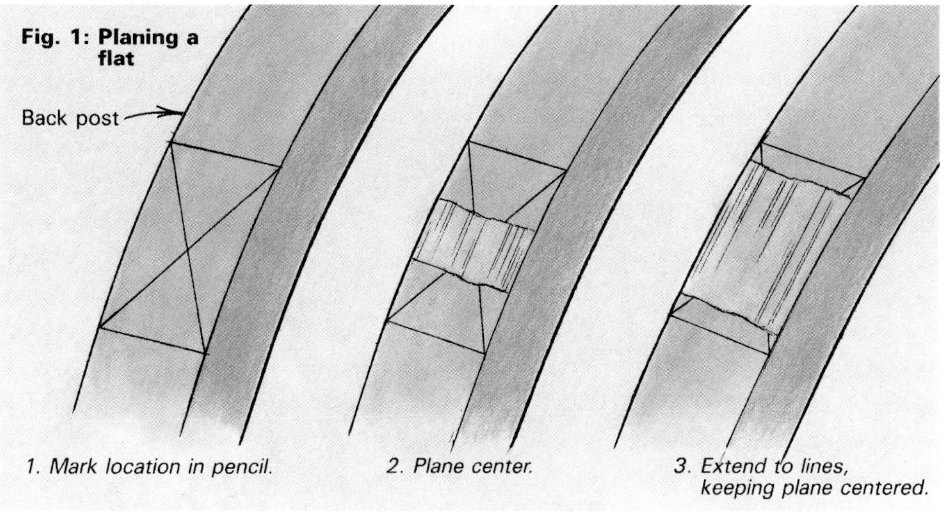

Fig. 1: Planing a flat

Back post

1. Mark location in pencil.   2. Plane center.   3. Extend to lines, keeping plane centered.

From *Fine Woodworking* magazine (September 1986) 60:38-45

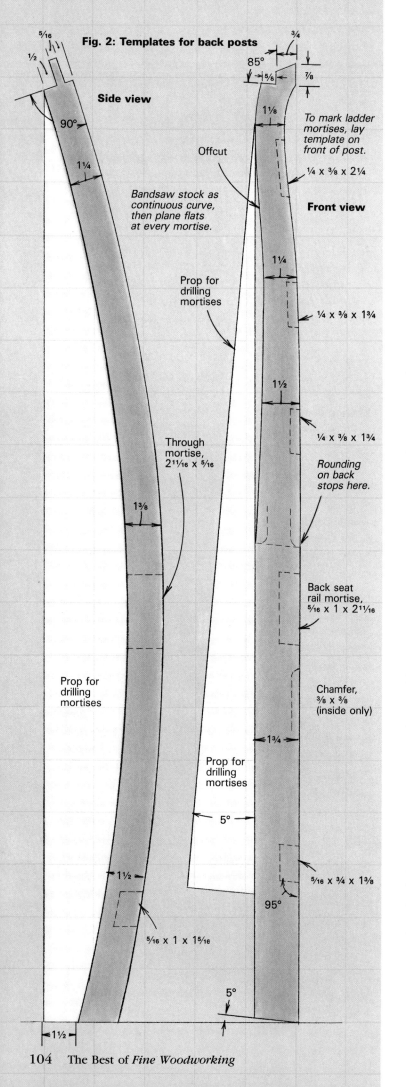

Fig. 2: Templates for back posts

Side view

5/16

1/2

90°

1 1/4

Bandsaw stock as continuous curve, then plane flats at every mortise.

Offcut

Prop for drilling mortises

Through mortise, 2 11/16 × 5/16

1 3/8

Prop for drilling mortises

1 1/2

5/16 × 1 × 1 5/16

5°

1 1/2

3/4

85°

5/8

7/8

1 1/8

To mark ladder mortises, lay template on front of post.

1/4 × 3/8 × 2 1/4

Front view

1 1/4

1/4 × 3/8 × 1 3/4

1 1/2

1/4 × 3/8 × 1 3/4

Rounding on back stops here.

Back seat rail mortise, 5/16 × 1 × 2 11/16

Chamfer, 3/8 × 3/8 (inside only)

1 3/4

5°

Prop for drilling mortises

5/16 × 3/4 × 1 3/8

95°

is not necessary to scrape the upper parts of the post at this time—the front surface will be molded with a scratch stock, and the rear surface will be rasped round after the front-view curves have been bandsawn. The main reason for filing the curves on the upper posts is to be sure they are continuous and even down their centerlines. The lower parts of the posts will remain square from now on; therefore, scrape the front and back faces, then plane the lower legs inside and out. Take care here—these will be the final surfaces on the finished chair.

Chisel tips—Now is a good time to shape the top tenon, taking the sizes from figure 2. Saw, then pare the tenon shoulders to the correct angle (set with a bevel gauge), and adjust its thickness to 5/16 in., a step easily done with calipers as a gauge and the proverbial "sharp chisel," a term that can use some explanation.

There is really only one trick to using a chisel—its back must be absolutely flat, and polished as smooth as the bevel. When this is the case, you can lay a chisel down flat on the work, bevel up, and pare high spots away without risk of digging in. If you find the wood tearing because of contrary grain, simply pare in from the side of the tenon, cross-grain, instead of from the end. When cutting shoulders, press the chisel into the knife line, overlapping the cuts along the full length of the joint, then pare off the chips to establish a slight ledge. With the ledge as a backup behind the chisel, heavier cuts can be taken without danger of the chisel "backing up" and damaging the shoulder line. You can form a perfect square shoulder this way, but in fact, all the joints in this chair are undercut, as shown in figure 4.

If your chisels seem sharp but won't pare flat, it is because the back is rounded. The rounding may be so slight that you can barely see it, but such a tool rides up over the fibers you want to cut, just as the raised tip on a ski rides up over snow.

When the post tenon is sized, clamp the front-view template to the front of the leg and pencil the curves. You can bandsaw the front profile by supporting the post on the offcut from the stock, just as you would to bandsaw any three-dimensional object.

With this done, mark and shape the flats for the ladders. The best approach is to clamp the two legs side-by-side in the vise for marking, to ensure that the flats will align.

Laying out mortises—Scribe mortises with a mortise-marking gauge and/or knife, then use the drill press with a slightly undersized bit to remove most of the waste. Relieving the wood this way reduces the chance of splitting. Finally, pare to the knife lines with a chisel.

Gauges and chisels are extremely precise "partners" in handtool woodworking. To explain, let me begin with a couple of definitions: The familiar marking gauge has a sharp pin that scratches a single line—the pin can be set and locked a certain distance from the fence. A mortising gauge is similar to a marking gauge, but it has two pins that can be locked various distances apart to scribe parallel lines. The distance the pins are set apart represents the width of not only the mortise, but also the width of the tenon that will fit it. The distance the pins are set from the fence represents the distance the joint is from the face of the work. If you always run the fence along the outside faces when scribing, the two pieces will align perfectly when the joint comes together. Why? Because the final cuts are made to the line by starting the edge of a chisel directly in the scribe mark. This halves each scribe line down the middle, with a built-in precision that would require painstaking setup time on a machine.

The man who made this chair some 200 years ago set his mor-

Fig. 3: Parts of a Chippendale chair

As in most period chairs, parts vary slightly in symmetry and dimensions throughout.

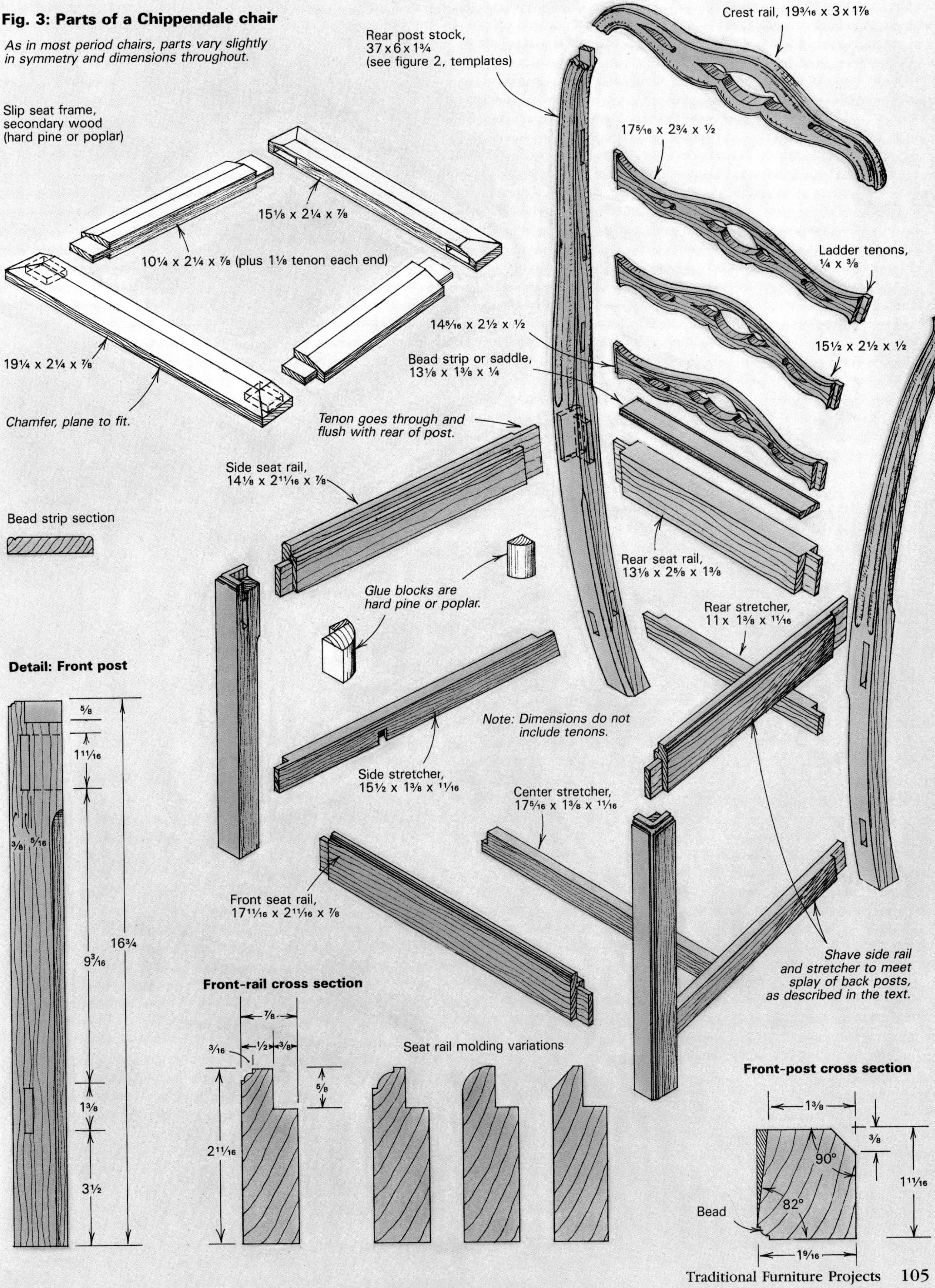

Crest rail, 19 3/16 x 3 x 1 7/8
Rear post stock, 37 x 6 x 1 3/4 (see figure 2, templates)
Slip seat frame, secondary wood (hard pine or poplar)
17 5/16 x 2 3/4 x 1/2
15 1/8 x 2 1/4 x 7/8
10 1/4 x 2 1/4 x 7/8 (plus 1 1/8 tenon each end)
Ladder tenons, 1/4 x 3/8
14 5/16 x 2 1/2 x 1/2
15 1/2 x 2 1/2 x 1/2
19 1/4 x 2 1/4 x 7/8
Bead strip or saddle, 13 1/8 x 1 3/8 x 1/4
Chamfer, plane to fit.
Tenon goes through and flush with rear of post.
Side seat rail, 14 1/8 x 2 11/16 x 7/8
Bead strip section
Rear seat rail, 13 1/8 x 2 5/8 x 1 3/8
Glue blocks are hard pine or poplar.
Rear stretcher, 11 x 1 3/8 x 11/16
Detail: Front post
Note: Dimensions do not include tenons.
5/8
1 11/16
Side stretcher, 15 1/2 x 1 3/8 x 11/16
Center stretcher, 17 5/16 x 1 3/8 x 11/16
3/8
5/16
Front seat rail, 17 11/16 x 2 11/16 x 7/8
16 3/4
9 3/16
Shave side rail and stretcher to meet splay of back posts, as described in the text.
Front-rail cross section
7/8
3/16
1/2
3/8
Seat rail molding variations
5/8
Front-post cross section
1 3/8
3/8
90°
1 11/16
2 11/16
1 3/8
82°
Bead
3 1/2
1 9/16

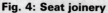

Fig. 4: Seat joinery

Section through posts and rails

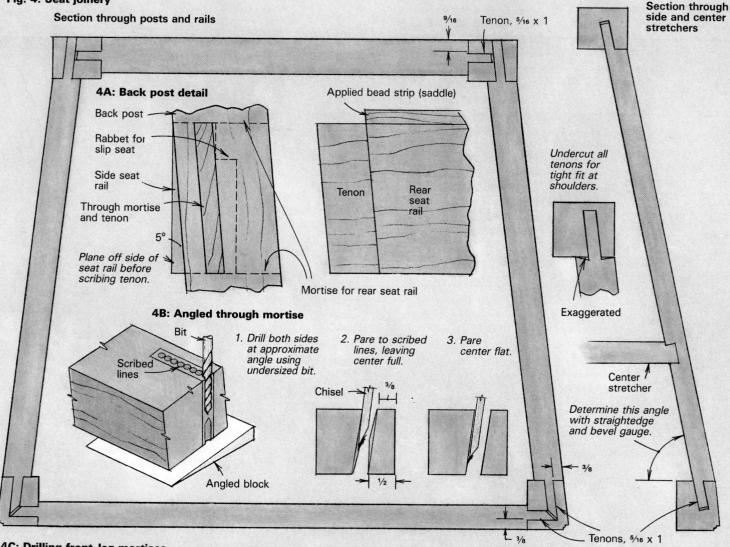

Section through side and center stretchers

9/16 Tenon, 5/16 x 1

4A: Back post detail

Applied bead strip (saddle)

Back post

Rabbet for slip seat

Side seat rail

Through mortise and tenon

5°

Plane off side of seat rail before scribing tenon.

Tenon

Rear seat rail

Mortise for rear seat rail

Undercut all tenons for tight fit at shoulders.

Exaggerated

4B: Angled through mortise

Bit

Scribed lines

Angled block

1. Drill both sides at approximate angle using undersized bit.

2. Pare to scribed lines, leaving center full.

3. Pare center flat.

Chisel   3/8

1/2

Center stretcher

Determine this angle with straightedge and bevel gauge.

3/8

3/8

Tenons, 5/16 x 1

4C: Drilling front-leg mortises

Mortise angles for seat rails can be drilled accurately as shown above. Side-stretcher mortises are drilled undersize, then trued with bevel gauge and chisel after dry-fitting the back, seat rails and front legs.

Bit

Side-rail mortise

Front-rail mortise

82°

Second leg blank, resting on angled face

Second leg, with angled corner up

82°

4D: Stretcher half-dovetail

1. Bandsaw half-dovetail, scribe on side stretcher.

2. Saw down corner to lines, then chisel waste.

Waste

Saw kerf

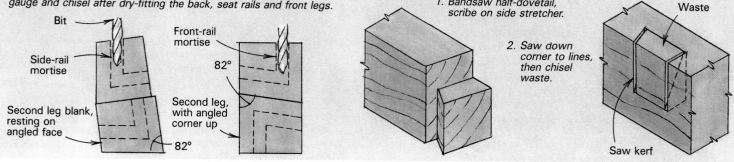

tising gauge to scribe two lines 5/16 in. apart, then he left it there. Every mortise in the chair is 5/16 in. wide, except those for the ladders. He probably had another gauge, set at 1/4 in., for them. On complex jobs, I've had as many as six or seven gauges working, each pre-set to a specific critical dimension.

Sizes and locations of the required mortises are shown on the templates, with details of their angles in figure 4. The one that looks trickiest is the through mortise for the side seat rail. This through mortise is a Philadelphia hallmark, and I expect that it caught on for two reasons: First, to the chair buyer, it looks strong. Second, chairmakers like it because it is actually easier to cut than a blind mortise—figure 4B shows the strategy: Drill in from both sides with the work supported on angled blocks, using

a drill considerably undersized. Then chisel to the lines on both sides, leaving the center of the joint to be pared out as the last step. With this method, an 18th-century cabinetmaker could simply eyeball the approximate drilling angle, as it was the final chisel cuts that would true it up. My drill press, therefore, is the equivalent of a brace-and-bit, not of a modern machine tool, which would call for elaborate angle jigs to cut directly to the line. It would be absurd to claim that a drill press is a handtool, but that's the spirit in which I use it.

Making an angled blind mortise is more difficult, but in this chair the drill press begins the correct angles and they can be pared remarkably true by simply angling the workpiece in the vise, as shown in figure 6, so that you are chopping perpendicular—any last adjustments can be made when the pieces are dry-fit together. As an aid for drilling and paring, the splay angle of the legs can be scribed on the front surface of the leg with a bevel gauge. Don't scribe the rear of the leg, or the marks will show in the finished chair.

Figure 4C shows strategies for ensuring the correct angles in the front-leg mortises. If you choose to, you can devise similar fail-safe tricks for the bottom mortise in the rear posts—which turns out to be the only mortise in the chair that's difficult to line up. I generally eyeball it using a bevel gauge to indicate the angle in top view, and positioning the post in the vise so that the side-view angle can be chopped perpendicular.

One piece at a time—The rear seat rail, as mentioned earlier, is the keystone that establishes the critical angles in the chair. Consider this lowly piece of wood for a moment. It is merely a length of mahogany with a tenon on each end. The shoulder lines are scribed with an X-Acto knife and a bevel gauge, roughed out with the bandsaw (by tilting the workpiece), then pared to the scribed lines with a chisel. This is *not* a difficult piece to make, nor, considered one at a time, are any of the rest of the pieces of the chair. Each may have its minor peculiarities, but I'll show you how to deal with them as we proceed.

The front rail is vertical and the rear leg splays. Because of this, the outer face of the side rail must be "twisted" to conform to the splay of the leg. The reflection in the photo, top right, shows that the rail is simply tapered on the diagonal to the necessary angle at the rear. Here's how to twist the rail:

According to the dimensions in figure 4, measure and scribe the twist angle on the endgrain at the back end of the rail blank. It wouldn't hurt to scribe the taper line along the bottom of the rail as well. A plane can then remove the wood down to the lines. Here is an example of another woodworking "partnership," that of a plane and a scribed line: As soon as the plane iron has cut down as far as the scribed line, the indented line appears as a feathery shimmer at the edges of the work, warning you that you have gone almost as far as you must—you don't have to keep looking at the edges of the work to see where you are.

Once the faces of the side rails have been planed to shape, laying out the tenons is straightforward. The rear tenon is angled, as shown in the photo at right, but because it is scribed with the mortising gauge against the tapered outside face, it is scribed, in effect, just like any other tenon—square. I simply tilt the piece to bandsaw near the lines. The chisel does the rest.

The side rails (and the front rail) will be rabbeted on their inner edges to contain the slip seat. You could do this now. I usually use an old wooden rabbet plane for the job, but on this chair I used my Stanley 45, for the sole reason that a lot of you guys out there might want to show this paragraph to your wives and say: "See, honey, I really *did* need to buy that tool!" Of course, this cut is a perfect excuse to use a tablesaw.

The seat rail edges and front leg, in this chair, were beaded with a molding plane. This beading is optional, because in similar period chairs it might have been a chamfer or a plain round. I'd rather see these alternatives on a reproduction than see a molding generated by a stock router bit.

The top of the front leg posts must also be rabbeted so the seat will fit, but this step is done with mallet and chisel after the chair is assembled. Notice that the glue blocks are large enough to support the corners of the seat, doing double-duty, as it were.

The stretchers are miniature versions of the seat rails and should prove no problem, but note that the side stretcher's angle

Top, the reflection on the side seat rail highlights the strategy for 'twisting' it to meet the splayed rear post—the surface is planed down along the diagonal. In normal lighting, the rail looks flat, with the twist more easily felt than seen. Lower photo shows the rear tenons on the rails (scribed marks darkened for clarity).

is more acute than the seat rail's. Notice, also, that they have only one shoulder on the tenons, so that the mortises can be wide, yet remain away from the face of the legs. This is typical chairmakers' strategy, keeping things strong. The single-shouldered tenon also shows up in chairs with a vertical splat, in case you would like one instead of the ladders, but the single tenon at the bottom of the splat must have its shoulder at the rear, while the tenon at the top has its shoulder at the front—otherwise there's no place to cut the mortises. Vertical splats are slipped into place after the rest of the back has been glued up. The saddle, which holds the splat at the bottom, is an applied piece, just as is the decorative bead in our chair. The saddle is glued atop the rear seat rail to secure the splat, which floats freely in its mortises both top and bottom—if you glue a splat it may split.

The center stretcher is fitted after the chair has been glued up—bandsaw the half-dovetail as shown in figure 4D, removing the saw marks with a chisel. Scribe the shape onto the bottom of the stretchers, then begin the sockets by handsawing down the

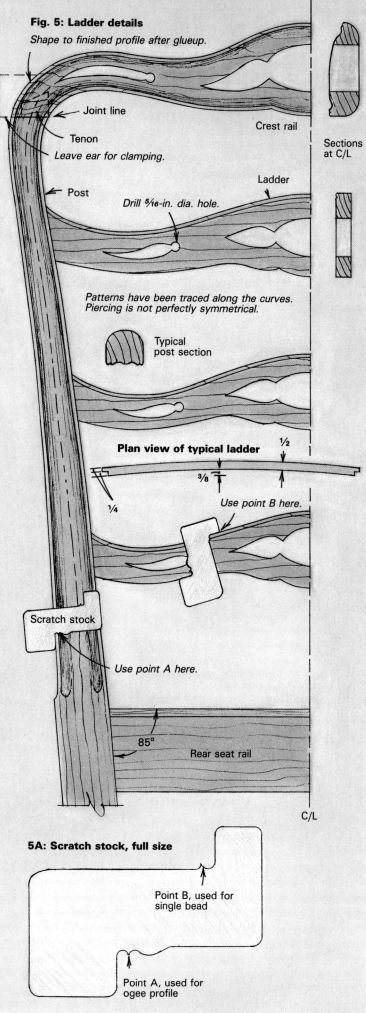

Fig. 5: Ladder details

Shape to finished profile after glueup.

Joint line

Tenon

Leave ear for clamping.

Post

Drill ⁵⁄₁₆-in. dia. hole.

Crest rail

Ladder

Sections at C/L

Patterns have been traced along the curves. Piercing is not perfectly symmetrical.

Typical post section

Plan view of typical ladder

½

⅜

¼

Use point B here.

Scratch stock

Use point A here.

85°

Rear seat rail

C/L

5A: Scratch stock, full size

Point B, used for single bead

Point A, used for ogee profile

Drawing: Lou Bassler

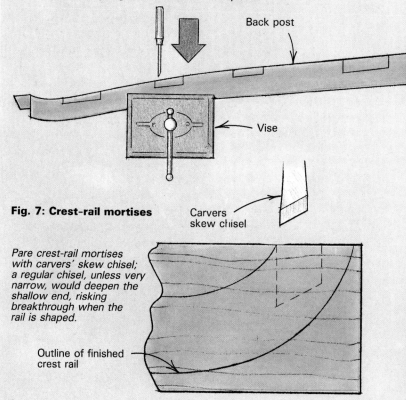

Fig. 6: Chopping angled mortises

To maintain correct angles, position post in vise so chisel chops vertically, following angle established on drill press.

Back post

Vise

Fig. 7: Crest-rail mortises

Carvers skew chisel

Pare crest-rail mortises with carvers' skew chisel; a regular chisel, unless very narrow, would deepen the shallow end, risking breakthrough when the rail is shaped.

Outline of finished crest rail

lines as far as you can go. Next, chisel out the waste. If you have never made a half-blind dovetail this way, you may be surprised at how easy it is.

The crest rail—The mortises in this rail are as large as they can be without breaking through the top. Lay out the mortises and the profile of the rail on a piece of squared stock, then relieve the mortises on the drill press, being very careful not to drill too deep at the shallow end. Pare them as shown in figure 7.

Cut the front and the top profile of the crest rail on the bandsaw, but leave a couple of "ears" at the ends for clamping, as shown in figure 5. I make the pierced decoration on the crest rail by drilling ⁵⁄₁₆-in.-dia. holes straight through, then using a power scroll saw to cut the rest of the curves (you could use a saber saw or a hand fretsaw). The back of the crest rail is rounded with rasps, files and scrapers to the approximate cross section shown. It is not possible to show drawings and photos of all these compound curves, but as a guide I might say that the back of the crest rail looks as if it were blown up with a bicycle pump, with hardly a flat spot anywhere. The backs of the ladders are eased somewhat, but are basically flat.

The fronts are beaded with a scratch stock. The one I used was made by a local machine shop from steel about ³⁄₃₂ in. thick, then tempered to 50Rc—about the same hardness as a planer blade. It is ground square, and can work in either direction without needing a burr (if you encounter contrary grain, just go the other way). One edge of the scratch stock has the profile for the back-post molding; the other edge has the profile for the single bead around the edges of the ladders (see figure 5A).

Sizes for the ladders, and their precise shoulder angles, can be taken off the back when it is dry-assembled, as I am shown doing in the top photo on the next page. The ladders are made in the

When sizing the ladders, above, a pair of clamps stabilizes the back posts. To pierce the back, left, first drill entrance holes for the scroll saw blade. The size of the drill bit used, in this case ⁵⁄₁₆ in., conforms to the design.

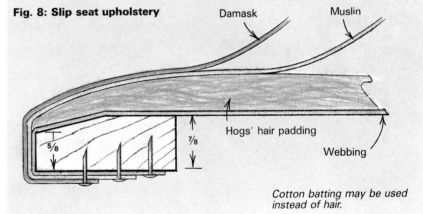

Fig. 8: Slip seat upholstery — Damask — Muslin — Hogs' hair padding — Webbing — ⁵⁄₈ — ⁷⁄₈ — Cotton batting may be used instead of hair.

same way as the crest rail, that is, they are marked out in the square, then shaped, pierced and beaded. Notice in figure 3 that the tenons have only one shoulder, located at the front.

Assembly—The back is glued up first and allowed to dry. The ladders, incidentally, are merely press-fit into place without glue. Then the rails, stretchers and front legs are glued and clamped to the back assembly. When this is dry, add the center stretcher, and fit the saddle (which is first beaded with the same scratch stock used on the ladders). Then cut the glue blocks to fit.

Make the slip seat as shown in the drawing, allowing a little room for the fabric—at least ⅛ in. on all sides. I prefer not to get involved with upholstery myself, as it would cut too much into my woodworking time, but there is nothing difficult about this seat. A cross section of the upholstery is shown in figure 8.

So, there's your chair, the first one, anyway. Now that you've got your confidence, my last piece of advice is to make them in batches from now on, the way they would have done it in the 18th century. You'll find that things go much faster. I'm not about to tell you how quickly I can make a set of six ladderback chairs—word might get out to my clients—so you'll have to find out for yourself. But I will tell you that 18th-century chair shops made a pretty good living, and there was a lot more competition then than there is now, that is, if you are talking about the real thing. It's a lot of trouble for a machine to duplicate the Chippendale look, so most factories don't really try—most of what you see as Chippendale these days is just mush. With handtools, though, the style is a piece of cake. □

Gene Landon makes furniture in Montoursville, Pa.

The New England Windsor Chair

A tradition captures the imagination of contemporary makers

by Jeremy Singley

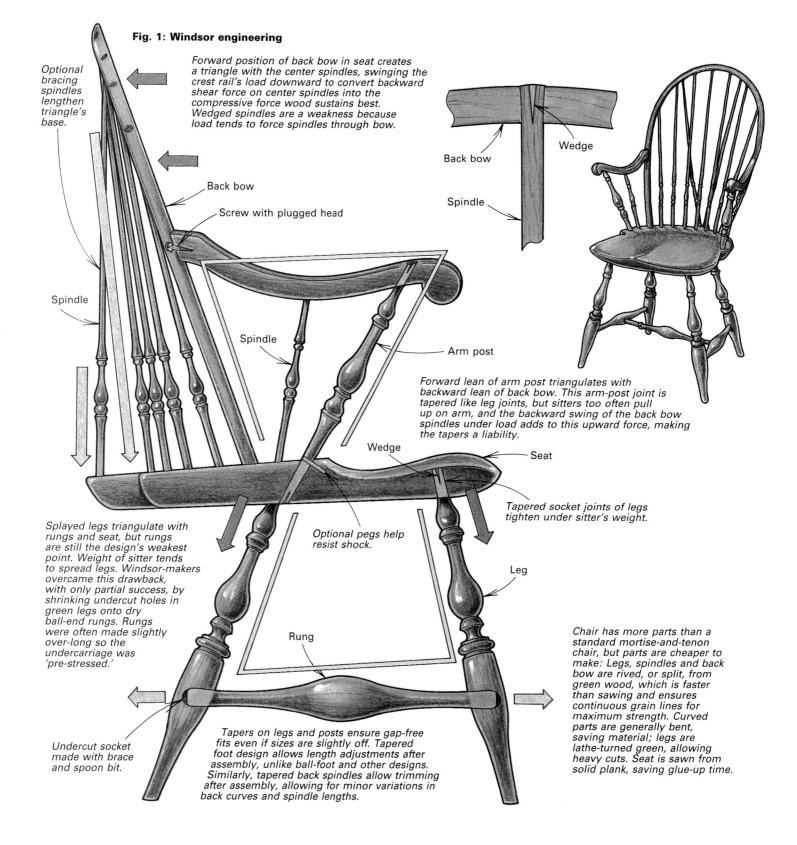

Fig. 1: Windsor engineering

Forward position of back bow in seat creates a triangle with the center spindles, swinging the crest rail's load downward to convert backward shear force on center spindles into the compressive force wood sustains best. Wedged spindles are a weakness because load tends to force spindles through bow.

Optional bracing spindles lengthen triangle's base.

Back bow

Screw with plugged head

Spindle

Spindle

Back bow

Wedge

Spindle

Arm post

Forward lean of arm post triangulates with backward lean of back bow. This arm-post joint is tapered like leg joints, but sitters too often pull up on arm, and the backward swing of the back bow spindles under load adds to this upward force, making the tapers a liability.

Wedge

Seat

Tapered socket joints of legs tighten under sitter's weight.

Splayed legs triangulate with rungs and seat, but rungs are still the design's weakest point. Weight of sitter tends to spread legs. Windsor-makers overcame this drawback, with only partial success, by shrinking undercut holes in green legs onto dry ball-end rungs. Rungs were often made slightly over-long so the undercarriage was 'pre-stressed.'

Optional pegs help resist shock.

Leg

Rung

Undercut socket made with brace and spoon bit.

Tapers on legs and posts ensure gap-free fits even if sizes are slightly off. Tapered foot design allows length adjustments after assembly, unlike ball-foot and other designs. Similarly, tapered back spindles allow trimming after assembly, allowing for minor variations in back curves and spindle lengths.

Chair has more parts than a standard mortise-and-tenon chair, but parts are cheaper to make: Legs, spindles and back bow are rived, or split, from green wood, which is faster than sawing and ensures continuous grain lines for maximum strength. Curved parts are generally bent, saving material; legs are lathe-turned green, allowing heavy cuts. Seat is sawn from solid plank, saving glue-up time.

From *Fine Woodworking* magazine (July 1988) 71:32-38

The work of Michael Dunbar, one of the leading makers in the rebirth of the handmade Windsor, demonstrates some of the adaptability of the concept: a shaped plank seat bored with sockets to accept an undercarriage and superstructure *that are lightweight yet strong. Rear, from left to right: continuous-arm chair, fan-back armchair, high oval-back desk chair, birdcage sidechair. In the foreground are two stools and a child's fan-back.*

Had George Nakashima taken his work less personally, my chairmaking career might never have begun. A woman who bought two of his very first captain's chairs, years before, feared to return them to their source for repairs because she knew the famed contemporary-style woodworker was known sometimes to revoke ownership of work he thought the owner had abused. Instead, she dropped them off, in pieces, at my daddy's shop one serendipitous day some 17 years ago. I was fascinated. The chairs were all of oiled walnut and showed signs of being handmade. The spindles bore heavy spokeshave marks like facets on a cut diamond, and the joints were precisely turned and pegged in place. But when the chairs were restored, I found them uncomfortable to sit in. My attempts to better them ensued, and I began developing my own versions of sleek all-hardwood spindle-back chairs.

It was years before I began to realize I was developing variations of Windsor chairs, a form that certainly didn't start in my lifetime or Nakashima's. My ignorance of the style's pedigree could only be a liability to my work, perhaps bordering on arrogance. I hit the books and talked to people who knew, and I was happily humbled.

The Windsor chair, a shaped solid-wood seat into which are socketed wood legs and spindles, appeared in England sometime in the late 17th century. While the Queen Anne designers were dogmatically building rigid chairs founded on their refined understanding of mortise-and-tenon joinery and the strength of materials, Windsor makers had begun drawing on an intimate knowledge of the *nature* of materials, much of it learned in other woodworking trades, to build comfortable, flexible chairs that could sell at half the Queen Anne price. Figure 1 on the facing page shows how these mass-producible parts work together as a team, like the parts of a suspension bridge or a bicycle wheel, branching together into a single tension/compression unit. Where the Queen Anne chair, built like a post-and-beam house, required eight or more braces (four disguised as ear pieces at the knees), the Windsor needed none. The whole chair was itself a brace.

Cherchez la femme?—It was a timely idea, and a woman may have been its inspiration. After the fall of Rome, only great men sat in chairs, or more properly, thrones—heavy, complicated and expensive. It wasn't until the 16th century that women, leading their own lives for the first time, demanded chairs of their own, specifically lightweight, portable chairs to take into their all-female bed-chamber social gatherings. Among these were the first crude precursors to the Windsor.

I sometimes wonder if they weren't collusions between the woman of the home and the one branch of the woodworking trade that was her domain. Historians generally agree it wasn't a city chairmaker who invented the Windsor. Some suspect a turner, and others a wheelwright, but as one who has repaired both old Windsors and old spinning wheels, I can say that to a spinning-wheel maker, building a Windsor would have been as easy as making the flyer 10 sizes too big and shaving the wheel spokes into spin-

Photo: Andrew Edgar; drawings: David Dann

Michael Dunbar

Dunbar uses traditional methods and tools to make his chairs, a low-overhead approach that produces two chairs per week and allows a comfortable profit.

dles. Everything else—the splayed, turned legs in tapered sockets beneath, the wheel posts (translated to arm posts) in similar sockets above, and even the ornamentation—is identical with the parts of Windsor chairs. In fact, a wheel's functional reels, rings and tapers translate into one of a Windsor's main production economies. All the decoration on a Windsor can be done by machine.

At any rate, wherever it may have originated, it was almost certainly near Windsor, England, that the design matured, for from the 1720s onward, it was to the southern counties, and Chipping Wycombe in particular, one went to buy these green-painted "stick" chairs that were becoming all the rage as garden seats.

Storming the colonies—With a name like "Windsor," the chair might have become synonymous with tea and crumpets, but by 1750 it was the American Windsor that was known worldwide. Given the circumstances, such a flourishing was inevitable. First, a burgeoning American population—in Philadelphia alone, from 13,000 in 1740 to 40,000 in 1776—had reached a degree of civilization that required fashionable chairs, and furniture then, as now, was not easy to ship.

Second, we had the wood. English Windsors were almost always all of hardwood, an expensive material not conducive to easy production. After centuries of shipbuilding, they had few large softwoods left, while we had—still have—whole forests of clear, straight pines, poplars and basswoods wide enough to make more than 50 18-in.-wide seat blanks per tree. (I can look out and count 10 in the Vermont woods outside my window right now.)

Third, we had the technicians. In the previous century, essentials were the priority, giving rise to a massive guild of turners and spinning-wheel makers. Many of these had by now begun to slip into the niches opened by the more genteel life-style, offering rush-bottom and banister-back chairs and daybeds among their wares, then advancing to Windsors as these began arriving from abroad. At first these domestic copies were considered stopgaps for those who couldn't afford the real thing from England (George Washington dismissed them as too flimsy "for common sitting" and ordered his from England), but by 1755, things British were already becoming tainted. Washington, in fact, eventually canceled his order and furnished Mount Vernon with American Windsors.

Finally, our developing democracy was a fertile social milieu for mass production, a concept in its infancy elsewhere. The rising middle class created such a huge market for mid-price furnishings, that advertisements from the 1760s onward described batches of *thousands* of Windsors—often all from one shop—for sale in major ports all along the coast, the West Indies and Europe. These chairs, made by the likes of Francis Trumble and Joseph Henzey, were often branded with the maker's name to prevent mix-ups during shipping, the beginnings of the "brand name." Virtually all of the early advertisements originated at Windsor "manufactories" in Philadelphia, the mid-century Windsor center of America. In fact, Philly enjoyed such a monopoly, that by the 1760s *all* American Windsors were becoming known as "Philadelphia chairs," a trend New York and New England makers found distressing.

They set out to rectify their subordinate position in the good old American way: by building a better product. By introducing crisply executed turnings, bold carvings and daring splays and proportions, the northern Windsor makers gradually weaned their neighbors from out-of-state shipments of standardized mass-produced designs. Along the way, their experiments toward a more appealing Windsor led to the development of the continuous-arm design, perhaps the boldest of them all and one apparently never made south of New York.

North of New York, today: Dunbar in Portsmouth—You can't research the history of Windsors very far without bumping into the name Michael Dunbar. Dunbar didn't just write about traditional Windsors, he built them—a lot of them. From 1970 to 1985 he built well over 1,000 chairs using the original methods and tools. Along the way, he wrote several books on the subject and became something of a Windsor guru, inspiring a subculture that now includes at least 100 Windsor makers across the country. Here was the man to see.

I met with Dunbar at the art museum at the Rhode Island School of Design (RISD), where we looked over the museum's collection of antique Windsors and talked shop. Much of what Dunbar said addressed modern misconceptions. "In the 20th century we're in love with wood, to the point where 'the natural beauty of the wood' has become a cliche. Everybody says: I want to make a Windsor chair, but I want to make it all out of walnut. But a Windsor is an engineered product—the wood has been selected for its properties, not for what it looks like." Which is why the old-timers chose only tough, resilient woods like oak, ash and hickory for their spindles. Besides having the strength to support and the flexibility to conform to the sitter, these woods rive and shave easily enough to enable a good worker to turn out a set in an hour. The legs and armposts were made of maple, beech or birch, woods that, when turned green, cut so cleanly an experienced turner could knock out a turning every three minutes. For the seats, they chose a single slab of clear white pine, basswood or poplar, wide enough to avoid the extra step of edgegluing and soft enough to saw and adze into shape easily.

These tricks work as well today as they did then, but we power toolers have become so conditioned to doing things by machine that we tend to work with machines even when it doesn't make sense, to the point where some of us end up reinventing the wheel.

Dunbar went on to say, "I once read an article by a fellow who began by saying: 'It may be more satisfying to carve out seats with an adze and inshave, but I run a production shop....' He then goes on to describe how he uses a chainsaw to rough out his seats, and his last sentence is: 'And doing it this way I can make a seat in two hours.' Hell, I can do it in half an hour using traditional tools! Which brings up a point about business. Too many people believe unless you've got the drill press, the jointer, the bandsaw, the lathe, etc., you can't be a woodworker. I make two chair seats a week using a $45 bowsaw. It takes me from five to seven minutes to cut out the two seats, after which the saw goes back on the wall 'til next Monday. A bandsaw takes up space and has to be cleaned off, and it costs a lot more than $45. It's ridiculous for two or even six chairs a week. You have to decide what level of production requires setting up machinery."

Dunbar is able to turn out two chairs a week in his New Hampshire shop because the Windsor was conceived not as a show piece but as a production piece, built of the easiest-to-work woods by the fastest methods. The unfinished product, a mix of wood colors with tool-marked surfaces, was brought together visually and made smooth with paint, which Dunbar feels adds to the challenges. "Anybody can take crotch mahogany and make it interesting. That's no real achievement; it's pretty to look at anyway. Now take a product that's going to be painted and make it look interesting. You've narrowed yourself down to a very tight range of possibilities, and one of them is line. I'm convinced that among the 'mysteries' of the trade, those things handed down by oral tradition, were instructions on consciously working in the element of line."

The Windsor is a composition in which each of the parts moves the eye to the next in a continuous linear flow. Because the eye is always moving through the chair, individual parts need not be perfect. Dunbar pointed out some alarming discrepancies on RISD's old Windsors. He suggested some chairs had one or two skinny legs because of rough blanks that were rived too small from the log, or because the turner tried to shave away a slipup with the skew chisel. Discards? Those legs were made the hard way: "Once we've got it chucked up and roughed round, there's no way we're gonna throw that thing away. It either blows up on the lathe or it goes on the chair."

You'd think the maker would at least have sorted his legs so that each chair had, say, two fat legs in the front and two skinny ones in the back, but generally in the period they seem not to have recognized that as a convention. "We've grown up with machine-made uniformity, but back then if a leg had a flaw (he points out a thumb-size knot hole on a leg's front), it went where it went and there was no conscious effort to turn it to the back."

The fact is, they didn't have the time, because these guys were making them by the thousand. The profit margin was too slim to allow for finickiness and still is, as Dunbar's experience shows.

"You learn these things the hard way. For the first five or six years in business, I'd make anything anybody wanted, until I realized I was losing my shirt. Finally I got kind of hard-ass about it. I made the kid's chair, the oval-back side chair, the sack-back and the continuous-arm, and that was it. Not only did you have to come to the shop to pick up the chair, you had to come in to order it, because I didn't want someone to order a chair and then come in and say 'My god, this isn't what I wanted at all!' So you'd come in, look at the model chairs I'd work from, and that's what you'd get." Dunbar's only display was in his kitchen. His deposits were nonrefundable, he refused to ship and he sold the chairs painted or unfinished only.

Buyers weren't deterred. Collectors who couldn't afford antique Windsors paid $450 each for his chairs, and he turned them out like a one-man production line. But he kept his sanity, too. "I almost always made them in pairs. I'd bend the backs on Monday so they'd be ready to go on the chairs by Thursday. I'd turn the legs and by the time I got done with the eighth one that was about all I wanted to turn. The same with the seats. Two was enough." Was it worth it?

"It's a wonderful way to make a living...."

Dunbar wasn't the first modern Windsor maker to revive the style—that honor probably goes to Wallace Nutting of a prior generation—and he wasn't the first living Windsor maker I'd ever met in person.

Sawyer in Calais—In the summer of 1982, I served on the jury at Frog Hollow Craft Gallery in Middlebury, Vt. Dave Sawyer, a tall, slim, prepossessing and affable gentleman with lantern jaw and expressive gray, bushy eyebrows had just lugged into the jury room two of his early efforts, a blue sack-back and a red youth chair. The chairs were okay, but they lacked charm. As the woodworker on the panel, my "no" vote was the clincher for Dave's rejection.

About six months later, he returned with a beautiful continuous-arm and one of the most beguiling and comfortable fan-backs I've ever tried—obviously a fast learner. The gallery has been showing his work proudly ever since, and Dave and I have been on close terms, visiting and following one another's work from time to time.

Sawyer graduated from the Massachusetts Institute of Technology with a mechanical engineering degree in 1959. He'd taken up the profession because, after helping his dad, a commercial artist, in his professional workshop since childhood and working in a boat yard while in high school, he knew he wanted to be involved in building things. He took a nine-to-five job as an engineering draftsman in 1963, but says: "It put me to sleep, so I gave it up. It was all pretty far removed from actually making something."

As an antidote to pencil pushing, he built an 8-ft. by 10-ft. house from scrap lumber in a week on six acres in Quaker City, N.H. Having no room for woodworking, he proceeded to make leather belts, then candles. After adding onto the house, he graduated to woodworking with a line of wooden pitchforks.

In 1970, a thousand or so pitchforks later, he built a shop. Having found a ladder-back he liked at a friend's house, he went into ladder-back chairmaking, a trade he chose because he "liked the idea of starting with a tree and a few hand tools one day and having a finished product the next."

Sawyer eventually took a trip to see Dunbar, who at the time was giving all comers measured drawings remaindered from one of his books. Dave took a set home and finally built his first Windsor, a sack-back.

Sawyer constantly experimented with improvements. He curved the back of his continuous-arm more deeply than those of antique models, making it more inviting to sit in, "more like sitting in a basket and less like sitting against a wall." A more daring experiment was to try an oak back on a butternut seat and cherry undercarriage (see the middle photo, next page). Showing through a clear oil finish, this makes a pleasing combination, and

Photo: Eric Borg

Photo: Jay O'Rear

Dave Sawyer

Dave Sawyer, left, captures the flavor of Windsor style in overall proportions as well as in crisp details. Sawyer's comb-back rocker, above, is a style that may have never existed in the period; rocking chairs were rare. Sawyer's reproportioning of the cherry legs, necessarily short and wide-splayed, is pleasingly well-balanced. The seat is butternut and the superstructure oak. The Windsor accepts stylish detailing without sacrificing its underlying integrity of structure. In the beginning of the 19th century, when things Chinese were in vogue, bamboo-pattern side chairs, such as the one above right, were popular. Simplified detail streamlined production.

since butternut is as easy to carve as pine, and cherry as easy to turn as the traditional white woods, it adds little to the construction time. Sawyer himself still prefers his Windsors painted, but says, "I like them both ways. A lot of customers like to look at wood, and I don't mind humoring them."

Sawyer's comb-back rocker, shown above, is truly an avant-garde chair, since there's almost no such thing as a traditional Windsor rocker, rockers being invented and popularized later. To me, it's an intriguing taste of where Windsors might have gone had they kept going. Always on the lookout for new ideas, Sawyer travels from Quebec to North Carolina to talk to his fellow craftspeople, constantly learning and often teaching about ladder-backs and Windsors. Ironically, he met one of his closest Windsor-making friends, Robert Chambers, just over the mountain in Corinth, Vt.

Chambers in Corinth—A fellow engineer, Chambers started really high-tech as an aerodynamic designer of jet missile engines. "I was making lots of bucks in aerospace but also suffering a big dose of questioning what I was doing. From the earliest times, I remember being with my father in his woodworking shop—he didn't make much furniture but was always doing something. I'd get a real craving to do something and find out right away if I did it right or not."

Chambers picked up a copy of Dunbar's old book. "I found it tremendously appealing that I could go knock some trees down one day, stand against the lathe with spray in my face the next, and in between fool with the design."

He took his first sack-back to Dunbar, who pronounced it one of the best first efforts he'd seen, but Chambers, his own harshest

critic, was convinced Dunbar was just being polite. He soon got a chance to try again when a friend asked if he'd make him a pair of sack-backs and four side chairs. It was then that it occurred to Chambers that he might be able to sell these things. "I made the decision to jump out of my comfortable position and move to Vermont," says Chambers. "I took out ads in a few trade journals, and since my prices were low ($175 to $275) and there weren't many other Windsor makers at the time, I got myself terribly busy, more than I wanted to be." He dropped the ads and cut back to take a teaching job at Vermont Technical School in nearby Randolph until, a year ago, he felt ready to regroup.

Meanwhile, his sack-back design evolved. He bent the back bow on his arm-crest form so that, with the same curve to both bends, the chair looked unified. He took the same kind of thinking further with his undercarriage layout.

Many Windsor makers, like Dunbar, "know all the angles" and simply eyeball their leg angles. Chambers prefers to stand a block with a guide mark on his seat blank to help him align the bit when he bores his leg holes, using a modern bit and brace rather than the spoon bit of old. Then, to ensure symmetry, he bores the rear leg holes using the block to set his side-view angles only. The rear legs' rear-view angles are always bored in the same planes as those of the front legs, like a rocking chair's, so they can be sighted directly from legs plugged into the front holes. Besides facilitating boring, this trick seems to serve equally well as a design formula, for the result, in Chamber's hands at least, is a chair with strikingly well-balanced proportions. All his Windsor styles, with their rear-leg tenons set well in toward the seats' center-lines, remind me of lithe dancers up on their toes.

Robert Chambers

Robert Chambers, left, here drilling tapered sockets with a reground spade bit, is a former aerospace engineer who continually refines his Windsor designs. Typical of Chambers' Windsors, shown above, is an uncluttered, unified look, much in contrast to some early chairs (example top left). Homely furniture from the past is a reminder that utilitarian forms weren't always built by design geniuses.

"Each time I go to make a chair, it's an opportunity to make it better. While some of my chairs are pretty close to standardized, most are variations on a theme.

"I accept a lot of the given," concludes Chambers. "I haven't invented any new styles, but I still find it a big challenge to put together something that works, that's pleasing, and harmonious with an earlier time."

Over all, it takes Chambers about 40 hours to build a continuous-arm from tree to paint. When I hinted this was a mite longer than the old-timers took, he replied, "I've hewed one side of a 26-in. 8 x 8 in an hour and a half, so I can see where it could be done in the six hours it was supposed to have taken 'those old-timers'—if you could keep it up. But, you know, a friend of mine told me once, 'Hey, Bob, I've seen an old photograph of some of those old-timers. They're about 26.'" Chambers is a bit more mature than that.

Both Sawyer and Chambers have restored "bodgering"—turning Windsor parts—to the fine art it once was. But to my eye, there's a man who has taken a step beyond.

Franklin in Easthampton—Born in Burlington, Vt., one of Peter Franklin's earliest memories is buying his first antique while accompanying his parents to an auction as a small boy. When he grew up, his interest in things old led him to a career as a contractor in Nova Scotia, where he restored buildings. But one winter day, standing on a half-finished roof in a freezing rain, he found himself asking, "Why am I doing this to myself?" A friend suggested an apprenticeship with a man who made Windsors in Bristol, R.I. Franklin made the move.

As an apprentice, Franklin made thousands of parts, but no chairs. Since there was a master turner in the shop, producing a leg every three minutes, Franklin was left to figure out the lathe on his own, after hours. After leaving his apprenticeship and moving to his present shop in Massachusetts, he continued to fine-tune the skill, beginning with a reproduction of a New England-style leg he'd measured from a chair belonging to a couple in Westchester, N.Y. He learned well. His turnings are so perfect it's hard to believe he hand-turns these patterns by eye, again and again, for every chair he builds.

His shapes are crisp, delicate, bold and daring all at once, but it's a feat he had to work a compromise to achieve. Franklin turns kiln-dried maple, which he chose for its great strength and density. "These turnings can be light in form yet retain great strength. Additionally, maple's density permits a sharpness of detail not possible in softer woods," says Franklin. By turning the wood dry, he avoids the crumbling and fuzzing of green stock, enabling him to turn clean curves with razor-fine rings and shoulders. He admits it's a trade-off, as it takes considerably longer to turn dry stock, particularly maple, than it does to turn traditional woods.

Franklin spent the first few years after his apprenticeship collecting designs. One of his best is a variation on a continuous-arm that had come into the Leeds Design Workshops, in the same building as his shop on 1 Cottage Street, for repair. After acquiring permission from the owner, he applied his standard routine. "I take a tape measure and paper and draw little lines corresponding to significant features. Then I walk away from the chair." The result is an interpretation, not an exact duplicate.

In the shop, Franklin tranfers the chair's seat outline to particle-

Photos above and below right: Peter Franklin

Peter Franklin

Peter Franklin, above left, who works with a couple of helpers, combines high production with snappy detailing that's almost audible. Franklin's settee, above right, is a Windsor form still evolving: The vibrant undercarriage appears to be impatiently waiting for the sedate top to catch up. Franklin's corner chair, at right, is a form that probably never existed, but it clearly carries on the tradition toward ever more buoyant design. The earliest Windsor precursors, drawing below, a handful of which survive from the 16th century, were mired in Gothic heaviness. Lightweight intermediate forms, photo below, realized the possibilities of tension/compression engineering.

Museum of Art, Rhode Island School of Design; gift of the estate of Mrs. Gustav Radeke

board and cuts it out on the bandsaw. Then he glues hardwood blocks at the leg locations and uses the leg angles he's recorded to bore rough guide holes. This unit becomes a combination seat pattern and boring jig. Or, if the seat shape is one he already uses, he may grab a finished blank from his stock, glue on the blocks and bore it directly so he can stick in whatever legs he was kicking around and see how it looks. It doesn't always look right, but Franklin is philosophical: "You can't be paralyzed by fear of ruining a good seat. You've got to take a chance, hold your breath and drill it."

Even if an experiment comes out looking good, it still may not be right, because for Franklin, the chief determinate is comfort. "The philosophy of the early makers was to make chairs to sit in. They weren't making art furniture or chairs to set aside in collec-

tions, and if it's not comfortable, you can't use it."

Nor were they pedagogues. Thus Franklin feels invention is justified. "I just built something that may never have been made before, a Windsor corner chair, for a show in Holyoke, Mass. If the original makers had had access to as many things as we do, I think they'd have been as whimsical as we. Just because you're working in traditional elements doesn't mean you can't incorporate new ideas into traditional design."

To my eye, Windsor design is not only flourishing, it's healthier than ever—a 200-year-old tradition that's just now getting its second wind. ☐

Jeremy Singley is an author and a full-time woodworker in East Middlebury, Vt., where he makes Windsors and other furniture.

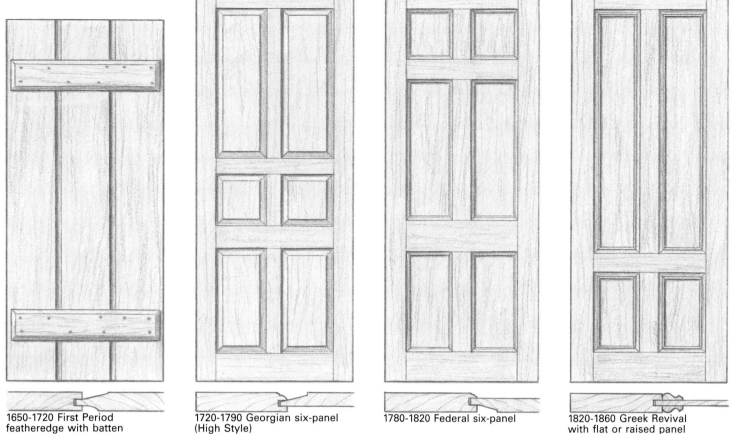

Fig. 1: Evolution of period doors

1650-1720 First Period
featheredge with batten

1720-1790 Georgian six-panel
(High Style)

1780-1820 Federal six-panel

1820-1860 Greek Revival
with flat or raised panel

Making Period Doors
Through tenons and scribed cope joints

by Malcolm MacGregor

The New Hampshire seacoast region where I live was one of the first to be settled by the early colonists. By the 18th century, Portsmouth was a busy port and a commercial center. Local merchants and sea captains invested their wealth in elegant homes, many of which still stand today. Thanks to a renewed interest in restoring these fine homes, about half of my woodworking business consists of making authentic period moldings, sash, trim and doors, mostly with traditional hand tools.

In this article, I'll concentrate on building frame-and-panel entry and passage doors. I'll also discuss the simpler doors found in humbler dwellings or in the less important rooms of more-formal homes. Over the years, I've acquired quite a collection of wooden molding planes, which figure prominently in the hybrid hand/power tool techniques I've developed. For tedious work—thicknessing and ripping stock to size or cutting a dozen mortises—I rely on power tools. But, I make all my moldings and panels with handplanes. Using the original 18th-century tools ensures authenticity.

There is always a great deal of variation in molding and panel details from house to house. I have at least a dozen thumbnail planes and 15 different panel-raising planes so I can duplicate any 18th-century look. These planes, plus about 400 molding planes, are sharp, set and ready to go: I don't have any time-consuming setup time or wasteful trial runs. For custom restoration work, I can beat any production shop hands down. Also, a hand-cut molding run on straight, clear pine approaches perfection: Corners and fillets are square and sharp and the wood needs little or no sanding.

Period door design—When most people think of early woodwork, an elaborately paneled wall complete with crown molding and chair rail comes to mind. But during the mid-1650s to early 1700s, often called the First Period, buildings were not ornate. Common houses were usually of timber-frame construction. Interior partition walls were made of floor-to-ceiling boards whose edges were molded in a pattern called featheredge, which is a very shallow, slightly curved bevel or panel section (see figure 1). The featheredge on one board usually fits into a groove in the edge of the neighboring board. Doors were simple affairs. Most consisted of two or more featheredge boards fastened together by clench-nailed battens. Butt hinges weren't widely used until about 1780, so these doors were hung on strap, H-and-L hinges.

I've seen many variations of batten doors, including entry doors made of three or four vertical boards on the exterior side clench-nailed to a layer of horizontal boards on the interior side. This double thickness (about 2 in.) makes a strong, weatherproof exterior door. Many other early doors were a refinement of the featheredge design: The edge of each vertical board was grooved to accept a loose spline, and instead of the featheredge, a bead or shadow molding was run along the joint.

By the 1720s, the early Georgian Period, many colonists could afford more stylish homes. Elegant fireplace surrounds and formal paneled walls and doors embellished with trim inspired by classical Roman architecture came into vogue. Despite the new style, the featheredge paneling and batten doors found use in back rooms and attics well into the 19th century. Georgian paneled doors typically had four or six raised panels set into frames decorated with thumbnail moldings. If the doors themselves were somewhat stylistically uniform, their settings certainly were not. The Georgian style allowed for many variations in trim. The joiner's toolbox and the client's pocketbook actually determined how elaborate the work would be. By the time the style reached its peak around 1770, a formal entry door might have been flanked by stop-fluted Corinthian pilasters capped by an elaborate broken pediment. Similarly, interior architraves (door casings) were trimmed in varying widths of classically derived moldings.

During the Federal Period, which began around 1790, the six-panel door became more widespread in New England. Figure 1 shows the proportions of a typical Federal pattern, commonly known as a Christian door because its frieze rail and intermediate stile form a cross. This design became so popular that it's usually what you'll get today if you order a machine-made paneled wood or steel paneled door. The stiles and rails of Federal doors were usually decorated with ovolo moldings. The panels were both flat and raised, but any raised panels were turned toward the least important side of the door. By about 1820, when the Greek Revival Period began, six-panel doors were still popular, as was the four-panel door shown in figure 1—a design more in keeping with the vertical scale of Greek Revival houses.

Making a paneled door—Despite variations in style, period paneled doors are all constructed the same way: Loose panels are set into a molded rail-and-stile frame, which is held together with wedged-and-pinned tenons, not glue. Apart from the joints themselves, the chief technical problem is mating the molded edges where rail and stile meet. In the modern woodshop, router and shaper cutters can cut a perfect-fitting cope joint in a few seconds. However, they cannot make doors in the traditional manner. These tools didn't exist in the 18th century, so a traditional joiner had to cut the cope by hand, using chisels and an in-cannel gouge whose radius matched the molded profile. I use the same method in my shop.

Before I get into joinery specifics, I'll offer some general comments on the door dimensions given in figure 2. In First Period houses, ceilings were usually quite low, thus it was not unusual to find doors as short as 6 ft. During the Georgian and Federal periods, doors got taller, nearing the usual standard for modern doors—6 ft., 6 in. to 6 ft., 8 in. Widths varied with the application. A typical Georgian passage door ranged from 26 in. to 32 in. in

width. The modern standard is 30 in. Main entry doors of the 18th and 19th centuries, although shorter than today's, were often just as wide at 36 in. to 48 in. If you are making a door for a new house, I'd suggest referring to the local building code. A replacement door should be sized to fit the original opening.

For passage doors, a rail and stile thickness of 7/8 in. works well with 11/16-in.-thick panels raised on one side, flat on the other. Very few period doors were raised and molded on both sides, primarily, I suspect, because a double mold-and-raise meant both sides of each joint would have to be coped, requiring twice as much work. Because of this, main entry doors are often a composite construction. This is actually two doors in one: a conventional frame-and-panel door clench-nailed to a separate vertical-board door. Besides being quicker to make, a composite door is up to 2 in. thick and is therefore more secure and weatherproof. If I'm making a regular paneled entry door without composite construction, the rails and stiles will be 1¾ in. thick to 2¼ in. thick. Single-raised panels are 7/8 in. thick; double-raised panels are usually two single-raised panels set back to back.

I begin a door by selecting stock. Period woodwork is almost always painted, so eastern white pine is the wood of choice. Pine is also soft enough to mold nicely with handplanes and compresses enough at the cope to produce a tight joint. I prefer quartersawn stock, or at least nearly quartersawn, for the rails and stiles because of its stability. In any case, to avoid warping later, select straight boards without wild grain. Figure 2 shows the overall dimensions for a typical Georgian passage door, and these of course, should be varied to match any existing original woodwork.

Layout and joinery—I begin construction by ripping and cross-cutting the rails and stiles. To reduce the chances of their splitting, the stiles should extend 2 in. or 3 in. beyond the mortise. This excess, called a horn, is trimmed flush after assembly. Through tenons are used, so the rails should be cut to a length that equals the total width of the door, plus 1/8 in. to 1/4 in. for trimming.

The panel grooves are cut first. I do this with a vintage plow plane, but it can be done with a router or tablesaw. Note that in a door with single-raised panels, the groove is offset, as shown in figure 2, detail A. This means that the molded side of the door has a deeper relief than the back, allowing enough thickness for the molding and positioning the groove so the panel's raised field is flush with the front faces of the rails and stiles. A double-raised door, with moldings on both sides, would be thicker (about 1 1/8 in.), with the groove centered. Once the groove is plowed, I mold the thumbnail molding with a handplane. This operation can also be done by machine, but to my eye, the results aren't as appealing.

In handwork, it's usual to chop the mortise before making the tenon. Since I use machines for both operations, I find it easier to saw the tenons on the tablesaw first and use them as guides for laying out the mortises. As figure 2, detail C shows, to allow for the cope, the tenon's back shoulder is offset by the exact width of the stile's molded edge, and the cheeks are offset within the stock thickness in such a way that the back cheek aligns with the back of the stile's panel groove. I lay out the 5/16-in. tenon with a mortise marking gauge, then measure and mark the offset shoulders with a square and knife.

I cut the tenons on the tablesaw, sawing the cheeks first by feeding the stock vertically against the fence. This is not a particularly dangerous operation if you keep the stock perfectly upright and your hands well away from the blade. The cheeks can also be cut using a commercial or shopmade tenoning jig. The offset shoulders also are cut on the tablesaw, using the miter

From *Fine Woodworking* magazine (July 1988) 71:60-64

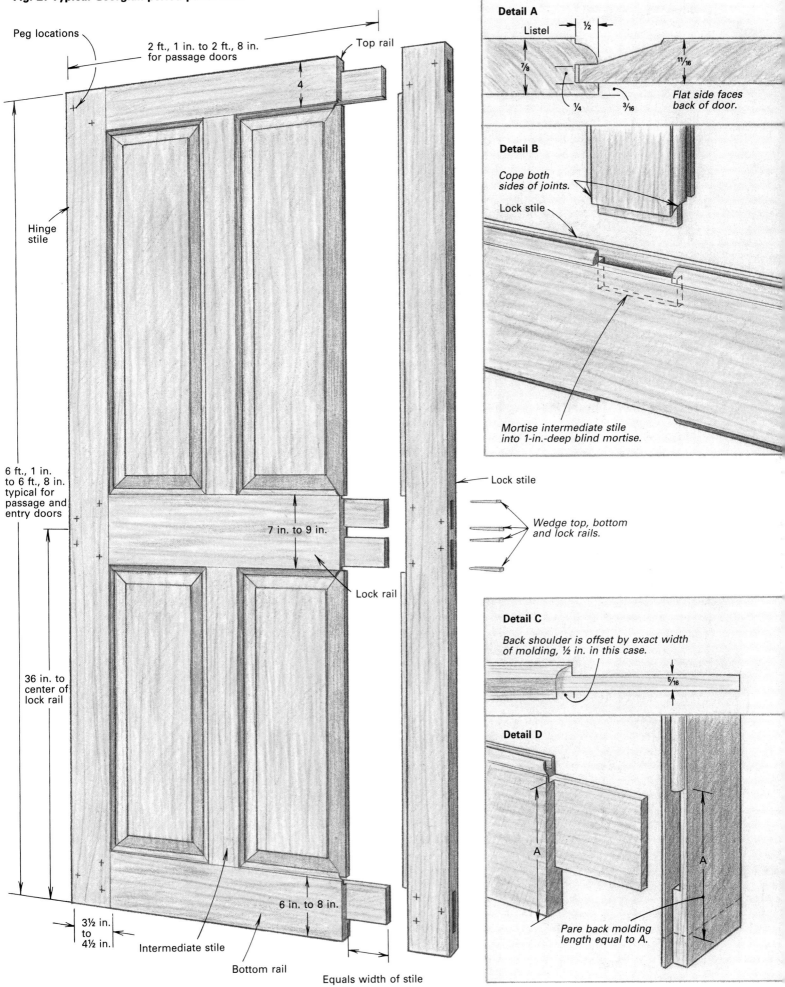

Fig. 2: Typical Georgian-period panel door

Peg locations

2 ft., 1 in. to 2 ft., 8 in. for passage doors

Top rail

4

Hinge stile

6 ft., 1 in. to 6 ft., 8 in. typical for passage and entry doors

7 in. to 9 in.

Lock rail

36 in. to center of lock rail

3½ in. to 4½ in.

Intermediate stile

Bottom rail

6 in. to 8 in.

Equals width of stile

Lock stile

Wedge top, bottom and lock rails.

Detail A

Listel

½

⅞

¼

³⁄₁₆

¹¹⁄₁₆

Flat side faces back of door.

Detail B

Cope both sides of joints.

Lock stile

Mortise intermediate stile into 1-in.-deep blind mortise.

Detail C

Back shoulder is offset by exact width of molding, ½ in. in this case.

⁵⁄₁₆

Detail D

A

A

Pare back molding length equal to A.

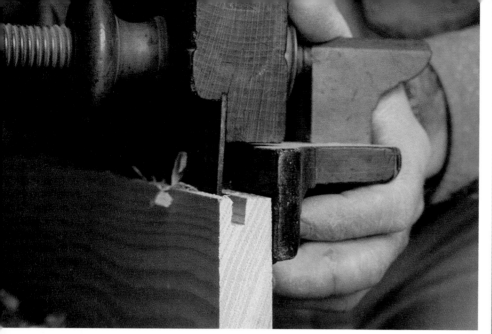

After the stock is ripped and cut to length, grooves for the panels are plowed with an 18th-century plow plane, above. The same operation can be done with a router or on the tablesaw. Left, the rails (and intermediate stiles) are tenoned on the tablesaw. The cheeks are cut first by feeding the stock vertically against the fence. Because the blade's vertical reach is limited, wasting up to the shoulder is done with multiple crosscuts, which are then pared off. The cope on the molded rail, right, is cut with a ½ in. in-cannel, in a series of shallow, slicing cuts. To ease the fit, it's undercut slightly.

gauge and with a stop block clamped to the fence, as shown in the photo above. Through tenons for doors are as long as the stiles are wide (usually at least 4 in.)—quite a bit more than a 10-in. tablesaw can cut vertically. To finish off the cheek, I make closely spaced multiple cuts when I saw the shoulders and then pare off the waste with a slick or chisel. The width of the tenons isn't critical, but traditionally, the wide lock rail has a pair of side-by-side tenons instead of a single wide one. Some craftsmen believe this is for wood movement, but I think the real reason is that the load in a door is carried not by the tenon cheeks, but by the top and bottom edges of the tenons. The more tenons, the stronger the door will be. Also, the space between the tenons leaves wood for the lock set to be mortised into, without weakening the joint.

After cutting the tenons, I position the rails where they'll join the stiles and mark the mortises directly from the tenons. With the same marking gauge setting I use for the tenons, I mark each mortise position on the outside edges of the stiles too. This way, when I cut the through mortise with a hollow chisel on the drill press, I can cut in from both sides. To allow room for wedges, the mortises should be about ⅛ in. longer than the tenons. While the mortiser is set up, I cut the blind mortises for the intermediate stiles, as shown in figure 2, detail B. The intermediate stiles themselves are cut to length and tenoned after the principal frame copes are cut and the door is test-assembled.

Cutting a hand cope—Two moldings can be joined at a corner by cutting or coping one to the exact reverse section of the other, allowing the moldings to nest together. It's time-consuming, but not difficult if you have a sharp in-cannel gouge (mine is ½ in. radius) that closely matches the molding profile. Before coping on a door, I'd suggest a few practice joints. I begin by using a chisel to pare off the molding on the stiles where the rails will meet them, as shown both in the photo above and in figure 2, detail D. The molding is pared off to a depth even with its fillet or listel.

I mark out the cope cut with a miter square. Although the joint isn't really a miter, it looks like one when it's done, and a 45° angle closely approximates the correct profile. The layout line (and the cut itself) should just intersect the very end of the rail at the point where the molding's listel or fillet meets the tenon's shoulder. Cut the cope with a series of shallow paring cuts until your gouge just reaches the layout line, then try the joint. Undercutting a bit as you approach the line will provide some extra clearance. If the cope won't seat, the offset back shoulder needs to be trimmed back a little with a shoulder plane. If the cope seats with an open back shoulder, deepen the cope until the shoulder pulls down. Remember, soft pine will compress at the cope, so a hairline opening at the back shoulder usually isn't a problem. Use the same method to fit the two copes that mate the intermediate stiles to the lock rail.

With the copes done, I test-assemble the door and check for proper fits. Test the door's squareness by measuring diagonally from corner to corner. There should be enough play in the joints to make minor adjustments. At this point, I measure between the top, bottom and lock rails, fillet to fillet, and add 3 in. to get the exact length of the intermediate stiles, which I then tenon and

MacGregor's associate, Stu Worthing, assembles the door. Assembly proceeds from the inside out by first inserting the intermediate stiles into the lock rail, followed by the panels and the top and bottom rails. Last in place are the lock and hinge stiles.

Above, wedges and pins lock the tenons securely without glue. The wedges are driven in above and below the tenons until they seat firmly. Below, pins made from rounded square stock are driven into ¼-in. through-bored holes.

cope. The tenons are 1½ in. long. When all the rails and stiles are in place, I determine panel sizes by measuring the actual frame openings, again fillet to fillet. I allow ¹⁄₁₆ in. on the length and nothing to ⅛ in. on the width, depending on the season, to allow for wood movement. I raise the panels with a wooden plane (see the profile in figure 2), but this operation can be done with machines as well (for example, with a router with a fence extension and a shopmade jig). After trying the panels in their grooves, I smooth-plane the fields, rails and stiles and sand as needed.

Final assembly–Since the door won't be glued, you can proceed directly from test assembly with the panels in place to wedging and pinning the tenons, assuming everything fits. You might be tempted to glue the tenons, but there's no need. I've seen old doors that have stood up to two centuries of wear and weather without a drop of glue.

I begin by clamping the door lengthwise to pull the intermediate stiles tightly against their shoulders. The intermediate stiles are not wedged or pinned, so the tightness of their shoulders depends on their being held slightly in compression against the lock rail. Clamps placed widthwise pull the rails home. With the clamps still in place, I use a razor knife to slice wedges from a scrap as thick and as long as the tenons. The wedges taper from about ³⁄₁₆ in. to perhaps ⅛ in. and are driven in at the top and bottom of each tenon. I tap the wedges in as far as they'll go without breaking off, then trim them flush with a backsaw. To further lock the joint, each tenon is pinned with a pair of round-cornered square pegs driven into a ¼-in. hole bored through both mortise-and-tenon cheeks.

To finish up, pare the pegs flush, finish the stiles and rails with a smooth plane and cut the horns off. The door is now ready to hang. Once hung, a couple of coats of primer followed by a coat or two of good-quality oil paint completes the job. ☐

Malcolm MacGregor operates Piscataqua Architectural Woodwork Co., in Durham, N.H. For more on doors, see FWW on Joinery.

The author builds period reproduction mantels, such as the one shown here, using antebellum mantels as inspiration. This blockfront mantel incorporates grooved pilasters, raised panels and a variety of moldings made with simple milling procedures.

Building Fireplace Mantels

Antebellum designs provide inspiration

by Ben Erickson

Fireplace mantels of the antebellum South range from rigid interpretations of classical architectural styles to more homely examples shaped by the whim of the homeowner and his builder's skills. To arrive at mantel designs for the houses I restore, I've studied 25 antebellum mantels in central-western Alabama, where I live. Built in the Greek Revival style that swept the young republic between 1825 and 1860, these designs have been a good source of inspiration, and when altered to suit modern building codes, they're perfectly suitable for new homes as well.

Even though Greek Revival is associated with strict rules of proportioning and detail, I haven't been able to develop universal design rules based on mantels I've seen. I suspect the local builders lacked formal architectural training and copied high-style pieces they had seen or heard about. I'm not the first designer to have problems determining proportions. Even Asher Benjamin, 19th-century housewright, author and architectural authority, was reluctant to formulate precise guidelines. "The proportions of chimney pieces," he wrote, "I am obliged to leave to the judgement of the workman, as no exact rule can be laid down that will answer for every room." Still, the following construction guidelines enable you to design and build a mantel to suit any fireplace.

Mantel anatomy—Mantels are embellishments meant to frame the fireplace, the focal point of the room in the days before central heating. The word mantel itself defines the entire ornamental structure surrounding the fireplace, not just the shelf above it. Figure 1 illustrates one type of mantel popular in the antebellum South, an elaborate design I call a blockfront. Figure 2 shows two more common styles. Although they have markedly different appearances, all of these mantels consist of four major elements: a field, a shelf, pilasters and applied moldings. Some designs incorporate a fifth element: a decorative entablature board.

The field is appropriately named, for it serves as the foundation to which the other parts are fastened. Basically, the field is an inverted U-shaped assembly made of three pieces—two vertical boards on either side of the fireplace opening and a horizontal board that spans the two. The field is made as a single unit, thus the mantel can be built on the bench and then attached to the wall. Field boards are traditionally solid wood, 1 in. to 1½ in. thick, with the horizontal piece tenoned into the verticals. In new work to be painted, you could just as easily use cabinet-grade plywood whose dimensional stability will reduce warping.

Figure 1 shows typical dimensions for fields in period work. But

Drawings: Lee Hov

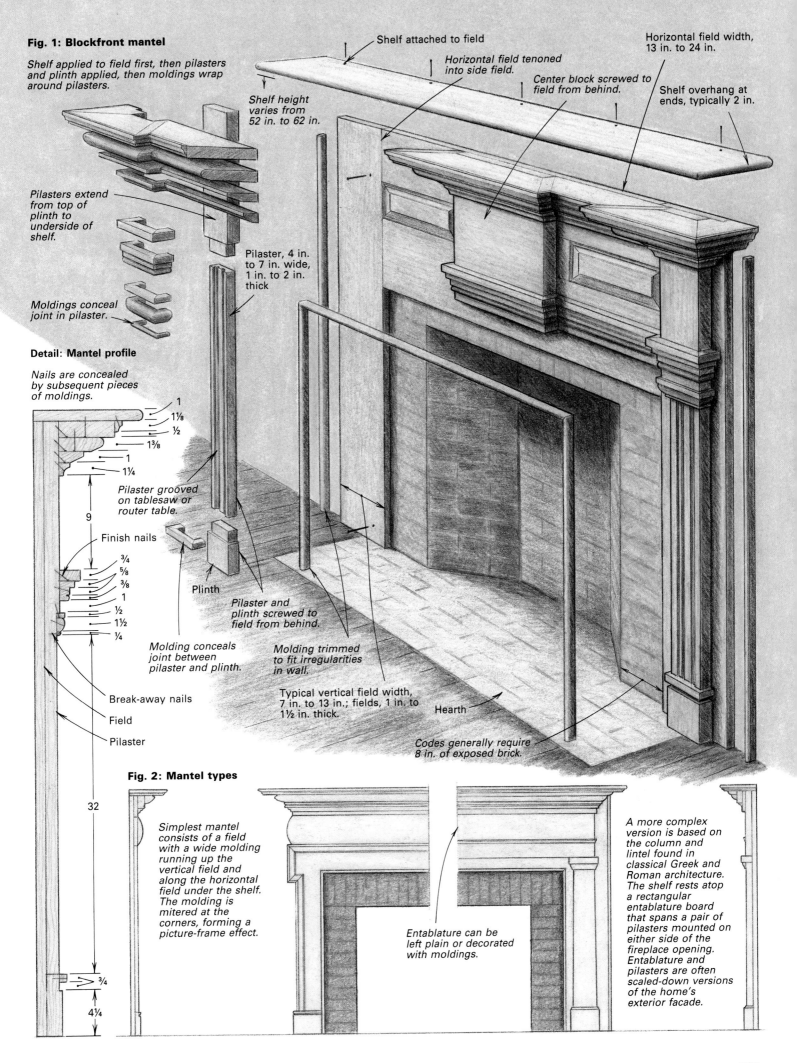

Fig. 1: Blockfront mantel

Shelf applied to field first, then pilasters and plinth applied, then moldings wrap around pilasters.

Pilasters extend from top of plinth to underside of shelf.

Moldings conceal joint in pilaster.

Shelf attached to field

Horizontal field tenoned into side field.

Center block screwed to field from behind.

Horizontal field width, 13 in. to 24 in.

Shelf overhang at ends, typically 2 in.

Shelf height varies from 52 in. to 62 in.

Pilaster, 4 in. to 7 in. wide, 1 in. to 2 in. thick

Detail: Mantel profile

Nails are concealed by subsequent pieces of moldings.

1
1⅛
½
1⅜
1
1¼

9

Pilaster grooved on tablesaw or router table.

Finish nails

¾
⅝
⅜
1
½
1½
¼

Plinth

Molding conceals joint between pilaster and plinth.

Pilaster and plinth screwed to field from behind.

Molding trimmed to fit irregularities in wall.

Typical vertical field width, 7 in. to 13 in.; fields, 1 in. to 1½ in. thick.

Hearth

Codes generally require 8 in. of exposed brick.

Break-away nails

Field

Pilaster

32

¾

4¼

Fig. 2: Mantel types

Simplest mantel consists of a field with a wide molding running up the vertical field and along the horizontal field under the shelf. The molding is mitered at the corners, forming a picture-frame effect.

Entablature can be left plain or decorated with moldings.

A more complex version is based on the column and lintel found in classical Greek and Roman architecture. The shelf rests atop a rectangular entablature board that spans a pair of pilasters mounted on either side of the fireplace opening. Entablature and pilasters are often scaled-down versions of the home's exterior facade.

From *Fine Woodworking* magazine (May 1988) 70:42-45

in designing a mantel around existing brickwork, the fireplace opening's size, building code requirements and the need to have the shelf at a convenient height above the floor may severely limit variation in field dimension, particularly the horizontal field. Ideally, the horizontal field should be one-and-a-half times to twice as wide as the verticals to allow space to accommodate the graduated bands of moldings beneath the shelf. If a field this wide isn't workable, use less molding or no molding at all, otherwise the design will appear too crowded. Consider building the horizontal as a frame-and-panel construction if it must be very wide.

The shelf is glued and nailed or screwed to the top edge of the horizontal field and to the ends of the vertical fields. Shelves I've examined vary in thickness from 1 in. to 2 in. and in width from 8 in. to 12 in. I've found that the average thickness and width, about 1½ in. by 9½ in., looks right for the majority of mantels I build. The shelf should be long enough to extend about 2 in. to 4 in. past the outermost moldings applied beneath the shelf. In some period mantels, the vertical fields extend above the horizontal field by the thickness of the shelf. The shelf is notched around the verticals and nailed or screwed into place. This gives additional support to the shelf, but it's not a necessity, as the moldings, pilasters and entablature add additional support. If you decide on a plywood field, reinforce the shelf joint with dowels or plates.

Pilasters are the tall, rectangular projections that, along with

Making mantel moldings

With a little ingenuity, you don't need a shop full of expensive machinery to make mantel moldings. I make most of the profiles I need with a molding head on my tablesaw and with standard and shop-modified bits on my router table. Remember, a mantel doesn't require hundreds of lineal feet of molding, just two or three yards of each profile.

I shape the large nosing beneath the mantel shelf with a set of matched cutters in a molding head. (Mine is a Sears model 9HT3218 with a 1-in. radius cutter.) With the cutter head set up (see figure 3), I tilt the arbor to get the radius I want and take several shallow passes with each cutter until I reach the necessary depth. I finish the cut with a regular sawblade tilted at an angle and then smooth to the final shape with a handplane and 120-grit sandpaper. If you don't have a molding head, this profile, along with many large convex shapes, can be rough-shaped on the tablesaw with multiple passes, then finished by hand. For all edge-shaping and sawing operations, use a featherboard to hold the work firmly against the fence.

The large cove moldings applied beneath the shelf are also made on the tablesaw by feeding the wood diagonally across a regular sawblade. Varying the fence's angle and/or tilting the blade controls the cove's shape. For a nearly circular cove, feed the stock at close to a right angle; a deep, elliptical cove will result if the fence is more parallel to the blade. Tilting the arbor will make one side of the curve steeper, and a smaller blade will give a tighter curve. I make shallow, slow passes, increasing the blade height about ¹⁄₁₆ in. per pass. A small cove can be milled into a large board and then sawn off, or a larger cove can be ripped down the center to produce two separate moldings, as shown in the photo at right. For more on tablesawn moldings, see *FWW #35* or *FWW on Woodshop Specialties*.

Through and stopped flutes for pilasters are made quickly on the router table. Stopped flutes are blind-cut by plunging the wood down onto the bit while holding one edge of the pilaster firmly against the router-table fence. To keep track of where to start and stop the cut, I mark reference lines on the back of the pilaster and align these with marks on

To cut a cove molding, run the workpiece along a fence angled to the blade. Make several shallow cuts, then rip the workpiece in half. Hold the work against the fence with a featherboard, using a push stick to finish the cut.

the fence showing the bit's precise position. The centers of the flutes are marked lightly on the workpiece's face, then the fence is set an appropriate distance from the bit's center. If your pilaster stock is warped or bowed, press it down firmly over the bit, otherwise the flutes will be too shallow and uneven.

For through flutes, pass the pilaster over the bit along its full length, allowing the flutes to enter and exit at the ends. This may sound like a shortcut, but it's perfectly acceptable. Many period mantels I've studied have pilasters decorated in this fashion.

For matching unusual period moldings, I regrind high-speed steel router bits to the shape I need. First, I regrind a ¼-in.- or ⅜-in.-wide, 60-grit grinding wheel to a curve. I shape the wheel using a star wheel or diamond-tip dresser, then coat a rabbet bit with layout die and mark the desired shape on the bit with a carbide-tip machinist scribe (Sears 9HT4078). Next, I slowly grind to the line, holding the bit with locking pliers and quenching often to prevent softening the steel. Finally, I hone the bit with a slip stone. The entire process takes about an hour and is a good way to press old high-speed steel bits back into service. For more on grinding router bits, see *FWW on Making and Modifying Tools.* —B.E.

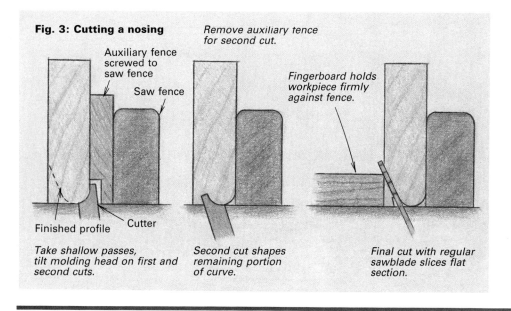

Fig. 3: Cutting a nosing

Auxiliary fence screwed to saw fence

Saw fence

Remove auxiliary fence for second cut.

Fingerboard holds workpiece firmly against fence.

Finished profile   Cutter

Take shallow passes, tilt molding head on first and second cuts.

Second cut shapes remaining portion of curve.

Final cut with regular sawblade slices flat section.

moldings, give a mantel its architectural presence. Pilasters are usually solid boards, 1 in. to 2 in. thick, glued and screwed onto the vertical field from the rear before the mantel is installed. Depending on how elaborate the mantel is to be, pilasters can be straight or tapered in width toward the top at a ¼-in. to ⅜-in. taper per foot of length. Pilasters can be left plain, reeded or fluted, as shown in the photo on p. 122, and can extend directly to the floor or be mounted atop a plinth block, as shown in figure 1.

Tiers of moldings usually extend beneath the shelf in step-like bands. Note in the photo on p. 122 that the moldings are mitered and return back to the wall or the field. The moldings, combinations of coves, rounds and ogees, are usually built up, but you could install a single-piece molding, such as a wide crown, instead. Although it's more work to fasten many individual pieces, it's easier to cut tight miters on them rather than fitting one large piece. For a less ornate mantel, you can skip the molding entirely, applying a rectangle of molding to the field that visually suggests a panel, as shown in the photo at right.

Building a mantel—Armed with the average dimensions of mantels I've studied, I begin with a scale drawing of the fireplace and hearth, roughing in the shape of the mantel around it. I alter the dimensions of the mantel's components until they look right. Check your local building codes before settling on a design. Most require a minimum of 8 in. of exposed brick between the mantel and the fireplace opening, and some require that the shelf be at least 12 in. above the opening. This is usually not a problem, but it's better to know it ahead of construction.

The overall width of the mantel should be such that the vertical fields extend to the outer edge of the hearth, though in hearths set flush with the floor, the fields can run past the hearth, onto the flooring. With a raised hearth, the fields must stop flush with or slightly inside the outer edge of the hearth. The height of the shelf above the floor can vary from 52 in. to 62 in., with 58 in. about average. In a floor-level fireplace with a low opening, 52 in. is about right; if the shelf is much higher than this, the horizontal field will be too wide and look awkward. Just the opposite is true for a fireplace with a raised hearth; a shelf height of 62 in. (above the floor) works well, otherwise the field will be too narrow.

Usually the facing bricks on the front of the fireplace are laid flush with the surrounding wall so the mantel can simply bridge the gap. Occasionally, facing bricks are laid with their full width standing proud of the wall, so the mantel must box them in. In these cases, side pieces must be glued to the back face of the vertical fields and the shelf must be wide enough to accommodate the thickness of the bricks. For this reason, it's best to do final measuring after the brickwork and hearth are completed. This avoids the unpleasant surprise of a beautifully built mantel that won't fit the wall. If the wall protrudes slightly past the bricks, take up the gap with molding applied around the inside of the mantel opening.

I assemble a mantel in the following sequence. First the field is glued and the shelf is glued, nailed or screwed on. Next, the pilasters and plinth blocks are butted under the shelf and screwed to the field from the back. If the mantel has an entablature board, it is screwed into place from behind and then the pilasters and plinth block are mounted below it. Finally, the moldings are mitered around the pilasters (and the entablature, if there is one). As shown in figure 1, the nails that fasten moldings under the shelf are hidden by subsequent moldings. I nail small mitered moldings with break-away nails (available from HGH Hardware Supply, Inc., 3912 2nd Ave. S., Box 31192, Birmingham, Ala., 35222) that are of very small diameters and extremely brittle. Driven in and left standing proud of the molding face, they can

Erickson built this mantel for a fireplace on a raised hearth. The fireplace mantel extends away from the wall approximately 4 in. to accommodate the fireplace's facing bricks, which were laid proud of the wall.

be snapped off about ¹⁄₁₆ in. beneath the surface of the molding with a sideways hammer tap.

The mantel is centered on the fireplace opening and nailed to the wall studs through the field at top and bottom with 16d casing nails countersunk and filled. If the filled holes will detract from the appearance of a natural finish, leave off one of the moldings beneath the shelf, attach the mantel to the wall where the molding will go and apply the molding to cover your tracks. The small finish nails fastening the molding will be less visible. To fasten the bottom of the mantel, leave off the plinth blocks at construction, then use them to hide your nail holes after installation.

After the mantel is attached to the wall, a ½-in.- to ¾-in.-thick molding, usually with a bead cut on the edge, is applied to the inner and outer edges of the field. I normally make two sets of moldings, one the exact size and one slightly wider than it needs to be. If the mantel fits snugly to the wall with few irregularities, I use the narrow molding. To accommodate a bumpy wall, I plane the wider molding to fit using a block plane. Unless there is a major irregularity, I don't scribe these moldings but plane them by eye until I get a perfect fit.

Mantels can be painted, stained or clear-finished. I generally use poplar for painted or stained mantels and walnut or mahogany for clear-finished work. Many antebellum mantels were painted black to resemble marble and to make them less likely to show soot, which was more of a problem in those days when fires were burned around the clock than today when they are used only occasionally. □

Ben Erickson builds furniture and millwork, including antebellum shutters, in Eutaw, Ala.

Further reading

The Classical Orders of Architecture by Robert Chitham. Rizzoli International Publications, Inc., 597 Fifth Ave., New York, NY 10017; 1985.

The Gentleman and Cabinet-maker's Director by Thomas Chippendale. Dover Publications Inc., (reprint third edition), 180 Varick St., New York, NY 10014; 1966.

The American Builder's Companion by Asher Benjamin. Dover Publications Inc., (reprint sixth edition), see address above; 1969.

Index

wooden, making, 31, 33
Human Factors Design Handbook (Woodson), cited, 13
Hutches, adaptation of, 61-63

I

Inlay:
  circular, pivot templates for, 41
  cutter for, 32
  fan, making, 40-41
  line-and-berry, 47
  scratch beader for, making, 41
  sealing, before finishing, 43
  sources for, 35, 43
  See also Marquetry.

K

Knots, resinous, dealing with, 51
Krutsky, Alex, on spice boxes, 44-47

L

Lamb, David, on Shaker casework, 71-76
Lamination, for curved rails, 32
Landon, Eugene E.:
  on Chippendale chairs, 102-109
  on Hepplewhite card table, 30-33
Latches, for cupboard, making, 80, 83
Lathes:
  post scribe for, 20
  See also Bits.
Layport, Ronald, on walnut chest, 64-69
Leather, for desk surfaces, installing, 50, 51
Legs:
  glued-up, 42, 43
  housed-dovetail tripod, 18-19
  inlaying, 32
  pivoting, making, 30-32
  for post-and-panel, 81-82
  square bench, making, 98, 99-101
  tapered, making, 23-24
  tripod pedestal, making, 26-29
Locks, tambour-activated desk, 56-57
Lynch, Carlyle:
  on brandy stand, 34-36
  on corner cupboard, 77-79
  on Hepplewhite bureau, 40-43
  on post-office desk, 58-60
  takes measurements, 8-11

M

MacGregor, Malcolm, on period doors, 117-21
Make a Chair from a Tree (Alexander), cited, 93
Mantels:
  anatomy of, 122-23
  making, 124-25
Marking gauges, use of, 103, 104, 106
Marquetry:
  small tabletop in, 34-36
  See also Inlay.
May, Warren:
  on Kentucky cupboard, 80-81
  on quilt cabinet, 61-63
Miter joints:
  beaded, shooting board for, 98
  "key"-strengthening of, 50
Moldings:
  bits for, making, 124
  for corner cupboard, 77-78
  for cupboard, 80, 82, 83
  gluing, 47
  for mantels, 124
  measuring, 10-11
  for small secretary, 67-68, 69
  on tablesaw, 124
  uses of, 13-14
  See also Beaders, scratch.
Mortise and tenon:
  beaded mitered, 73-74, 75
  for beds, 87
  blind, for doors, 77-79

for curved rails, 32
green-wood, 93, 94
mitered beaded, 98
pinning, 121
on tablesaw, 24-25
wedged, 118, 121
See also Mortises. Tenons.
Mortise gauges, use of, 103, 104
Mortises:
  angled, 106-108
  for carcase sides, 82
  crest-rail, making, 108
  on drill press, 120
  green-wood, 93, 94
  haunched mitered, 75
Music stands, making, 17-21

N

Nails, break-away, 124
Norwegian bench. *See* Sengebenk.

O

Odden, Phillip, on making Norwegian bench, 96-101
O'Hearn, Jeff, on materials list, 11

P

Pallardy, Jean, *Early Furniture of French Canada, The,* cited, 37
Patterns, Lucite for, 27
Patterson, Lance, on music stand, 17-21
Penetrating-oil finishes:
  applying, 79
  and lacquer mix, 83
  and varnish mixture, 76
  See also Tung-oil finish.
Philadelphia and Chair-Maker's Book of Prices, The, cited, 103
Phyfe, Duncan, tool box of, 8-11
Planes:
  plow, using, 119, 120
  scrub, using, 37, 38
Plans, sources for, 43
Polygons, method for, 85-87
Post-and-panel construction, for cupboard, 81-83
Pulls, making, 76

Q

Quilts, cabinet for, 61-63

R

Raised panels:
  making, 98-99
  profiles for, 117
  rounded, 72
  See also Frame-and-panel.
Ramsey, Charles George, and Harold Reeve Sleeper, *Architectural Graphic Standards,* cited, 13
Rasps, patternmakers', source for, 18
Restoration, of Hepplewhite card table, 30
Routers:
  dado jig for, 16
  end-mill bits for, source for, 43
  See also Bits.

S

Sawyer, Dave, makes chairs, 113-14
Schuerch, Peter, on chest, 37-39
Screws, brass, steel fitting for, 79
Scribers, for lathe, 20
Secret compartments, in secretary top, 65, 67
Secretaries:
  small many-drawered, making, 64-68
  See also Desks.
Sengebenk, making, 96-101
Settees, Windsor, 116

Shaker:
  bureaus, 12-14, 76
  Canterbury Shaker Village, 76
  casework, 70-76
  pedestal table, making, 26-29
  and Sheraton style, 71
Sharpening, of carving tools, 100
Shellac, applying, 76
Shelves:
  for cupboard, 82
  mortised, 62
  nailed, 77
Shooting boards, for miters, 98
Singley, Jeremy, on Windsor chairs, 110-16
Spice boxes, making, 44-47
Spindles:
  boring, 18
  glued-up stock for, 18
  hollow, turning, 18
  with square hollow, 17-18
Steam bending, of green wood, 93
Stenstrom, David, bed by, 89
Story sticks, using, 73

T

Tables:
  alignment pins for, 25
  brandy, making, 34-36
  corner blocks for, 24-25
  curved rails for, 32
  finish for, 25
  Hepplewhite card, making, 30-33
  locks for, 25
  round extension, making, 22-25
  Shaker pedestal, making, 26-29
  slides for, installing, 24, 25
  See also Aprons. Legs. Tabletops.
Tablesaws:
  bevel cuts on, 27-28
  beveling on, with molding-head cutters, 86-87
  moldings on, 124
  mortise and tenon on, 24-25
  taper jigs for, 23, 85-87
  tenons on, 36, 119-20
Tabletops:
  attachment methods for, 58
  breadboard ends for, mitered, 72
Tambours, interlocking, making, 52-53, 55, 57, 58
Tapers, cutting, 23-24, 85-87
Templates, Masonite routing, 55
Tenons:
  angled, making, 36
  offset, 75
  round wedged, 47
  on tablesaw, 119-20
Tool cabinet, Duncan Phyfe's, 8-11
Tung-oil finish, source for, 69

U

Upholstery, for slip seat, 109

V

Varnish, and penetrating-oil mixture, 76
Veneer:
  scorch-shading, 35, 36
  sources for, 35
Veneering, of card table, 32

W

Walnut, black *(Juglans nigra),* highlighting stain for, 69
Wood:
  green, book on, cited, 93
  green, working with, 92-95
Woodson, Wesley E., *Human Factors Design Handbook,* cited, 13
Worthing, Stu, assembles door, 121